May's Boys

Beryl P. Brown

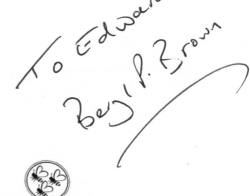

To Edward

Beryl P. Brown

THREE BEES PUBLISHING

British Library Cataloguing-in-Publication Data
A catalogue record for this book is available from the British
Library.

Paperback ISBN 978 1 9163375 1 0
ebook ISBN 978 1 9163375 0 3
ebook ISBN 978 1 9163375 2 7

Published in Great Britain by Three Bees Publishing, 2020

This is a work of fiction. Any similarity between the
characters and situations within its pages and places or
persons, living or dead, is unintentional and co-
incidental.

Cover design by Spiffing Covers

About the Author

Beryl P. Brown has won numerous prizes for her short stories. She graduated as a mature student in 2017 with a Master's degree in creative writing.

After living for many years in rural Dorset, she, her husband and a large Dalmatian moved to a small 17th century cottage on the Suffolk/Essex border.

Beryl can be contacted via www.berylpbrown.uk

Author Note
Certain terms, which are unacceptable today, are used in the text purely to preserve the authenticity of the era.

For my mother, May,
whose name I have borrowed.
1927 – 1992

Chapter 1

May crouched over the handlebars; the night was as dark as the inside of a coal sack.

'Who goes there?'

'Watch out,' she shouted, swinging sharply left. The bike nosedived into the bank, pitching May forward. She shot out a foot to stop herself from falling and barked her shin on the chain guard.

Rubbing her leg, she said, 'Ephraim, what the heck are you doing in the middle of the lane?'

'Friend or foe?'

He was such a pompous idiot. 'You know exactly who I am.'

He switched on his shielded torch. 'Can't be too careful, May. WI meeting were it?'

He knew there had been a WI meeting; his wife never missed one.

'We heard a bit of news. I'm sure Mrs Potts will tell you later but—'

'Mrs Potts issen' one for gossip.'

May covered a derisive snort with a cough. Ephraim and Isabella enjoyed making everyone's war so much harder. What would the sanctimonious little twit do when ARP wardens were stood down? No doubt he'd find some other reason to strut around the village.

'Ephraim, Dr Haskett is giving me a lift to Southampton tomorrow,' she hesitated. 'I'm worried. They've already had two doodlebug hits but there's a rumour about a new kind of flying bomb. Silent, so you can't hear it coming. Have—'

'You'd do better to bide quiet, May Sheppard. Careless talk costs lives. Mr Churchill would tell folks if such a thing existed,' he said. 'You'd best get on – that lad needs a close eye kept on him.'

'Ephraim, please stop using Cliff as a whipping boy. Yes, he caused a few problems when he was first evacuated *five years ago*. You're like a cracked record.' She wrenched the bike around, mounted and forced him to jump back as she pedalled off.

A barn owl floated soundlessly over her head as she pushed her bike up the garden path. She thought of the silent flying bombs and shuddered. At least Cliff had drawn the thick curtains, all she needed was another run-in with Ephraim. She heard his whiney voice in her head, 'Put that light out, May Sheppard.'

The meagre beam of her torch was just enough to light her way around the cottage to the back door. Roll on the day when there was no need for blackouts and dim-outs.

Hanging up her coat, she let the warmth from the range envelope her after the cold of the October night. The smell of the onion and cheese pudding she'd left for Cliff to put in the oven made her mouth water.

'Cliff?'

No reply. She opened the door at the bottom of the stairs and called again. Where was he? The terror she'd felt the night she thought he'd been caught in an air raid rekindled every time he was out after dark.

The brown metal pie dish held the remains of the onion pudding. Cliff had already eaten two-thirds – she encouraged him to take the lion's share, letting him think she had a small appetite. She sat at the table and piled what was left on to a willow-patterned plate. Last night she'd caught sight of her jutting hipbones in the wardrobe mirror; the elastic of her knickers stretched like a rope bridge between two mountain peaks.

Despite the hardships and deprivations, life without Cliff was unimaginable. Had she made the right decision to work on her father-in-law's farm rather than join up? Of course. If she'd been in the Forces, she wouldn't have had the chance to provide a home for an evacuee. For Cliff. That had changed her life, and the decision they'd now made to apply for his adoption was what they both longed for.

As she emptied the kettle into the enamel washing-up bowl, her thoughts turned to the ordeal facing her the following day. Apart from the threat of flying bombs, there was the prospect of meeting Cliff's mother, Lynette. How was she going to broach the subject of adoption? The woman might not take kindly to being asked to formally give up her son, notwithstanding that she hadn't contacted him for four years. A sense of dread welled up at the thought of the scene that might follow.

The age-spotted clock over the range showed ten minutes to nine. Where was Cliff?

She turned the knurled knob on the wireless. Its window glowed amber as she waited for the set to warm up.

The announcer was reading the news headlines when the back door banged open. Bringing in a blast of cold air, Cliff bounced in, face radiant. 'Auntie May,' he said, 'look what I've got us.'

She felt a surge of pleasure at his appearance, even as she noticed his muddy boots on the clean lino. She turned off the wireless.

With a flourish, Cliff brandished a brace of pheasants. Dead wings flapped open as he held up the birds by their clawed feet. She had an image of Ephraim's face glowing with vindictive delight.

'Where did you get them?'

The smile left Cliff's face to be replaced with that guarded look she hadn't seen for a long time; that look he'd had when he first came to the village. Although he was often up to mischief – climbing over fences, scrumping apples and building dens with precious firewood – he was accused by Ephraim of being behind everything from water leaks to fuel thefts. How the weaselly warden would relish adding poaching to Cliff's misdemeanours.

She felt a tightness in her chest; her job could be in jeopardy if he'd poached from the farm, but she shouldn't have snapped. She should have waited for him to explain. The sound of the crackling fire and the ticking of the old clock filled the silence.

'Well?'

'I din't poach 'em.' He always reverted to his backstreet accent when he was upset.

Damn. 'I didn't say you did. But where did they come from?'

'A friend.' He dumped the birds on the table, kicked off his boots and walked to the stairs door. 'I thought you'd be pleased. I'm goin' to bed.'

'Cliff—'

The door slammed. The stairs creaked as he climbed them.

She was as bad as Ephraim. Picking up the birds, she wiped a smear of blood from the table and carried their dead weight to the icy scullery.

Chapter 2

Cliff kicked the bedroom door shut. After all the talks she'd given him, telling him it was a bad thing to take what didn't belong to you, how could she think he'd pinched the pheasants? She thought he hadn't learned anything. Maybe he'd be better off with his mum.

Auntie May had stood up for him in the beginning, when Old Potty had threatened to call the coppers after he'd pinched his apples. Potty'd said he'd been going to win a cup with them, and he wanted Cliff to pay.

He had nothing. His mum would have killed him if he'd been sent back to Southampton owing money. He'd been really scared, but Auntie May told the old misery guts that he'd never seen fruit on trees before and hadn't known they belonged to someone.

She'd shamed Old Potty. Said how bad he'd look trying to get money from an evacuee. In the end he'd piped down, but, now, *she* thought he'd nicked something. He knew you couldn't just take things. Especially when stuff was rationed and there wasn't enough to go round.

The room was icy. He ripped off his clothes and dragged on his pyjamas. The springs twanged as he leapt into bed still buttoning his pyjama jacket. He slid his feet between the sheets. The warm sheets. He wriggled his toes into the fluffy jumper wrapped around the stone hot water bottle.

Auntie May had put a bottle in his bed. He hadn't even washed. He would have done, and he would have told her about the pheasants, if she hadn't decided he'd been poaching.

His mum never checked that he'd washed or cleaned his teeth, even on the nights she wasn't out when he went to bed.

He heard the clatter of the latch as Auntie May closed the scullery door. He shouldn't have slammed out on her. He liked it that she was always there; it was a snuggly feeling, like the hot water bottle.

Sometimes, back in the city, he'd wet the bed rather than go out to the privy in the dark. The shouts from the street scared him as much as the black shadows in the yard and more than the thought of the clip round the ear he'd get when his mum found the wet sheets.

Auntie May hadn't got cross when he'd wet the bed. She got a rubber sheet and gave him a guzzunder to pee in, but he wasn't scared here and, after the first week, never needed it. Some evacuees had to wash their own sheets if they peed the bed. One boy was thrashed.

He turned over and wriggled down the bed. He was never scared here. He closed his eyes and remembered the night he'd heard his mum talking to a man in the front room as he crept downstairs to the privy. He was passing the living room door when the man opened it and grabbed his arm.

'What d'yer think you're doin' yer little devil?'

He was terrified and couldn't speak. His arm hurt and he'd stretched his toes down to try to reach the lino as he was hauled upward. The man smelt of beer and cigarettes and he had crusty patches under the grey stubble on his chin.

His mum hurtled from the front room. She dragged the man off, looking like the cat he'd found hissing and spitting in a corner of the yard.

'Leave him be,' she snarled, pulling the man away.

She jerked her head in the direction of the back door. 'Go,' she mouthed to Cliff.

He ran across the yard, his pyjama trousers slapping wetly around his thighs.

He should have told Auntie May about the pheasants. The story would have been easy then. Now it was like a huge mountain he had to get over: saying sorry, making her believe he wasn't a poacher. He tugged the eiderdown up to his chin and wrapped his feet around the jumper. Maybe she wouldn't ask about them again.

Chapter 3

From the minute the desolate Western Docks came into view, May was certain she'd made the journey in vain. How could anyone be traced among these wastelands?

It was after eleven by the time the doctor dropped her off. The journey to Southampton had been a nightmare of hold-ups, with military vehicles and British and American Army ambulances all having priority over civilian traffic.

The street where Lynette Erwin lived at the beginning of the war was a scene of destruction. Shards of homes stood as stark one-dimensional monuments to life before the first bombs fell on the city.

A weak sun glinted off the barrage balloons that floated above the city like a school of silver whales. She shaded her eyes, looking up and remembering the threat of flying bombs. Did the blimps protect against doodlebugs, or the new silent weapons if they existed?

She trudged up the road, wishing she'd worn her other shoes. Her navy leather courts were already spattered red with brick dust. Both her pairs of shoes had been repaired many times and, because she used most of her own coupons for Cliff's clothes, she had no hope of replacing them.

She approached an end wall from which the rest of the house had been ripped away. A ragged ledge was all that remained of the upstairs floorboards. Above it, an intact mirror hung by one corner, reflecting the open sky. As she moved past, she was startled to see the adjoining house seemingly undamaged. She banged on the door and a shower of powdery green paint flaked off. The woman who tugged the door open was probably in her mid-forties but looked a decade older. Her complexion was sallow beneath the paisley-patterned turban that covered her hair. She wore a faded wraparound overall.

'Yes?'

'I'm sorry to bother you, Mrs erm…'

'Wallbanks.'

'Mrs Wallbanks, I'm trying to find Lynette Erwin. She used to live at number eleven.'

The woman looked her up and down. Everything May had on was pre-war, patched and mended over and over again but, compared with this woman, she looked like a fashion plate. The one time she'd met Lynette, the peroxide hair and red lipstick had labelled her what she was: a docks prostitute. She'd turned up, on a whim, at May's cottage. She wanted to take Cliff home, saying he was a city boy and needed to be back there with his mother.

The reason she'd wanted her son was obvious. To send him out stealing – the only way of life he'd known before the evacuation.

Looking at Lynette's former neighbour, May realised she would have been wise to have dressed down if she hoped to get help from anyone here.

She tried a different tack. 'I'm May Sheppard. Mrs Erwin's son is fostered with me in Crompton Parva.'

Mrs Wallbanks's frown retreated and her eyes lit up with eagerness. 'Cliff? Is he all right?'

May explained that they hadn't heard from Cliff's mother since she'd told them she'd been bombed out of this street. A scribbled note and a half crown had come at Christmas 1940. They were the last things the lad had received from his mother.

'Mrs Erwin didn't let us know where she'd moved to. Have

9

you any idea how I might find her?'

Mrs Wallbanks put a hand on the doorknob. 'I heard she'd gone up Millbrook – or was it Shirley? Up that side a Soton, anyway. I ain't seen her for years.' Her lip curled. 'She got quite partial to the Yanks.'

She began to pull the door shut but then added, 'You could try the Rest Centre. A lot went there after the Blitz.' She closed the door.

May stared at the peeling paint. Mrs Wallbanks hadn't said where the Rest Centre was but she didn't dare disturb her again. She continued walking along the ruined street. Lynette Erwin had clearly not changed her occupation and didn't seem very particular where she sold her favours. What had made her take to that kind of life? Seth had been May's first love and her experience of sex began and ended within their all too brief marriage.

At the end of the street she turned right towards the docks. A hand-painted sign on the door of a redbrick hall read "WVS Canteen".

Inside, she bought a cup of tea from the volunteer behind the makeshift counter.

As she drew a rickety chair across the bare wooden floor, the grey-haired assistant left her urn to come and wipe the table. She said, 'Waiting for your fella? On a ship is he, dear?'

May hated telling people whose families were giving their lives for their country that her husband had died in a freak farming accident before the war. It made her feel as if she had no claim to grief.

'I'm a widow,' she said, lifting the thick white beaker. 'I'm trying to find someone from here who was bombed out in November 1940.'

The woman finished her wiping, ignoring the greasy streaks

the cloth had left on the ringed table. 'Not an easy job.'

Standing in the doorway as the woman pointed out the way to the Rest Centre, May heard the sound she dreaded: the wail of an air raid siren.

The woman sprang into action. 'The shelter's this way,' she said, slamming the door and grabbing May's arm. 'If it's a doodlebug, it'll likely get there before us.'

May ran alongside her. Could she hear the tell-tale engine of a V1?

At a road junction a group of people were staring at the sky, nervously asking questions they clearly did not expect to be answered.

'Can you hear it yet?'

'Where is it?'

'Is it still running?'

May waited as the WVS woman instructed the watchers to get to the shelter across the road.

'No point, love, it's here. Look,' said a man squinting into the sun. 'Just pray the noise don't stop.'

Everybody fell silent as the bomb flew almost overhead, silhouetted like a black crucifix against the sky. May held her breath, praying the engine wouldn't cut out and cause the thing to come down nearby. The droning ran on. There was a communal sigh, like a sharp breeze, as the plane continued inland.

'Looks like Salisbury's in for it,' someone said.

May thought of the people who would hear the motor cut and have only fifteen seconds before they knew their fate.

It was two o'clock when May arrived at the heavily sandbagged police station. Her feet were sore and her legs ached from scrambling along rubble-strewn pavements and backtracking after finding roads closed off.

Tracing Cliff's mother was becoming an endless quest. Someone at the Rest Centre remembered Lynette and thought she'd moved to a flat in Millbrook. It was a part of Southampton May's rudimentary knowledge didn't include. She was asking directions when an off-duty ARP warden interrupted. He told her the only flats he knew of in that area had received a direct hit from a parachute mine.

The Rest Centre staff gave her a cup of tea and a cheese sandwich and the warden suggested she make enquiries at the police station. 'Old Bill Wicks has been a copper around here for donkey's years. He may remember her.'

At the desk, she asked whether PC Wicks was on duty. She was told to wait, and sat on a hard bench opposite a wall plastered with dog-eared posters. The sulphurous reek of cooked cabbage was thick in the air. After some minutes, a rotund policeman appeared, dabbing at his mouth.

'Apologies, madam, we just got a delivery of bully beef and I'd missed my break.' He pushed his thick glasses up the bridge of his nose. 'What can I do for you?'

May explained she wanted to locate Cliff's mother.

'I haven't seen Lynette Erwin for years. I heard she got a bad name for herself with the other girls because she'd only fraternise with the Yanks. Not that that would bother Lynette. She always had her eye on the main chance and the Yanks are pretty free with their money.'

May asked whether he knew where she'd been living when he'd last seen her.

'We'll have it on record from the last time we pulled her in. I'd have to check the files and they're in underground storage.

12

Give me your address, and I'll drop you a line. I think it may have been down where the flats got the parachute mine. If so, very few were pulled out alive.'

May stared at a faded poster, *Join the Wrens and Free a Man for the Fleet*. If she'd taken that option, she wouldn't be facing the possibility of telling an eleven-year-old boy that his mother had been killed.

Chapter 4

When May opened the door, she instantly knew the house was empty. The warmth of the kitchen wasn't enough to ward off the chill of the car journey and she shivered as she wondered where Cliff could be.

It's only six o'clock. Stop panicking and stop making assumptions, she told herself. She began banging around pots and pans. Cliff should have been here, waiting for news of her trip. Disappointment vied with relief that she didn't have to decide how much to tell him right away.

She checked the bread crock. The heel of a loaf and a few saved crusts. Maybe make a bread and date pudding if she could stretch the remaining sugar ration? It would mean resorting to the foul saccharine in their tea.

She was weighing out the pudding ingredients when she heard the click of the latch. Her stomach lurched. How was she going to handle this? She had to support him over Lynette's disappearance but, if they had a battle over the pheasants, it would make that so much harder. Parenting clearly wasn't all picnics by the river on a sunny day, and she was halfway to signing up for a lifetime's commitment. Alone.

Cliff seemed to be taking an age to come in, and, with a heavy heart, May swung open the door. On one leg, a boot half off, he was struggling to steady the three eggs he was holding in his cap.

'I wasn't sure when you'd be back, so I helped Mr Arrowsmith with the hens. He gave me these.' He looked at her uncertainly. He had straw in his hair, the tattered jacket he wore was too short in the sleeves and he smelt of the henhouse. He's like a scarecrow, she thought, taking the eggs from him.

'Come here.' She put an arm around his shoulders in a lop-sided hug. 'Thank you. I know Mr Arrowsmith will be grateful. He finds it hard to fit in my work when I'm away.'

He'd helped Tom of his own volition. The curmudgeonly old devil wouldn't be able to find fault with that.

She put the eggs on the dresser. 'I'll use one of these for the bread pudding.'

They sat at the table with steaming cups of tea. Cliff looked down, running a nail along the pattern on the oilcloth. 'Did you find her?'

May told him about the journey on roads clogged with military vehicles. Usually he was eager to hear what she'd seen, but this time he just nodded.

'I met Mrs Wallbanks—'

'Did you see my house?'

Hell. The houses were just heaps of matchwood and it was impossible to identify individual homes.

'Mrs Wallbanks's house was the only one that seemed unharmed.'

His face fell.

'Is Mrs W all right?' he asked. 'She used to look after me sometimes when Mum was out.'

Before May could reply he went on, 'Didn't she know where Mum was? She always knew everything – Mum called her a nosy ol' biddy.'

'She wasn't sure, but she sent her love to you.' She felt her face flush at the lie and dipped her head to sip the hot tea. 'While I was in the city, a doodlebug flew over.'

Cliff stared at her, eyes wide. 'Did you see it? Did the engine stop?'

'It flew on, thank goodness.'

'Was it scary?'

'A bit. But there wasn't time to be frightened – it was like a big black crow flying over.'

She told him about asking at the police station.

Cliff sat very still. May added hastily, 'They're often asked about missing people in wartime.' Damn. Why didn't she think? This was like tiptoeing across quicksand.

Sitting close together at the table, cooking smells filling the kitchen, the scene reminded her of a day soon after he'd been evacuated. He'd come home from school white-faced and silent. She'd not pestered him, there had still been a distance between them and he had yet to learn to trust her. She'd discovered a bit about his background from the things he'd said, and was appalled at the way he'd been left in an empty house while his mother went about her business.

She was at the stove stirring a rabbit stew when he'd blurted out his question. 'What is a whorehouse, Auntie May?'

The wooden spoon slipped from her fingers and splashed into the saucepan. Thankful that she had her back to him, she made a show of replacing the lid and rinsing the spoon, before sitting next to him at the table.

'Why do you want to know that, Cliff,' she asked, trying to keep her voice even.

He told her in a rush, his words tumbling together, 'Buster Johnson. I thought we'd be pals, both coming from the docks an' all, but 'e's a bugger.'

She bit her lip. The way he said it, like a navvy, was incongruous in this slight child in hand-me-downs.

'Please don't swear, Cliff. What did Buster do?' She knew the boy. Older than Cliff, big and raw boned, she was sure he'd bully younger ones given the chance. In the cramped village school, the children were in mixed-age classes and there was no way of protecting the youngest from being intimidated by their older peers.

'I was tellin' 'em, me mum works in a docks warehouse, but Buster started larfin' an' yelling, "A warehouse? Whorehouse more like." I didn't know what he meant, but all the other kids copied him, larfin' an' pointing at me.' May saw the glisten of tears as he bowed his head.

He mumbled that Mrs Parrot had to box the ears of a couple of the lads before the hubbub died down. No one would confess how it started and the whole class was to miss playtime for a week as punishment.

The original teacher who'd come with the evacuees joined up shortly after arriving in the village. Mrs Parrot, the local schoolmistress, was left to cope with a big class, many of them belligerent city children. Her only methods of control were physical punishment or detention, and it was an open secret that the timid little woman was frightened of her pupils.

Crossing her fingers under the table, May told him that sometimes, when men were away from home, they liked to have someone to kiss and cuddle with. 'Maybe they are frightened of what's ahead of them in the war, or maybe they are just lonely, we will never know. But your mum helps them to feel less scared or alone for a little while.'

He'd seemed to accept it, and, from then on, they only referred to his mother's occupation as "war work".

Now, another dilemma. How much should she say about Lynette's disappearance?

Cliff was fidgeting, desperate to know about his mother.

'A very nice policeman, PC Wicks, is trying to trace your mother's address. He'll write when he's checked the records.'

Coward, she told herself at Cliff's crestfallen expression, but she couldn't say Lynette might be dead. If she was, would the authorities let Cliff stay with her?

He turned to her, his face pale and anxious. 'If we can't find her, you won't be able to adopt me will you?'

He looked so pathetic. A lonely child longing for roots.

'It's early days, Cliff. Let's give the police a chance. Everything is muddled up in the war. People lose touch. We'll just hope we get some news soon.'

She desperately wanted Cliff to be her son but, if Lynette turned up, could there be another bridge to cross: would Cliff decide he wanted to go back to her, leaving May alone again?

'Come on. You lay the table and I'll dish up the liver. The pudding's nearly done.'

Every day when he got back from school, Cliff crashed into the kitchen and asked whether there had been a letter from PC Wicks.

Looking at him, collar askew, knees beneath his shorts burnt an angry red from the wind, eyes full of hope, she wanted nothing more than to make things right for him. She dreaded telling him there was no news and seeing his disappointment.

As the boy was so concerned about finding his mother, she hadn't mentioned the pheasants. They'd made several good meals and a pot of stock, helping to conserve the rations.

Chapter 5

May ran through her report for the WI Annual Meeting while she got on with her work in the poultry yard. Isabella Potts had never forgiven her for being elected President the previous year. Isabella had ruled the branch for years and, since being ousted, she and her cronies had developed a habit of sniping in stage whispers during meetings.

May remembered proudly announcing that Cliff had broken all records for collecting old newspapers. The papers were sold on to pay for wool to be knitted into comforts for the Forces. As May read out a letter from a CO thanking the members, Isabella hissed, 'That urchin's got a penchant for ferreting out people's property. It's in his blood.'

Trying not to falter, May requested a round of applause for the collectors and knitters. The enthusiastic response had been very gratifying. Now, the Annual Meeting had come round again. Rumour had it Isabella was planning a comeback and the dreaded election was imminent. Last year had surely been a fluke; she'd only agreed to put her name forward to give the election a sense of fairness and could still recall her amazement when she'd won.

Mucking-out a henhouse, she imagined standing up in front of the members and accepting election defeat from a gloating Isabella. A bubble of defiance welled up. Meetings had had a much better atmosphere this last year. Some of that must be down to her.

She shoved the pitchfork hard into a pile of straw, flung it in the wheelbarrow and bumped it savagely across the rutted yard to the dung heap.

Leaning the empty barrow against the wooden partition in the barn, she took a deep breath of the summery scent from the hay stacked beyond and relaxed. She would do her best to hold on to her position tonight. Not just for the sake of the members, but because she enjoyed it.

Cliff wasn't back by the time she changed for the meeting. She chose her charcoal costume, which had a straight skirt but, thanks to the dim-out, no one would see it hitched high as she cycled.

Had she got everything? Report, bag, torch? Drat. She'd snagged one of her best stockings. She couldn't sit on the stage with a ladder on view to everyone. She ran upstairs.

Coming down after finding her only replacement, she found Cliff in the kitchen.

'I thought you'd be at your meeting,' he said, avoiding her eye.

She had a sense of déjà vu. 'Where have you been, Cliff?'

'Just out.' He kept his eyes downcast. 'What's for me tea?'

'Where? I need to know – I'm responsible for you.' She sounded like Isabella. 'Tell me when I get back, I'm late.' Pulling on her coat, she added, 'There's a rabbit casserole in the oven.'

As she let herself out, she trod on something soft. A brace of pheasants. This had to stop. Tom Arrowsmith wouldn't hesitate to sack her, family or not, if his pheasants were being poached.

Most of the WI members were in the chilly room when May arrived. She was flustered and dishevelled and nipped into the outside privy. She pulled off her beret and, in the weak light, used her side combs to tidy her hair. Squinting into the cracked mirror, she dabbed on a touch of pink lipstick. Feeling nervous, but presentable, she entered the room, mounted the steps and took her seat centre-stage. Would this be the last time she conducted a meeting?

The membership gave her report rousing applause. The elections were to follow. The Secretary, Doreen Douglas, announced that there were two candidates for President; May was up against Isabella.

Dressed for a wedding, her rival began her speech. May tried not to let her eyes wander in the direction of the faded poster, which had caused so much resentment when she'd pinned it up during the reign of Queen Isabella. It was one of a batch and, after a meeting, Doreen had asked May to choose a couple to display in the room. The walls were already plastered with food charts, exhortations to dig for victory and to make do and mend, but she'd squeezed in a dramatic picture of a woman and child avoiding being run down in the blackout because they'd eaten carrots. Not finding space for a second poster, she'd looked around until she spotted the ideal position: at the side of the stage, facing the hall.

It was at the following meeting that tittering began amongst the audience as the President took her seat. Isabella had chosen one of her more flamboyant outfits that day: a cerise pink dress with navy accessories and a newly acquired pink feather stuck rakishly in her navy hat. More like someone you'd see on a city street than a country village. Divining she was the butt of a joke, Isabella brazened it out until the refreshment interval. May saw her surreptitiously check what had been out of her eye-line and, ostensibly busying herself serving tea, she didn't miss the thundercloud look on their leader's face as she read,

*To Dress Extravagantly In War Time Is Worse Than Bad Form,
It Is Unpatriotic.*

Her lips twitched at the memory, although hostilities had worsened from the moment Isabella discovered who'd pinned up the poster.

The laborious speech continued, with Isabella undermining successes achieved on May's watch. 'Of course, the newspaper collection received a courteous response from the army this year – the powers that be are concerned that everyone will stop making an effort, as we've been doing it so long. They are using the personal approach as a way of stimulating renewed effort. My contacts at Regional HQ tell me every branch received a thank you letter.'

There were mutters of surprise amongst the audience. May kept her face immobile. Treat it with the contempt it deserved. Isabella would love a reaction.

She stopped listening. Her mind was on what Cliff had been up to. If those pheasants came from Elem Farm woods, it could be the final straw for her and Tom. She could spend the rest of the war working in a munitions factory. Surely the boy wouldn't be poaching. She'd taught him better, hadn't she?

'I'll now collect the ballot papers.' Doreen made her way around the hall.

May stared over the heads of the audience at the green and white lampshades, shaped like coolie hats, dangling from the roof. They swayed, pendulum-like, in the draught.

'Thank you, ladies,' said Doreen. 'The Treasurer and I will count the votes.'

Get a move on. May felt beads of sweat on her forehead and smiled ruefully at Isabella, who ignored her.

'Well, there's no doubt. By a majority,' Doreen said, 'Mrs Sheppard retains the post.'

May stood up and reached out a shaky hand to Isabella. After a fleeting touch of a flaccid hand, Isabella left the stage.

May was freewheeling down the hill towards home without being able to remember any of the rest of the meeting. Elated, she tugged the combs from her hair and laughed aloud.

Too soon, she reached the cottage gate. A sense of foreboding descended. The pheasant issue had to be addressed.

Chapter 6

In the drizzly half-light, last night's elation was forgotten. The confrontation had been put off again because Cliff was in bed early, but it hung above her like the grey clouds overhead.

How did real parents cope with their children? May carried feed to the quiet corner where one of her favourite hens, Gracie, had chicks.

It was late in the year for chicks and most of the hens left on the farm in winter were slow laying. They were mostly only kept for the Christmas market and a new batch was bought in for spring. Gracie was prolifically broody and May saved her again and again from the seasonal cull, pleading her maternal value rather than her laying qualities.

The chicken coop was inside a wire pen but it was not right; the wire was bent. Something had forced its way underneath. She looked closer. The coop's hatch cover had been wrenched away. Claw and teeth marks pointed to only one culprit: a fox. Bits of yellow down were scattered around. She ran to the coop and reached in.

'Ow!' Gracie pecked the back of her hand, drawing blood. This was not like the gentle dignified creature who came to call. Was the hen injured? May tipped out some meal and stepped back. Slowly, Gracie emerged and began to peck at the feed. She seemed to have a few missing feathers but, otherwise, appeared unharmed. May moved towards the coop. The hen flew at her, squawking. She'd have to fetch some gloves; something was very wrong. As she was about to turn away, a single bedraggled chick emerged from the hatch. Gracie swept

24

it under her wing and glared at May.

In the couple of hours she had off in the afternoon, May cycled into the village to post some letters. Pulling up beside the shop-cum-post office, she heard voices from the pathway around the corner.

'That's right, Cliff Erwin. When he came to the village, he was a little savage. Stealing and getting into all sorts.' Isabella's voice. 'You had to warn him, didn't you, Ephraim?'

'Ah, 'e—'

The bike clattered as she flung it against the wall. How dare they. She seized her bag and stalked round the corner. David Mountjoy was striding away up the path, lifting his hat.

She ignored the pleasantries and saw the shock on Isabella's face turn to affront when she said, 'What were you saying about Cliff?'

'Mr Mountjoy were—' Ephraim began.

'We were having a private conversation with the Squire,' said Isabella, her mouth snapping like a rattrap. 'Come on Ephraim, we need to get back. You're on duty tonight.'

Ephraim hesitated, nodded to May and followed his wife up the street.

May attacked the hall floor. Suds sloshed across the black and white tiles and she wrung out the water, twisting the mop violently. She could barely remember her conversation with the postmistress, Ephraim's sister, Victoria. She'd been in no mood for the woman's usual petty-minded prying and gave short shrift. Another Potts in the enemy camp. Too bad.

Setting the chairs upside down on the table, she started on the kitchen floor. What did she know of Ephraim before he became an ARP Warden? Seth had grown up knowing him.

She remembered him saying it couldn't have been much fun working under Ephraim at the quarry. He was the foreman and had a reputation even then, for being over-pedantic.

Running the carpet sweeper over the rug in the sitting room, she recollected that, sometime between Seth's death and the outbreak of war, Ephraim had left his job in a hurry. It was whispered he'd received a golden handshake, but that was unsubstantiated gossip that could have been put about by the Potts themselves. Rumours were rife in Parva and it was wise to treat them with scepticism.

She walked backwards down the stairs, using a brush to sweep the treads. What had Ephraim and Isabella got hold of about Cliff? Was it the poaching? Had they passed it on to the Squire?

Poaching from the Squire's estate was far worse than from Tom's farm. Temporarily removed from Crompton Park, now a military hospital, David Mountjoy and his family were living in the Lodge for the duration. Not only did he still control the woods and parkland that had been in his family for generations, he was also a magistrate.

There was nothing left to clean and she had to face the ticking time bomb delivered in the afternoon post.

The envelope was brown and typewritten and the only clue to the sender was the Southampton postmark. She flipped the letter over and over as she sipped tea from one of her favourite cups. She and Seth had unpacked the bluebell-patterned tea service a few days before their wedding. The table at the farm had been deep in presents, wrapping paper and string. How happy they'd been, looking forward to living in their little cottage and discussing the prospect of starting a family after a few years.

That was not to be, but things change and fate had given her the prospect of becoming a parent. This letter could reveal how easy, or difficult, that was going to be.

She slit open the envelope with the vegetable knife. At the top of the letter was the Southampton City Police crest.

Dear Madam

Further to your visit to Southampton Police Station some weeks ago, I have made further enquiries regarding the whereabouts of Mrs Lynette Erwin.

Having consulted the records from the Millbrook area, it seems all the casualties from the bombed flats that were the last known residence of Mrs Erwin, were elderly people.

I regret that I can find no further information regarding Mrs Erwin's current domicile. Should I hear of anything that may help her son to trace his mother in the future, I will write again.

I remain your obedient servant.

Yours faithfully,

PC William Wicks

As she shut in the hens for the night, her mind churned with the possibilities the letter held for Cliff and herself.

Gracie was still protecting her chick; May had mentally christened him Lucky.

'You make a better mother than Lynette Erwin, any day,' she told the hen.

'Auntie May?'

Cliff had come up behind her.

'What were you saying to Gracie?' he asked.

'Nothing special – I chat to her all the time. She's a good listener.' Even as she smiled, she felt heat in her face but she

27

hoped, in the gloaming, Cliff wouldn't notice. 'I'm finished. If you get my bike, I'll lock the gate.'

The lad gave her a long look but said nothing and strode off to fetch the bike. As she watched him walk away, May noted ruefully that the gap between his shorts and his wellingtons was widening daily.

Chapter 7

'How did he take it?' Rose glanced over her shoulder towards the kitchen door. Cliff was outside in the lavatory.

Rose was the only person who knew about the hoped-for adoption. She was a loyal friend and May's only confidante. She tried to describe Cliff's pinched face and haunted expression when she'd told him his mother had disappeared without trace.

'At least we know she wasn't harmed when the flats were bombed,' she'd said, trying to offer him some comfort.

The bleak prospect of the childless life she feared had brought the pricking of tears to her own eyes but she forced them down, put an arm around Cliff and focussed on lifting his spirits.

'Let's give it until the New Year before we do anything. PC Wicks and Mrs Wallbanks know we're looking for her.'

When she'd finished telling Rose the story she said, 'I made a jam roly-poly for pudding and that seemed to take his mind off it.'

Rose laughed. 'Boys and their bellies.'

The latch rattled and Cliff came in, rubbing his arms. 'It's flippin' cold out there,' he said, stretching out his hands towards the open range before sitting down at the end of the table, picking up his pen and resuming his homework.

Facing May from the other armchair, Rose said quietly, 'Have you heard the news? The RAF finally sank *The Tirpitz*.' She stared into the flames. 'I know they're the enemy, but my heart goes out ter those poor matelots. Drowned, or burned alive.'

May sighed to herself. Rose was her own worst enemy. A compassionate soul who spoke her mind, she often landed herself in trouble. May dreaded a recurrence of the situation they'd had when Rose vociferously empathised with the aircrew of the Heinkel that crashed on the outskirts of the village.

She looked across at Cliff. He seemed to be engrossed in his composition – sucking the end of his pen in between scribbling words in his exercise book.

'You know you can say anything to me, Rose. Len being in the Navy must really bring their suffering home, but be careful you don't antagonise your in-laws again.'

May recollected trying to engineer a reconciliation with Len's parents who'd refused to speak to their daughter-in-law. Rose had been right, many people had been more concerned about the loss of two cows killed when the plane crashed, than about the loss of the German crew. Nonetheless, it proved a marathon task convincing Len's fiercely patriotic parents that Rose's sympathy for the dead wasn't disloyal to their son. Unfortunately, they had never since seemed to welcome their daughter-in-law.

'It's all right, May, I'm not going ter spout my views round the village again,' Rose said.

The picture of the twisted plane was imprinted on May's memory. She could still recall the smell of the acrid smoke hanging in the air when she discovered Cliff, a bucket at his feet, taking half crowns from the swarm of sightseers who descended on the site. About to ask what he was up to, she was pushed aside by Ephraim shouldering his way through the crowd. Red in the face, he'd growled that Cliff was always up to no good and had now turned to fleecing the public.

His jaw had dropped as Cliff held the bucket out and asked him whether he would take the money and make sure it went to build more Spitfires.

Unfortunately, looking stupid in front of an applauding crowd had only served to strengthen Ephraim's animosity towards Cliff.

'...I just want this slaughter ter end,' Rose was saying.

Cliff was listening, pen poised.

'Just think how far we've come,' said May. 'The war can't go on much longer. Paris is free and nearly all the Americans have gone from around here.' She turned to Cliff. 'Not so much free candy now, is there?'

Cliff saluted and drawled, 'No, Mam.'

Rose stood up to leave.

'What are you two doing for Christmas? You're welcome ter come over ter us.'

Thinking about Christmas didn't hurt like it had when she'd been on her own after Seth died. Then, she had wanted to spend the day anywhere but in their cottage. Now, with Cliff, it had become a family occasion they both looked forward to.

'Thanks Rose, we'll think about it. I'll invite Tom here, but he tends to avoid the cottage. I expect he'll go to his sister in Dorchester for Christmas dinner. We'll both have to work – the animals have to be fed and Tom is very fair about giving the land girls time off.' May pulled on Seth's old mac.

The women walked down the path to Rose's bike propped against the gate.

Rose put a hand on May's arm. 'Don't fret about this Lynette business. You and Cliff belong together. It'll work out.'

She sighed. 'Thanks. I've got a few weeks' breathing space before I have to make any decisions.'

She watched Rose's bicycle until the white mudguard disappeared into the night.

Chapter 8

Rain had been incessant for days and work had become an endurance. May was sick of wet coats and boots clogging up the kitchen. With Christmas approaching, the remaining hens had to be culled for market. The job of choosing which were to go was a task May detested only slightly less than wringing necks.

'You'll be safe, have no fear,' she told Gracie. The hen's wet feathers gave her a bedraggled look, but she cocked her head and her yellow eye watched May as if she were following every word.

Carrying her pitchfork, May closed up the wire pen. 'That's you done, Gracie. One of the land girls will shut you up tonight. I've got to spend the afternoon organising the Christmas Fair.' She smiled as the rust-red bird turned her back and headed for her coop.

The WI ran the fair every Christmas. As usual, members were making cakes and puddings to sell. May was donating a couple of jars of the jam she'd bought on ration. Cliff complained he wasn't allowed to eat it, but it was from the communal preserving sessions and would sell at a premium.

The memory of the smell of strawberries bubbling away in the makeshift jam factory dispelled the dreariness of the waterlogged fields on the ride home and took her mind off the rain dribbling under her collar.

Head down under a soaked headscarf, she dashed to the back door and stopped dead. Someone was sheltering in the covered way between the house and the lavatory.

'You made me jump,' she said.

Wearing a camelhair coat, with a navy pillbox hat perched over drooping blonde victory rolls, the woman turned to face her.

'I've been waitin' for ages, Mrs Sheppard.'

The dampness on May's back felt like a sheet of ice.

'Mrs Erwin.' Her voice sounded too high. She cleared her throat. 'I wasn't expecting you.'

The woman strode in as soon as the door was open, forcing May back into the rain. Inside, Lynette headed straight for the range and, while May peeled off her mac and kicked off her muddy boots, she warmed her gloveless hands.

'Please sit down and let me take your coat,' May said.

For a second, Lynette looked wary then, pulling her coat protectively around her, she sat at the end of the kitchen table. 'I'll keep it on, ta. It's lovely an' warm an' I got chilled to the bone waitin' out there.' She stroked the soft caramel-coloured fabric.

Something about the fine texture told May it was real camelhair. Half-belted, with horn buttons, it was clearly a very expensive coat and far too big for Lynette. With its padded shoulders, May couldn't dispel the image of a black market spiv sitting at her table.

'I'll make tea,' she said. 'The kettle won't take long. If you'd let me know you were coming…'

'Didn't know when I'd get a lift,' Lynette said. 'Don't mind if I smoke, do you?' She opened her navy handbag and took out a pack of Lucky Strikes. 'Got a match?'

May lit a taper from the range and held it to the cigarette.

Lynette breathed out a trail of pungent smoke. With her collar turned up and her eyes narrowed from the smoke, she seemed to fancy herself as a film star. 'You don't smoke do you?' she said, her nose pointing to the ceiling.

'No.' May plonked the ashtray, which she kept for guests, on the table, noting that Lynette's snooty demeanour was marred by the layer of caked powder that coated her, admittedly attractive, features.

The boxy handbag, standing on the corner of the table, looked new. Soft leather. The kind May hadn't seen anywhere outside of the fashion pages, since the beginning of the war. Black market? A Yank splashing his money around?

Deliberately, she laid out the everyday cups and saucers.

'Do you take sugar?'

'Ooh, yes please.'

'I'm afraid it will have to be these,' she said, thumping down the bottle of saccharine and feeling a pang of satisfaction as she saw Lynette's disappointed expression. She set the tea on the table and sat opposite Lynette, who puffed away and stared into space.

She said, trying to put a sarcastic tone in her voice, 'Cliff is well.'

Lynette's eyes flickered over to her. 'Yes, April Wallbanks told me.'

'You knew I'd been looking for you?' Why hadn't Lynette made contact as soon as she'd heard? Cliff had been fretting for weeks.

'The police thought you might have been caught in the Millbrook bombings.'

At the words, Lynette's tea, halfway to her mouth, slopped on to the tablecloth. May rose to get a cloth. 'Cliff was very worried about you until we heard that you weren't one of the casualties.' It wasn't quite the truth, but Lynette deserved to feel guilty.

'Why d'you go to the coppers?' Lynette's voice rose and

pink spots appeared through the powder on her cheeks. She took a long drag on her cigarette.

Why antagonise her? She was going to ask her to part with her son for good. Upsetting her was not the way to go about it. May mopped the table and sat down, hiding her trembling hands in her lap.

'Mrs Erwin,' she began, taking a deep breath. 'We hadn't heard from you for so long—'

Lynette started to protest.

May kept her the tone of her voice low. 'I can't imagine what it was like living in a city so relentlessly bombed. We've only had one direct hit here, and I was shocked when I saw your old street. Moving around and losing all your belongings must've been terrible for you.'

Lynette seized on it. 'You've no idea...'

'You must be so glad that Cliff was safely out of it?'

'A course.' Lynette replied hastily. 'You've done a marvellous job, Mrs Sheppard.'

'Cliff' is very happy here. He's really taken to country living.'

'That's good. And I'm sure it's all down to you,' said Lynette twitching her scarlet lips into a sweet smile that didn't reach her eyes. 'You'd make a wonderful mum.'

This was too easy. She was up to something. Did she know May wanted to keep Cliff?

'Have you planned where you'll live when the war ends and Cliff comes home?' May held her breath.

Lynette exhaled and narrowed her eyes as the smoke drifted up. 'I'm not sure what me plans are at the present moment.'

Damn. 'It would help Cliff to know what's in store for him – school and so on,' she gabbled.

'He's okay in the village school, isn't he?'

36

Lynette was enjoying this. Making her squirm. She plunged on, 'It's unsettling for him. His evacuee pals are talking about going back to Southampton, and he doesn't know what to say. He feels out on a limb. As a mother, I'm sure you can understand that. He needs some idea of where his future lies.'

Lynette's smile faded. 'That is something I want to talk to you about.' She stubbed out her cigarette. 'I wondered if you'd be able to keep Cliff a bit longer – after the war's over, I mean. I won't be set up for some while, and also—'

'Yes, yes, Mrs Erwin I would. I'd like to adopt Cliff. He's very keen and all we need is your agreement.' She stopped. Lynette's eyes had lit up and a sly grin was creeping across her face.

'I see. Want him for good do you? I don't know about that. Losing my son for ever...'

May could have bitten off her tongue. She'd let the cat out of the bag and given away the lever of indebtedness she'd tried to wield.

'I suppose we might be able to do a deal.' Lynette smirked.

A deal? Sell her son? Before she had a chance to say anything, Lynette went on, 'As it happens I have a favour I want meself.' She stood up. 'I might see meself clear to sign Cliff over if you agree to take this off me hands for a couple a years.'

She pulled open her coat. May stared at the distended belly, speechless.

Two things happened simultaneously: a car horn sounded outside and the back door opened.

Chapter 9

Cliff shoved open the back door. An afternoon off school – as long as Auntie May didn't make him go back.

'I hurt me knee — *Mum*?'

His mother was standing at the kitchen table, but, as soon as she saw him, she sat down, tugging her coat round her.

The room smelt of smoke and a red-stained cigarette end was squashed into the ashtray.

'Hello, Cliffy,' his mum said.

Auntie May was on her feet. 'What have you done to your knee?'

Blood had seeped through the bandage. He unbuttoned his mac and Auntie May took it from him. What was his mother doing here? She hadn't come to get him, had she?

His legs felt funny and he grabbed a chair and plonked down on it. Auntie May pulled his leg straight and began fussing with the bandage.

'Football again?' she asked.

'Tackle,' he answered, without really knowing what he said. Was she going to take him?

'Your mother has come to see how you are, Cliff.'

That's what she'd told Auntie May, but she could fool her – she was good at lying. What would he do if she sprang it on them that he had to go back?

He glanced at his mother. She looked the same – yellowy hair under a hat he'd never seen before. The collar of her coat was turned up even though the kitchen was warm and her face was shiny where her powder had cracked.

'How are you, Cliffy?' she said, putting on a smile.

'Awlright... thank you.'

Auntie May unwrapped the bandage. Mrs Parrot was no good at first aid. She just stuck on a bandage and sent you home.

'You'll live,' Auntie May said. 'I'll get another bandage from upstairs.'

If she was going to take him, she'd tell him now they were alone. He remembered those urgent whispers hissing in his ear as she pinched something from a shop and hid it in her pocket, 'Keep quiet. Say a word and I'll box yer ears.'

He stared at the floor. His mouth felt dry. He couldn't get a drink, he felt frozen to the chair. His mother drummed her fingers on the table. He heard her breathe in and waited for the words he was terrified of hearing.

'So, yer like it here do you?'

He released his breath. 'Yeah, it's great. I've got tons a friends and I help Auntie May all the time,' he gabbled. 'And I collect the eggs at the farm – they wouldn't be able ter manage wiv out me.'

'Hmm.' She fiddled with a button on her coat. 'You like football then? Never knew you could play.'

How would she know – he was five when he left, and she'd only seen him once since.

Auntie May's footsteps sounded on the stairs. She'd say it now.

But she held up a blue handbag. 'D'you like my bag?'

It could have been a sack for all Cliff cared.

She went on, 'A present. Real leather. Matches me best shoes.'

Auntie May opened the kitchen door.

'Right,' she said, dabbing something bright yellow on his

knee before rolling on the clean bandage. 'It might sting for a little while, but it's only a graze.' She tied up the ends. 'If it wasn't such a foul day, I'd send you back to school but, as your mother's here...'

The car horn sounded again. A long blast.

His mother used the voice she put on to make people think she was posh. 'My lift. The Captain will have finished his business. He needs to get back. He's on duty.'

'But Cliff's just arrived.' Auntie May's voice was sharp. 'You can't go, we haven't—'

His mum said something about writing to her and she took it the terms were acceptable. Were they sending him back? Or… was it something good?

'Auntie May, what about the adop—'

'It's all right, Cliff, I'll tell you later,' she said, rushing to follow his mother to the door.

'The rain's stopped. Good, sports cars are no fun in the wet,' his mother said, laughing and marching on towards the gate.

Cliff tried to jam his shoes on as he ran behind them.

'By the way,' his mother called over her shoulder, 'there were some dead birds on the step. It turned me up, lookin' at corpses. I put them in your lavvy.'

Auntie May didn't take any notice, just pushed Cliff ahead of her, nearer his mother, who was standing at the gate watching something up the lane.

Old Potty's missus was cycling towards them. She was staring at his mum but, when she got near, she flicked her gaze away. She mumbled something as she rode past.

His mum shrugged. Cliff squeezed past her to look at the car. It was shiny red, like a pillar-box, with a canvas roof and a spare wheel on the boot.

He was trying to see the badge when Auntie May said, 'Say

40

goodbye, Cliff.'

His mother was already in the car and he bent down to speak through the window. The driver, wearing American Army uniform, raised a hand in salute and started the car.

Cliff tried to return the salute, but it turned into a half-hearted wave as he stepped back when the car revved up. His mum looked at him and put on her red smile.

'Bye, Cliffy.'

Chapter 10

As they walked back up the path, Cliff implored May to tell him about the adoption.

She needed space to think. If she told him what he was longing to hear, she committed herself to taking on a baby. She knew nothing about babies. How would she feed it? Care for it? What about work? She couldn't bike with a pram. The farm was only half a mile away, but what about in snow? She hadn't asked Lynette when the baby was due, although by the look of her, it must be within a few weeks.

'What did Mum say – can you adopt me?' he said again.

How could she handle this? He needed an answer. As they went to go indoors, she remembered something Lynette had said and snatched open the lavatory door. Two pheasants lay on the stone floor.

'What are these?' she shouted.

Cliff's shocked expression hit her like a slap. He mumbled something inaudible, yanked open the back door and left it swinging. After the sound of his shoes being thrown on the floor, the stairs door slammed.

She slumped on to the wooden lavatory seat. She was no better than Lynette. All the boy needed was reassurance about his future, and she attacked him about bloody pheasants. She pushed the cock bird with her foot. Its head flopped sideways. The brilliant red and iridescent green feathers were dulled in death, and its eye seemed to be closed against her alone.

She had no one to talk to; Rose was working in the munitions factory, Tom thought she was mad taking Cliff on as an evacuee – how he would react to another child she had no idea, but it wouldn't be good. There was no one else.

She was shivering. When had the rain started again? She left the lavatory and closed the door on the birds.

When she had stoked up the range and made two steaming cups of cocoa, she called Cliff.

His face was pinched – were those tear stains? The bandage on his knee had slipped and hung down his leg at half-mast.

She enveloped him in her arms. The tip of his ear was cold against her cheek. All the sensible things she had planned to say evaporated. She'd do anything for this abandoned child.

They sat either side of the roaring range. The comforting smell of chocolate wafted from the cocoa as they drank. Cliff was silent, his eyes wary over the rim of the cup.

'I'm sorry your mother couldn't stay longer.' May said.

'She don't care about me, does she?'

'She has her own way of doing things. I'm sure she cares but—'

'Will she let you adopt me?'

What she said now, she could never go back on.

'She says she'll write to me giving permission, but—'

'So you can?' He was half off his chair, cup canted towards the rug.

'Mind the cocoa. Yes – so long as we get the letter.'

'Hurray.' Cliff stood the cup on the fender and flung himself at May.

Emerging from the bear hug, she studied him. He had a grin as wide as a banana; the happiest she'd ever seen him.

'There is something else, Cliff.'

His smile faded. 'Them pheasants.'

'No. Well, yes, but not right now. Your mum, she… well,

you know what she does?'

'Her war work?'

'Yes. She… she's going to have another baby—'

He stared at her, face blank.

'That's why she's givin' me away?'

Damn. She'd handled it all wrong.

'No, Cliff. She wants me, us, to look after the baby.'

He stared at her. 'We're gettin' a *baby*?'

How absurd was this? If Seth hadn't died this could be about her own child and her own baby. She stopped her thoughts dead. Cliff soon would be her own child.

She said, 'Apparently, yes, we're getting a baby.'

A knock on the door as darkness fell brought welcome relief. She was feeling overwhelmed by Cliff's incessant bombardment of questions: where would the baby sleep, could he give it a bottle, would it be his brother or sister? Most of the questions she hadn't even considered, and they underlined the immensity of what she'd been forced into.

'Don't say anything about the baby,' she whispered to Cliff as she went to the door. 'Hello, Doreen. Come in.'

Doreen brought the smell of the damp afternoon with her.

'Oh no. I've forgotten the Christmas Fair meeting, haven't I?' May said.

Doreen, May's right hand in running the WI said, 'Don't worry, hen, I covered for you. Believe it or not, Isabella warned me you might not be there.'

'Isabella?'

'She saw you with Cliff. Evidently he'd injured his leg, and she thought you might not make it to the meeting.'

Isabella had impressive eyesight – she'd seemed to be staring at Lynette.

'That's a turn up for the book.'

'Completely out of character. You'd better watch out – she might be up to something,' said Doreen.

'Probably going to report me to the HQ for non-attendance,' said May with a laugh. 'Cup of tea?'

'No thanks, I won't stay. I just wanted to see whether Cliff was all right – and it seems he is.'

Cliff was reading *The Beano*, curled up by the fire, his injured knee forgotten.

'Just a knock at football,' said May. 'He'll be fine tomorrow. What happened at the meeting?'

Doreen handed her a carbon copy of the minutes she'd taken. 'All organised, as far as I can see. Unless you want to change anything, it's all in place.'

One job dealt with. Now all May had do was organise her life around a babe in arms.

Chapter 11

Saturday morning, the day before Christmas Eve, was busy. The WI Christmas Fair opened at ten o'clock, and members had been busy in the village hall since eight – setting up tables, laying out stalls and getting the temperamental urn to boil.

May felt a sense of pride as she looked around the hall. Brightly painted newspaper chains criss-crossed the ceiling and holly and mistletoe decorated window ledges and lamps. The piece-de-resistance was a fir tree, donated by the Squire and decorated with red and green crackers made by the schoolchildren. The scent of pine seemed to bring Christmas to life.

All the members had contributed to the Fair. One woman, wearing what were clearly men's suit trousers cut down, was enthusiastically unpacking her homemade shampoo. The green sludge, in assorted bottles and jars, didn't look as if it would swell the funds to a large degree. If no one else bought a bottle, May would have to – just to maintain morale.

She'd reserved the job of ticketing the tombola donations for herself. She'd be able to weed out some of the worst horrors. She had learned that, in the President's job, diplomacy was a priority. She buried a three-legged china sheep, a milk jug with a chipped spout, and a balding fox-fur tippet in the emptied boxes under the table.

Isabella was fussing around her perennial stall, claiming prime position by the doors once again. She sold hand-knitted dolls, tea cosies and potholders, made by the knitting circle, alongside her own striped tank tops that were notoriously unpopular. The cognoscenti came armed with ingenious excuses to sidestep Isabella's pushy sales tactics.

In the kitchen, teacups were being clattered about and minor squabbles were breaking out over which of the biscuits – strictly one per person until they ran out – to put out first. Most were indistinguishable, other than by shape, although Doreen's Crunchies always carried the tang of dripping.

Satisfied with the tombola, May set off to do a final check before opening the doors. She felt a tap on her shoulder. Rose. She looked concerned and drew May aside.

'Cliff's outside. You need ter speak to him. He's in a state and won't tell me why.'

Was he hurt? Had he done something? Got caught poaching? Across the room Isabella was looking pointedly at her watch, in between glaring at Rose, who wasn't a member and, theoretically, shouldn't be in the hall before it opened. May turned her back on Isabella. Rose wasn't one to panic and if she thought it necessary to come in, Cliff must be very upset.

'I've got to check on this lot and get the doors open,' she said. Other stallholders were looking at her expectantly.

'He won't wait. He says he's got ter get back.'

Rose's face was filled with concern. May trusted her judgement. She'd supported her completely when she'd told her about Lynette's baby, calming her panic with generous suggestions.

'You can borrow my old pram,' she'd said. 'And I've hung on ter some baby clothes – just in case – but, ter be honest, that's not likely ter happen, no matter when Len gets back.'

May was embarrassed by the frankness, but grateful for the offer.

'Any help you need, just ask. My two haven't done so bad, so I can't be that terrible a mother. You'll be all right. Look how Cliff's turned out.'

The reassurance went a long way to helping May adjust to the situation and she'd begun to imagine her new role as a mother of two.

She checked quickly round the hall. The kitchen assistants were chatting, their cups and saucers laid out in front of the hatch. Isabella was making minute adjustments to her display and a few others were still rummaging in boxes or shoving empty bags under their tables.

'Doreen, can you take over, please, I've got something I have to attend to.'

Doreen frowned and looked at her watch. 'But…,' she began until, seeing May's face, she said, 'Yes, of course.'

May followed Rose out of the side door. As she pulled it closed, she spotted Isabella staring after her, disapproval written large on her face.

Cliff dashed towards her, shirt-tail hanging below his jacket, socks concertinaed round his ankles.

'I'll leave you to it,' Rose said, and went to join the queue at the front door.

'What is it, Cliff? You said you were coming later. I'm really busy.'

'Me mum's sent—'

'The letter? That could have waited.' Despite her words, May felt a twinge of excitement. Could this be it: permission to adopt Cliff?

'No. It's… It's…'

May's spirits sank. 'What?'

The doors had been opened and people were jostling to get in. The clothes on the jumble stall were a big draw and everyone wanted first pickings.

'I need to be in there. Spit it out, Cliff.'

He gulped before mumbling, 'The baby. It's at home. And it's yellin'.'

Chapter 12

May shook her head. What was he talking about? There'd been no word from Lynette, and she hadn't agreed to take the baby without the woman's formal confirmation that she could adopt Cliff.

'Is your mother there?'

'A Yank brought it. In a jeep. Then he drove off.' Cliff mumbled.

This couldn't be happening.

Cliff was wringing his handkerchief. He said, 'I had to take it. He just put the box in the kitchen and went.'

She said, 'It's all right, Cliff. It's not your fault and you did the right thing coming to get me.'

She couldn't take it in. She had to do something – a baby was alone.

The fog in her brain cleared enough to let her get down to practicalities. 'Take my bike and get home as fast as you can. I'll be right behind you and we'll sort out what's going on.'

Cliff heaved May's bike out from the lean-to. 'You won't be long, will you?' he asked. The bike seemed to dwarf him.

'No. Just go.'

He rode off, standing on the pedals, crouching over the handlebars.

May raced back inside to a barrage of chatter and clatter. She felt utterly disorientated. Where was Rose?

Doreen appeared next her. 'Good, you're back. Are you all right, hen? You look terrible.'

'I've got a problem at home – nothing I can't sort out,' she lied, Doreen wasn't above gossip. 'Have you seen Rose?'

'She volunteered to do your tombola – much to Isabella's disgust.' Doreen raised her eyes. 'You get off. I can cope here.'

'Thanks. I owe you a favour.'

Rose was shaking a metal pail full of folded tickets. 'Five gos for sixpence. Wonderful prizes,' she called.

May ran up just as a boy pushed his sixpence into Rose's hand. Rose held out the bucket, and the boy dipped in, rooting to the bottom.

'What was it, May? Is Cliff all right?'

'She's sent the baby,' May whispered.

'I've got a five,' said the boy.

Rose ignored him.

'But you haven't heard from her, have you?'

'No. But it's in the cottage *in a box*. I don't even know how old it is.' May ran her hand through her hair. 'Can I borrow your bike? Cliff's gone back on mine, but I can't leave him on his own.'

'I've got a *five*,' the boy waved his ticket at Rose. 'Can I 'ave me prize? It's that one.'

Distractedly, May and Rose watched him point to a flat greaseproof packet tied with twine. It contained two of Doreen's greasy biscuits, and they shared a grimace.

'Take the bike,' Rose said. 'I'll sort out some things to bring over later. Forget about this place, it's running like clockwork.'

At that moment, the crash of breaking crockery briefly silenced the hubbub around them. May turned towards the kitchen with consternation.

'Go,' Rose said. Turning back to the stall, she beamed at the boy. 'Right, young man.'

***

She could hear the baby crying before she got to the door. She burst into the kitchen where Cliff was kneeling on the floor, trying to rock an open cardboard box. Her wedding dress had arrived in a box like this. She remembered the prickle of excitement she'd felt as she lifted the lid on a snowfall of satin and lace.

'I can't make it stop,' Cliff said, moving back as May knelt beside the makeshift cradle.

A moth-eaten shawl covered a body that was furiously kicking its legs in time with its yells of frustration. How could such a tiny being produce such a tremendous noise?

Was the baby ill, or just needing attention? An only child, May had had little to do with babies, but her instinct told her this one might be hungry. With relief, she spotted a feeding bottle and a tin of dried milk wedged into a corner of the box.

The baby was lying on its side, face obscured by the white knitted bonnet that had slipped over its face.

'Come on, little one.' She lifted the bundle. It was surprisingly heavier than the feathery hens she picked up every day.

She moved to a chair and breathed in the milky-sick smell of the baby. The crying stopped as she gently unwrapped the shawl.

'Cripes!' So this was why Lynette wouldn't keep the baby. Its brown eyes were brimming. Brown eyes set in a face the colour of the peaty whisky Seth used to drink.

Never had she imagined this.

'It's a darkie,' said Cliff, leaning forward to stare. 'It can't be me mum's.'

Could he be right? Was there some mistake? Different scenarios somersaulted though her head: mix-ups at the hospital; the Yank being asked to take more than one baby.

'Get a grip,' she told herself. She was clutching at straws. It was *Lynette Erwin* they were talking about. A prostitute at the docks. Her baby could be any colour.

Hoping to cover the tremble in her voice, she said, 'It's just a sweet little baby, Cliff. Of course it's your mother's. I expect its father was one of the black Americans.'

He stared at the baby, who was wearing a flannelette nightgown and mittens. May held her breath as it lifted an arm towards Cliff. She watched with relief as he took its fist in his grubby fingers, pulled off the woollen mitten and lightly touched the pink seed-pearl nails.

'It needs its nappy changed,' she said feeling dampness under the little body. 'Go and get a blanket, please, Cliff.'

He pounded upstairs. May felt the softness of the tiny black hand gripping her little finger. 'Your mother never ceases to surprise me,' she said gently, looking down at the child, a smile on her lips. 'What am I going to do with you?'

Cliff spread the blanket on the table. May laid the baby on it, pulled up the nightgown and unpinned a ragged nappy.

Cliff peered in as the nappy fell open.

'A boy!' he said, 'He's my brother.'

'Yes, he is Cliff.' Should she explain about half-brothers? Not now. He knew well enough they didn't share a father.

She began rummaging in the box. 'We need nappies. Was there anything else? A bag or something?'

'No, but I think the Yank said there was a letter.'

May lifted out the hand towel that had been underneath the baby. Below it were two greyish nappies, a vest, another nightdress, a washed-out matinee jacket, a tin of zinc and castor oil ointment and a scruffy brown envelope.

'Let's get him changed,' she said, laying the envelope aside.

The baby squirmed as May struggled with the nappy and its fearsome pin. She gently eased his arms into the fresh nightdress and gingerly turned him on his stomach to lace up the back. He seemed so fragile.

She bundled the wet clothes together. There was going to be a great deal more washing from now on.

Cliff held the baby, as delicately as if he were one of Gracie's chicks, while she rummaged for the bottle in the box. Thick glass, with raised graduations down the side and a rubber teat on top, the bottle was empty, but a scrawled note, on brown tape stuck to the side of the milk tin, read: *4 x 2 fl. ozs. a day*.

When the evacuees first arrived, several mothers came with babies. In an attempt to involve them in the community, they were encouraged to bring their infants along to WI meetings, and May had often been in the kitchen when bottles were made up. She searched her memory for what the women had done, as she tried to decipher the print on the blue and white tin.

The bottle and teat had to be sterilised. She immersed them in boiling water. Likewise the china jug, into which she tipped milk powder using the little metal scoop inside the tin. She added hot water, measured in the bottle. The teat was tricky; the bottle skittered about as she tried to stretch the rubber over its thick rim, and she was scared she'd overturn it and have to start again.

Eventually, it was in place and the bottle cooled in cold water. She dripped a creamy spot on to the back of her hand and dabbed it with her tongue. It was sweet and warmly comforting.

The baby had begun to yell before the bottle was ready and Cliff willingly handed him over. He watched, rapt, as the milk disappeared and the baby gradually lapsed into sleep.

Chapter 13

The contents of May's bottom drawer lay over her bed. Her selection of jumpers and cardigans was fast decreasing. Those that hadn't fallen into holes, or felted up and would only fit Cliff, were shapeless and virtually threadbare. How did it feel to wear something that you, or someone else, hadn't had for at least five years?

She'd sort out the clothes later, the drawer was needed downstairs.

Using a pillow in the bottom, a cut out piece from the mackintosh sheet she'd used when Cliff had first arrived and a pillowcase on top, she made a cosy bed for the baby.

Wrapped in his own shawl, she laid him in the drawer and set it behind the armchair where he'd be warm and out of bright light.

Cliff was occupied with *The Beano.* With a cheese sandwich in one hand, May shook out the contents of the envelope from Lynette. A Ministry of Food pamphlet, a green ration book, a clothing ration book, an ID card, a document folded in three and a handwritten letter on thin, lined paper tumbled on to the table.

First the document. It was the baby's birth certificate. He had been born on the ninth of December. His mother's occupation was shown as housewife. Father unknown. The baby's name was Spencer Erwin.

Two weeks old and she'd parcelled him up like last week's leftovers and sent him off. Was it even legal? But then, all these evacuee children were torn from their families and she'd sent him to join his half-brother. No matter May hadn't actually agreed to take him, Lynette knew her well enough. Knew she'd never leave a child in need.

The scrawled letter was short.

Dear Mrs Sheppard

I'm sending the babys papers so you can get his rations. He was an easy birth and don't cry much. He had the bottle from the beginning.

I'm leaving Blighty to live with my fiances family in the States. He's being invalidid out and we'll marry when he gets there. They are landowners in South Carolina, so I cant take Spence with me.

I'm sure Cliffy will love his little brother. Send him Merry Christmas from me.

Yours truly

Lynette Erwin (Mrs)

P.S. I will write about the adoption when I'm setled.

May snorted and threw the letter down.

Cliff looked up. 'What's that?'

'A letter from your mother.'

'Wos it say?'

'What *does* the letter say, Cliff.' He lapsed into poor English whenever the subject of his mother came up. 'The baby is called Spencer. Your mother wishes you Merry Christmas and—'

'Has she writ about the adoption?' He got to his feet.

How was she to tell him Lynette was moving thousands of miles away?

'Wrote. Has she wrote about the adoption?' he asked, panic in his voice.

May sighed. What did grammar matter?

'She says she'll write when she's settled. The thing is Cliff, she's moving. To America. And she's getting married to an American serviceman.'

'But what about me?' He looked terrified. 'She don't want to take me, does she?'

His eyes filled.

'She hasn't said that. She's going to write again. As I said.'

'I don't want ter go. I want ter be here with you and Spencer.' A tear ran down his face.

She pulled him to her. 'It's all right. You're not going anywhere. We'll sort this out.'

But how?

She put the birth certificate and letter in the dresser cupboard. The cardboard box was outside. She couldn't bear to look at it. A box. For a baby. Perhaps a pine drawer wasn't much better, but it wasn't something to be thrown away after use.

There was a rap on the door. Cliff opened it. Rose was outside, holding the handle of a low, dark blue pram.

'Hello, Cliff.' she said.

May saw her scanning around the kitchen. 'The baby's behind the armchair. Come in quick or he'll be in a draught.'

'I'll leave the pram here – the wheels are a bit muddy,' said Rose. 'Can you give me a hand with these, please, Cliff?' She pulled back the rain cover and revealed a pile of baby clothes and two bulging bags.

'Where did all this come from?' May asked. Surely Rose would have unpicked the boys' outgrown woollies and reknitted the wool into something else? She told Cliff to put the clothes on the table. Rose laid the bags next to them and a satin-edged shawl slid out.

'I'll explain, but first, Bob and Peter are having a game of football down by the pond. If Auntie May says it's all right, Cliff, you could go and join them.'

Cliff looked expectantly at May.

'Yes you can go. Put on your coat and scarf and try not to fall in the pond.'

'Thanks, Mrs Gale,' he said, as he grabbed his coat and rammed on his boots. He slammed the door.

The baby gave a little whimper.

'I must take a gander,' said Rose.

'You'll get a surprise.'

'Don't tell me she's sent you twins?' said Rose with a laugh, pulling back the shawl.

'Almost,' said May.

'Christopher Columbus!' Rose stared at the sleeping baby. She ran her hand tentatively over the cloud of soft black hair. She said, 'Lynette doesn't do things in small measures does she? What are you going ter do?'

'You don't know the half of it,' said May, going to the dresser and taking out the letter. 'Read this.'

They sat at the table, May tapping her fingers while Rose read the letter.

'So, the fiancé isn't the father?'

'I don't think so. I think I'm meant to see that she's got to hide that she's consorted with a black,' May said.

'South Carolina, that's the Deep South – *Gone with the Wind*, country, isn't it?' Rose asked.

'I think that was Georgia, but they act the same as far as I know.'

'You reckon she's found Rhett Butler, then?'

'I don't know. She's film star crazy. I'm just glad she didn't call the baby after Rock Hudson.'

They howled with laughter. Something released inside May and she felt things slide into perspective. She leaned back in her chair and rolled her shoulders. Gradually the tension in the muscles relaxed and the ache in her back eased.

'I've got to tell Tom,' she said, 'and I'm worried about his reaction. I don't know how I'll work once Cliff goes back to school. I'll have to walk and take the baby in the pram. Gosh I'm sorry, I haven't thanked you for it, or the clothes, or even made you some tea. It's only the first day and I've already gone to pot.'

'You sit still,' Rose said. 'I'll put the kettle on. You're welcome ter use the pram and the clothes. I kept them against my better judgement and despite Ephraim demanding to take the pram for salvage. I'm saying it's a loan, although my hopes of having a little girl are fading every month this war drags on. I'm forty next year.'

'I'm sure when Len gets back...' What did she know. Maybe if she'd had children herself...

'Don't fret about me. We need ter think about this baby.' Rose picked up the bottle from beside the sink. 'Did she send enough dried milk?'

'There's a tin of it and she sent his ration book. I'll sort it out after Christmas.'

'That's soon enough. You don't want to face that now. It'll be bad enough walking a brown baby around, never mind Christmas and Tom and—'

May rubbed her shoulders; the ache had begun again.

Chapter 14

Pockets of mist hung between the blackthorn hedges in the lane, occasionally clearing in the open gateways to reveal the fallow corrugated fields beyond. She yawned. Her glove left moisture on her face and, by the time she wheeled her bike into the barn, her headscarf was clammy and limp.

'Morning,' she called to the indistinguishable land girl mucking out the loose boxes while the Clydesdales pulled at their hay.

'Hello,' a voice called back. May could see a turbaned head bobbing around beyond Blossom's roan back. 'I borrowed your barrow. Ours has got a broken wheel. Tom said he'll fix it by tonight. Can you use the skep?'

May sighed. The last thing she felt like doing was heaving around heavy baskets of chicken dung. 'Right,' she said. 'D' you know where Tom is?'

'Dairy, I think.'

'Thanks.'

She picked up her pitchfork and shovel and lifted the large wicker basket from the nail on the beam. She'd have to speak to Tom about the baby. She dreaded it. Taciturn at the best of times, he resented Cliff's demands on his daughter-in-law's time no matter that it never interfered with her work. How he'd handle news of a babe in arms was anyone's guess.

She'd long ago become accustomed to the smell of chicken manure, but this morning, after a broken night and no breakfast, lugging the brimming skep on her hip to the dung heap, she felt queasy. With relief, she up-ended the basket and stepped back, forearm over her mouth and nose, as the malodorous load tumbled on to the steaming heap.

'Pah!'

'You all right, gel?'

She hadn't heard Tom's rubber boots on the frozen path.

'Morning, Tom. Yes, just a bit of ripe stuff.' She forced a laugh. Damn. She'd wanted to be more prepared.

'Come up and get your bird before you leave. He's in the dairy, all ready for 'ee.'

That made it even more awkward. She had to thank him for his annual Christmas gift and tell him about the baby.

'Thanks. I won't forget. Will you be in the dairy later?'

'Reckon I will, gel.'

'Righto. I'll finish here and then come up.' She picked up the skep. 'You'll be all right to shut them in tonight?'

'I'll tuck 'em in, don't you fret.'

'Thanks.'

She stacked the tools in the barn. The hens were fed, watered and had fresh bedding. She called, 'Merry Christmas,' to the invisible land girl, whose reply drifted out from the harness room, and wheeled out her bike.

She took the track past the hayricks and the potato clamp, pushing the bike along the edge. The mud, poached by the farm horses, was frozen into ridges. The hoof-shaped hollows were crusted with opaque ice, which shattered on impact and sent a jet of arctic water up an unwary leg. What would Seth have made of his stepfather still using horses? He'd almost succeeded in convincing him to get a tractor before he'd died, but, after that, Tom wouldn't hear of change. In a macabre way, Tom had the last laugh as many mechanised farms had to bring

61

their horses out of retirement because of the fuel shortages. Not that Seth could have foreseen it.

'Ugh.' She reared back, her feet slipping, as a large brown rat shot out almost underfoot. She shuddered as she righted herself. Rats were the bane of the henhouses; always after spilt feed. She hated the brutes.

The dairy was attached to the farmhouse. Seth had told her his mother had made butter and cheese there but, after her death, it had become a general cold store and Tom used it in December to dress a few chickens for the table.

The ancient cream-painted door creaked as she entered. A dozen or so trussed chickens squatted on a marble slab, each with a label strung from a clawed foot. The air was heavy with the tang of raw meat.

Tom was wearing his habitual cap and the brown overall, spattered in dried blood and tied with string, that came out every year.

'All finished, gel?'

'Yes. Bedding'll last two days and I'll give them a good clean out on Boxing Day.'

'That for the bird?' he pointed to the holdall that May was carrying. 'Give him here, I'll stick him in.'

May handed over the leatherette bag that she'd lined with newspaper. She watched Tom lower in the flaccid body.

'You and the boy'll have a good feed off that 'un,' he said, lifting his cap to scratch his pink scalp.

She pulled a package from her pocket. It was wrapped in holly-printed paper. 'Thanks for the bird. This is for you from Cliff and me.'

'That's very good of you, gel.'

He'd guess it was tobacco. It always was.

'Before I go, I've got something to tell you.'

He looked wary. She bit her lip. The holdall stood like a barricade on the slab between them.

'You remember Cliff's mother, Lynette Erwin?'

His face clouded. 'That doxy.'

She smiled at the archaic word. 'She's had another baby and, to cut a long story short, I'm looking after it because she's going to America to get married.'

Tom glowered. 'How old is this child?'

May looked around. Her back ached and she was exhausted. There was nowhere to sit, so she backed up to the wall and slumped against it.

'It wasn't exactly my choice, but it is wartime and I couldn't ignore a young baby. He's Cliff's half-brother, after all.'

Tom lent over the table. 'You have obligations. You agreed to look after my flock. How old is it?'

'Two weeks.'

Tom's face changed from florid to an alarming purple. If he had a heart attack, would she remember what to do?

'Two weeks? It'll need tendin' every hour o' the day. It's out of the question.'

She'd known he wouldn't take it well. She still had to tell him the baby's colour and he wouldn't take that any better. He'd refused to have a Polish refugee working on the farm just because he wasn't British.

'I can manage if—'

'Are you mad, gel?' He thumped his fist on the slab. 'What do you know about babbies?'

'Cliff will—'

'How could you care for a babby and that boy *and* look after my hens?'

She pushed forward, glaring across the inert birds. 'Do you

63

think it's easy for me, Tom? I do my best. Cliff has changed since he's been with me. He's a lovely boy. Seth would have been proud to have him as a son.' Tom lurched as if she'd hit him with a brick, but she couldn't stop. 'He's looking after his brother now, and he will do all the holidays. The decision has been made. I won't neglect your blasted hens. I never have. I work damn hard but if you'd rather get the land girls to do my job, then do that.'

She snatched up the holdall and made for the door. Over her shoulder, she said, 'By the way, the baby's black. So put that in your pipe and smoke it.'

Chapter 15

Frosty Christmas-morning air tingled in her nose and the remnants of sleep evaporated. The latch on the lavatory door was rimed with ice crystals, like iron filings on a magnet. Inside, the asbestos roof did nothing to keep out the cold and May wondered whether she could have the scullery made into an indoor bathroom after the war. If she had any money coming in.

She'd heard nothing from Tom. No surprise. He was a proud man and she would be the one to extend the olive branch – if only for the sake of keeping food in the children's mouths. How strange, "children", as if she was a real mother.

It was only seven o'clock and Cliff was still in bed. She stoked up the range, placing logs and coals piece by piece with the tongs to avoid waking Spencer. He'd been fed at five and, with luck, would sleep a while longer. She was getting to know his habits and had a growing feeling of attachment.

Cliff would want his presents straight after breakfast, so she lit the fire she'd laid in the front room. The Christmas tree – a pine branch she'd rescued when one of the land girls snapped it off with the muck cart – was hung with Cliff's homemade decorations. Milk-bottle-top stars and pipe cleaner snowflakes dangled precariously on cotton threads. They'd set the bough in soil, in a paper-covered bucket, in the bay window. The fairy, who'd seen many better days, drooped wearily at the top.

Beneath the tree lay a meagre pile of presents. She'd been worried she hadn't anything to give Spencer. He wouldn't know, but Cliff might feel his brother had missed out. When she'd got back from work on Christmas Eve, Cliff had cycled into the village and returned with a mysterious parcel which he hid behind his back, but he handed May a brown paper package.

It was from Rose and inside was an ivory-coloured teething ring. It had a little duck dangling from it, and Rose had tied a piece of sky blue ribbon around the neck. A note said, 'Knew you wouldn't have anything for the baby. I'd seen this left on the white elephant stall. Now Isabella believes I'm expecting!'

Rose never let her down. Soon she'd need her even more; Spencer was sure to be the target of Isabella's barbed tongue.

Chapter 16

Cliff opened his eyes. Something was different, something exciting. Was it Saturday? He sat up. His stocking! It was Christmas Day.

He threw off the covers, and the rag rug skidded away as he lunged over to the fireplace.

One of Seth's old socks leaned against the grate. He didn't believe in Santa Claus anymore – Buster Johnson had told everyone it was make-believe a couple of years ago – but he and Auntie May pretended on Christmas Eve.

There was a thin layer of ice on the inside of his window and Jack Frost's handprints patterned the outside making his room a white cave. Cold seeped through his pyjamas, and he scrambled back into bed pulling the covers over his legs.

He shoved his hand into the stocking, using his fingers to guess what the little packages contained. Some hard and round things. Marbles, had to be. He pulled out the parcel and ripped the paper. Half a dozen glassy marbles rolled on to the eiderdown. One was milky white with a red and blue centre. Wizard. He jumped out of bed, kicked away the rug and peered into the wardrobe mirror, holding the marble in his eye socket. He pulled faces and growled. The monster eye was certain to scare the girls at school.

Next, a bag of gold-foil-covered chocolate coins. He ripped the foil off the farthing and shoved the chocolate in his mouth. Only one packet left. What was this? Through the paper he couldn't tell. It seemed hard and spikey. He tore it open. A puzzle made of two pieces of shiny metal knotted together.

How did they come apart? He fiddled and twisted the puzzle. It was impossible.

'Cliff, are you up?' Auntie May's voice was hushed.

'Yes.' He grabbed his dressing gown, shoved his feet into his slippers and raced downstairs clutching the puzzle.

'Ssh. Spencer's still asleep.'

Auntie May was pouring hot water into the teapot. The table was laid for Christmas breakfast and he could smell the nuttiness of a fresh loaf. A dish of bramble jelly sat next to slab of marge in the china butter dish that had a cow on the lid. The first time he'd seen it, he hadn't known what it was because his mum had always put marge out in the paper.

'Merry Christmas, Auntie May. Thanks for the stocking,' he said, keeping his voice low.

'Merry Christmas, Cliff. Sit down and we'll try and get our breakfast before the baby wants his.'

Auntie May sliced the loaf. 'I don't think we'll go to church this morning. I don't want to take Spencer out in the cold yet and I don't think it's fair to leave you minding him on Christmas Day.'

Cliff spread margarine on his bread, one eye on the puzzle he'd laid by his plate. 'Um. I don't mind, if you want to go,' he said, flicking over the puzzle with one finger.

'Can you leave that until after breakfast, please.'

'Sorry.' He pushed it away.

'I'm afraid, I haven't got anything for you this year from your mum, but we'll open our presents once I've got the chicken in the oven and the baby fed.'

'I didn't expect nuffin' from me mum,' he said. Rats, he'd been hoping for another half crown.

He knew the real reason Auntie May didn't want to go to church: Spence. People had said things about the black soldiers who'd come with the Yanks. They'd say things about Spence and his mum, too. Especially Buster. He'd be ready for him though. He was a big brother now and no one was going to hurt Spence.

Something must have happened already. Yesterday, when Auntie May got back from work, she had the red patches on her cheeks she only got when she was really angry. Like she got when Old Potty and his missus called him a guttersnipe.

The sitting room was warm and smelt like the woods on the hill. He looked around. Paper chains from each corner of the room met in the middle, where the bunch of mistletoe he'd climbed a tree to cut hung from the lampshade.

The feel of the room, the smell of the tree and seeing Auntie May in the armchair with Spence on her lap made him feel mushy inside.

He cleared his throat. 'Can we open them now?'

'Go ahead. Choose one.'

He looked at the heap of presents. He could see three with "Cliff with love from Auntie May" written on them. He picked up the smallest and laid it beside him. Before opening it, he pulled a flat parcel out from beneath the pile and handed it to Auntie May.

'I hope you like the paper,' he said, 'I got it from Miss Potts.'

Auntie May read out the message on the Santa Claus label he'd stuck on with brown tape, 'To Auntie May with love from Clifford and Spencer Erwin.'

She gave a little cough and looked down at Spencer, before beginning to pick at the tape to save the paper. She got the first end undone and peeped in. She must have seen the book. He couldn't sit still. What if she didn't like it?

'Open yours,' she said, starting on the other end.

Cliff tore round the tape, saving most of the paper, which he recognised from last year. He couldn't help watching Auntie May. She had to like it. She had to.

At last the tape was undone. Cliff held his breath as she revealed the back of the book. She turned it over, a frown on her face. His heart sank.

'My goodness. Francis Durbridge. And it's the new one, *Paul Temple Intervenes*. Thank you so much.'

She always listened to the Paul Temple stories on the wireless and she'd never let him read the battered book she kept on the shelf in her bedroom, in case it fell apart.

She got up, clutching Spence, came over and kissed his cheek. He felt himself blush, but he was pleased. Thrilled. It had taken months of saving – not to mention persuading Mrs Gale to order it for him; he knew Spinster Potts would tell on him if he tried to order it himself.

Now that was over, he concentrated on opening his own presents. At the end, he had a decent pile including a tin spitfire and the new *Beano* Annual, which had a picture of Big Eggo and Koko having a pillow fight on the front. Mrs Gale had sent him some gloves made with all different colours of wool, like her boys wore. He'd need to get them muddy pretty quick.

'Can you open your brother's one; he's a bit too small.'

His brother. He'd got a brother! He picked up the last present and crawled over to Spence.

'Let's see what you've got.' He glanced at Auntie May, who nodded. He ripped the scrap of paper away. It was a teething ring. He shook it, and something inside the little silver duck rattled. Spence gave a big grin.

Auntie May said Spence only had wind, but he knew his brother recognised his first Christmas present.

Chapter 17

Cliff tried to fix the two bits of metal puzzle together. It was as hard as getting them apart had been. Giving up, he stuck them in his pocket.

He mooched around the tidy kitchen. Something was wrong with Auntie May. She always left for work on time but, this morning, she kept finding things to do, even though Cliff said he'd wash up and sweep the floor. He promised to chop some logs if Spence didn't wake up.

Having a brother wasn't quite what he'd thought. Spence slept most of the time, and when he wasn't sleeping he was yelling for food or wanted his nappy changed. The clothes-horse stood in front of the range, hung with nappies and tiny clothes. Steam rose and made the windows foggy.

He wiped a patch of glass with the thick red curtain. The sticky tape was starting to peel off in some places, and he licked a finger and tried to re-stick the criss-crosses to the glass.

Outside it was cold and bright. Just the day for a game of footie by the pond. He looked at Spence in his pram. Fast asleep. Could he risk leaving him for half an hour? He could run there and back and have a short kick around; some of his friends were sure to be out on Boxing Day.

Better not. Auntie May would be livid if she found out, and he wouldn't like Spence to wake up alone. Sometimes he woke in the night himself and, for a few moments, thought he was back in Southampton, his mum out and the shouts of sailors on shore leave waking him. Usually what woke him was the screech of the barn owl, hunting the garden.

He put the broom out in the scullery and emptied the dustpan. Hanging around the house was boring. What if he took Spence for a walk? But if he met old Potty or his miserable missus, he'd be in trouble. They'd be sure to ask where he got Spence and, like as not, they'd think he'd pinched him.

Nothing for it. He pulled on his boots and, after jamming the toe of one of his slippers under the door to stop it closing, made his way round the back to the log pile. He looked forward to the job; letting the axe fall under its own weight, splitting the wood along the grain. Mr Arrowsmith had felled a pine in the autumn and brought them round a great heap of wood. Auntie May complained it spat out sparks as it burnt but, as it was chopped, its zingy smell filled his nose, reminding him of summer days in the woods.

He aimed the axe and proudly tossed another two perfectly even logs on the heap. The shaft of the axe was smooth on his hands. It had been Seth's, and Auntie May often told him his logs were as good as the ones Seth had chopped. What was Seth like? Would he and Cliff have got on? Seth and Auntie May might have had their own children by now and, if Seth hadn't joined up, they might be looking forward to having the evacuee out of their way. Where would he have gone now his mother was moving to America? He picked up a gnarled log; one he had been avoiding as too difficult to get the axe in safely. He heard his mother's 'Bye Cliffy', in his head and swung the axe. He brought it down with all his might.

The log began to split but the blade caught a knot and sheared off, sending a piece of wood flying upwards. The blade drove deep into the chopping block and he ducked to avoid the missile that shot past his head and smashed into the dustbin, sending it clanging backwards into the wall.

Immediately a wail came from indoors.

'Bugger.'

Auntie May had forbidden swearing but, as the man of the house, surely he must be allowed. He put down the axe. On his way to Spence he landed the bin a hefty kick and, giving a double V for Victory sign, yelled, 'Goal.'

Auntie May was back earlier than usual, but she seemed unhappy.

'I did these,' Cliff said, as soon as she'd hung up her coat. He pointed to a plate of doorstep chicken sandwiches in the centre of the kitchen table. 'I remember we had 'em last Boxing Day.'

He put the kettle on to boil and they sat down. He'd laid out knives and small plates. There were a few crumbs on the gingham cloth from where he'd cut the loaf and the slices were a bit uneven, but the sandwiches smelt good.

He rested his arms on the table and watched as Auntie May took a bite.

'Elbows off, please, Cliff.'

'Sorry.'

'These are lovely. A nice surprise. Thank you,' she said. 'How has Spencer been?'

'I fed him and changed his nappy – it really ponged.' He wrinkled his nose.

Auntie May patted his arm. 'I'm sorry you have to do it, but with me working…'

'It's okay,' he said. 'He does sleep a lot, doesn't he?'

Auntie May laughed. 'Thank goodness. I'm not sure how we'll cope once he starts running around.'

He'd prefer it when Spence started doing something. He laid down his sandwich and looked down at the cloth. There was a smudge of marge on one of the blue squares. 'Can we take

Spence out in the pram this afternoon?' He crossed his fingers under the table.

Auntie May didn't answer straight away. She was looking at the pram where Spence's brown cheek was just visible between his bonnet and the shawl.

'It's not too cold,' he said. 'We could cover him up well.'

Auntie May sighed. 'We'll have to do it sometime, I suppose. And I'm not working this afternoon.'

Cliff twisted his fingers harder.

'When I've had another cup of tea, I'll get changed,' she said, looking down at the jodhpurs she'd worn to work.

Why was she wearing trousers? She normally only wore them in snow and she'd told him ages ago Mr Arrowsmith didn't approve of women in trousers. That was strange because the land girls wore them all the time. One day, when he was buying *The Beano*, he'd overheard Spinster Potts and the other old biddies whispering about the unladylike clothes "they lan' gels" wore.

Auntie May said, 'All right, we'll walk up to the pond and, yes, you can take your football.'

Hurray! He released his fingers and stuffed the last of his sandwich in his mouth.

The hard rubber tyres bumped over stones and potholes as Cliff pushed the pram along the lane. He thought Spence would be sure to wake but he slept on, his blankets pulled up so far he was almost invisible under the pram hood.

Auntie May was walking beside him. She'd put on the bluey-grey coat that reminded him of wood pigeons. She looked like she did for her meetings – just to go to the pond. Cliff tried talking but she wasn't really listening, so he gave up and concentrated on avoiding the worst of the potholes. He was a Spitfire pilot dodging enemy gunfire.

'You'll make that baby sick.' Auntie May took the handle from him and steered the pram sedately across the junction into the village street. As they reached the first of the houses, Cliff saw she was peering around; she must be looking out for Old Potty. Cliff was ready for him. He'd give him an earful if he said anything about Spence.

They were nearly at the pond. It was set beside the road, in a triangle of grass opposite the village green, which nowadays had vegetables growing on it. People said there had been a cricket pitch before the war.

A spaniel came trotting along the footpath and stepped delicately around the pram. Cliff stroked the animal's coat. He would love to have a dog. One like this maybe: brown and white with long silky hair. The dog sniffed at his hand and gave it a warm lick. Should he ask Auntie May about a puppy again? He knew the answer. Not enough food for us let alone a dog. And now there was Spence.

'Isn't that Bob and Peter?'

Cliff looked down the street. Two figures lolloped into view pushing and shoving each other off the pavement. He waved an arm and the boys waved back.

'I'll get my ball.' he said, reaching under the pram for the muddy leather football lying in the wire tray.

Auntie May pushed the shawl down and he watched as she laid the backs of her fingers against Spence's cheek. 'Warm as toast.' she said, tucking in the covers before rotating the pram on to its back wheels to face home.

'Be back before dark, Cliff.'

He crossed to the patch behind the pond where the grass had been churned to mud by the boys' feet. He dropped the ball and ran backwards, lining himself up for a kick. He stopped, mid stride, as he heard a familiar voice.

'Mrs Sheppard?'

Old Potty had stopped his bike alongside the pram. Been out nosin' around, as usual, thought Cliff.

'What's this, then?' Old Potty pointed to the pram.

Cliff saw Auntie May hesitate and he ran over. He stared into Old Potty's face. Stared at his gingery-grey moustache that lay like a dead field mouse above his lip. He felt brave; Auntie May was there and Old Potty didn't seem so scary when he was in his civvies. In any case, he had to defend Spence.

''e's my bruver,' he said.

'Your ma's had another babby? Why isn't she looking after it?'

Cliff saw Auntie May flush and open her mouth to speak, but he gave her no chance.

'She's gone to America.'

'Emigrated?' He spat out the words, staring at Cliff.

'Spence's livin' wiv us.'

'Cliff…' Auntie May began.

'Spencer is it?' Potty's lip curled. 'Suppose 'e looks like Spencer Tracy then?'

He leaned in, peering under the hood. Cliff wanted to kick him. Tell him to leave his brother alone.

'Mr Potts, he's asleep. Please don't—'

Before Auntie May could say anything more, Old Potty tugged down the cover.

'Christ.' He recoiled as if Spence had bitten him. Cliff wished he had. Even more so when Old Potty turned his squinty little eyes on Auntie May and said, 'A black bastard? Livin' here in't village? Well, Mrs Sheppard, I don't know what folk are going to make of this. Hassen you thought about what you've taken on?'

76

The red blotches appeared on Auntie May's face. She said, 'Mr Potts. How dare you? What I do is my business. It's still wartime you know. I'm sure even you and Mrs Potts wouldn't leave a young baby in need.'

Cliff wanted to cheer, although he'd never heard Auntie May's voice so harsh. Old Potty's face was bright red and he looked as furious as if Auntie May had left all the lights on in the blackout. He snorted down his nose and swung his leg over the crossbar.

'That one'll be trouble, May Sheppard. You mark my words,' he said, his foot fumbling for the pedal. 'Just like his brother.'

Cliff watched as Auntie May pushed the pram down the road. Should he go with her? She looked so alone, her shoulders drooping, as she walked away. Sometimes he hated his mother. She made everyone do things they didn't want. It should be her looking after Spence and giving a mouthful to nasty men like Old Potty.

He didn't often think of living with his mum now. Living with Auntie May had been the happiest time of his life. Not once had he been scared, even during air raids he always felt that he'd be cared for. Protected.

In Southampton, his mother used take him to the market. It was bustling with people pushing and shoving shopping bags in his face. Voices shouted things he never understood. The man selling dead rabbits had them draped over the table. Cliff could never drag his gaze away from their staring eyes or the congealed pools of blood that lay spattered on the ground below their heads.

While his mum smiled and joked with the stallholders, Cliff was supposed to pinch stuff from the stalls. She'd told him, if he got caught he was to say he had been going to ask his mum to pay, but forgot.

One day, he'd slipped a block of cheese into her basket when a huge woman from the next stall started yelling, 'That nipper's nicked some cheese, Jeff. Right off your stall 'e took it.' She pointed at Cliff with a sausage-like finger. The man his mother had been laughing with dashed around the stall towards him.

Terrified, he'd tried to hide behind his mother, clutching her skirt in his fists. She grabbed him by the arm, 'Did you nick something?' she snarled, tugging her skirt free.

He didn't answer, just looked at the ground where crumpled squares of tissue paper from the orange boxes on the stall opposite, swirled around his boots.

''e dropped it in yer basket,' said the fat woman, jabbing her finger towards his mum.

Feigning disbelief, his mum reached into the scruffy basket and pulled out a crumbly chunk of cheddar. 'What d'you do that for?' she said, cuffing Cliff around the ear.

Cliff began to snivel. 'I was goin' to ask you to pay—'

'It's too bloody late,' his mother hissed. 'Shut up.'

She smiled up at the man, her mouth red with thick lipstick. 'Sorry, 'e's only three.' Cliff was four. ''e don't know no better.'

The stallholder's joviality had vanished. He glared at Cliff and told his mum, 'You'll have to pay for that love. It can't go back on the stall. Not now that brat's had 'is mitts all over it.'

By the time they got home, Lynette half dragging him as she strode away in a temper, it had been drummed into Cliff that it was all his fault: he was too dim to learn; he couldn't even nick a bit of cheese without been spotted. Did he think she could afford that much cheese?

He could still hear the snarl in her voice as she slammed down a plate and said, 'It serves you right. You're only getting' bread and marge for the rest of the day. Maybe next time you'll think about that and not let them see yer.'

That evening, when she left to go to what he and Auntie May now called her "war work", she didn't bother to tell Mrs Wallbanks, next door, that he was at home on his own. He'd been too scared to go across the yard and he'd wet the bed, earning another clipped ear the next morning.

He couldn't wish all that on Spence.

'You playing or what?'

He looked round. Bob and Pete were waiting. They both wore the green knitted balaclavas that made their heads looked like Brussels sprouts.

'Yeah. Who's in goal?'

'What was up with Old Potty?' Pete asked, while Bob ran over to stand between the two lumps of stone that stood in for goalposts. 'He nearly ran into Bob an' me.'

''e's just a misery guts,' said Cliff. 'Come on. Goal kick.'

Chapter 18

Tears stung her eyes and she could barely see the lane on the opposite side of the crossroads. From the moment she'd seen Spencer she'd known it would be bad, but she'd hoped she could rise above the stigma.

Spencer woke as she jiggled the pram through the kitchen door. Resolve to protect him flooded through her as she gently lifted him and laid him in the crook of the arm. She carried him to the small chest of drawers she and Cliff had brought down from the box room and placed under the window. The folded towel on top kept the baby warm as she unpinned the wet nappy and replaced it with a fresh one from the drawer. Thank God for Rose; she'd never have managed with just the few nappies Lynette had sent.

'Now, little one,' she said, 'time for your feed.'

She laid him back in the pram while she made up the milk. The tin was looking depleted; she'd have to go to the clinic for more. Don't let me run into Ephraim again, she thought. He'd probably spread the news. There was nothing he and Isabella liked more than being able to spread gossip, the more malicious, the better.

As she fed Spencer in the warmth beside the range, he clutched at her finger holding the bottle. His hand was no bigger than a cat's paw. She felt a surge of love; this was Cliff's brother, not just a brown baby or Lynette's by-blow. She was responsible for a family: two young boys who depended entirely on her. She wasn't going to let them down.

Cliff looked nervously around the kitchen after closing the back door with uncharacteristic care. Poor lad, he must be worried about her.

'Good game?'

'Yes,' he said, with a relieved smile, as he padded over to the pram. His toe was poking through his left sock.

More darning, May thought, her hands in a mixing bowl.

Cliff held out a finger and beamed down at this brother. 'Hello, Spence. You know I'm back, don't you?'

May dribbled water into the fat and flour mixture. At last Cliff had something of his own. A blood relative who was here and who could respond to love he was desperate to give.

'Some boys from school came out to play footie. I scored twice,' he told her, his hand hovering over the bowl as she tipped the ball of dough on to the marble rolling slab.

'Here you are.' She nipped off a small piece of pastry. 'The rest's for the pie. Will you draw the curtains, please? We can do without Mr Potts looking in at us tonight.'

Cliff dragged the jacquard curtains across the window. 'Why didn't Old Potty—' he looked at May, who raised her eyebrows. 'Mr Potts. Why didn't he and Mrs Potts get an evacuee like everyone else?'

May brought the rolling pin to a stop. Why didn't they? There had been some resentment about how they got away with it early on, but that had been forgotten in the general chaos of billeting, schooling and coping with the emotional turmoil of dozens of uprooted children. She shook her head. 'I don't know, Cliff. I really don't know.'

He shrugged and headed up to his room.

She slid the pie into the oven and went into the scullery to collect potatoes. The dingy room was only warm when they lit the copper on washday, or when they heated water to use the

81

tin bath in front of the range. She detested the smelly paraffin heater they lit when they washed out there, night and morning, and in winter they spent as little time there as possible.

She opened the hessian sack, which Cliff complained made the scullery smell like the farm's spud clamp, and took out a couple of potatoes.

Tom had avoided her since their spat on Christmas Eve. If she was honest, they'd avoided each other.

Even though the land girls wore trousers, it was childish of her to wear them just because he disapproved. There was little he could do about the girls, little he could insist on for her really, but she'd always tried to respect him. Not only was he her employer, he was also her father-in-law.

She rubbed the potato skins with her thumbs, and clumps of soil fell into the pail she kept for the compost heap. The cream enamel bowl clanged as she dropped in the potatoes and ran water on them from the heavy brass tap that sat a foot above the sink.

With the bowl on the kitchen draining board, she began to peel and cut up the potatoes. What was she going to do about Tom? She couldn't afford to lose her job, and she knew he couldn't afford to lose her – he always said the hens went off lay when she wasn't around.

But how was she going to manage caring for Spencer when Cliff went back to school? He was in the newly separated top class now, and the day was an hour longer than the lower classes. She couldn't take Spencer out on cold dark evenings to shut up the hens, and if she waited until Cliff got back it would be too dark to find them. The fox wouldn't hesitate to pounce if he discovered chickens out after dark.

She tipped the potatoes into a pan and added a scrape of dripping.

The new pullets wouldn't be arriving for a few months, so there wasn't too much mucking out and feeding to be done. The remaining birds roamed the farmyard, topping up their meagre rations with whatever they could find. The search for the few eggs that might be laid didn't take her long – she knew their hiding places as well as the hens.

She put the tin in the oven before checking on the baby. Sound asleep. She stacked the cooking utensils in the kitchen sink, added soap and poured on hot water from the kettle.

She'd have to walk to work with the pram, but the barn would be warm and dry. The girls were often in and out, and most of the time she was in earshot herself. She could manage if Tom agreed to let the land girls shut up the hens at night until the evenings got lighter and the new birds arrived. All she had to do was persuade him.

'Morning, May. Foggy again.'

'It's so thick, I could hardly see where I was going,' she said.

Sally, the senior land girl, met May in the doorway of the barn. She was leading Blossom. May rubbed the mare's nose when she snuffled at her bike basket, knowing it often held carrot or apple peelings for the horses.

'Not today, old girl. Sorry,' May said. 'What is it this morning, Sally? Muck carting?'

Sally was wearing a green land army sweater and brown jodhpurs, and all that showed of her blonde hair was a stray curl by her ear. The rest was hidden under a tartan turban. She pulled the horse away from May. 'Yes, muck carting, worse luck. It's good 'n ripe, so my feet'll keep warm. Cliff not helping today?'

'No, he's busy,' May called, as Blossom's massive hindquarters disappeared around the side of the cart shed.

'Babysitting,' she added silently.

Tom hadn't appeared by the time she finished work. She'd have to look for him. Most likely he'd be with Sally and Blossom. She scanned around when she got outside the farmyard but fog blanketed the fields. The muffling silence made her feel isolated from the rest of the world as she walked along the rutted track.

At an open gateway, the metal gate long gone for salvage, she followed the cart tracks into the field. Was that the sound of voices? She trudged over the broken ground, from which flax had been pulled earlier in the year. Once the muck was spread, the field would be ploughed. What would Tom be planting here this season? Potatoes? More flax? She was distanced from such decisions nowadays. Seth had always discussed his plans for the farm and seemed to value her ideas. Tom kept his own counsel.

Manure. An unmistakable smell. It hit her before she discerned the figures forking the steaming muck as Blossom patiently plodded along. She could make out Sally on top of the cart. Two other land girls were spreading the muck with pitchforks as Sally heaved it down. Tom was walking at Blossom's head. At least he wouldn't be able to escape.

She said hello to the girls. One of them offered her a fork to join them, but she laughed and made her way up to Tom. Over the creaking harness and the squelch of the wheels, the girls wouldn't be able to hear what they said.

'Hello, Tom.'

'Morning, gel.'

'Did you have a good Christmas?'

'Nice enough.'

He wasn't going to make this easy. 'I wanted to clear the air after Christmas Eve,' she said.

He patted Blossom's neck and made a show of adjusting her noseband. May waited, stepping out alongside him, matching her stride to his and echoing the rhythm of Blossom's shaggy hooves.

'Reckon you got enough on your plate at the minute,' he said, finally.

Was that an apology, or a forerunner to giving her the sack?

'I can manage, with Cliff's help, but once he goes back to school I won't be able to do the afternoons. I can't bring the baby out in the cold. He'll be fine in the mornings in the barn, if you agree. I'd get the work done and, until the lighter evenings, you'd just need the girls to shut in the hens at night.' She turned to face him.

Ignoring her, Tom looked over his shoulder and called to Sally, 'Hold up, gel.' He circled Blossom away.

The girls stepped aside, rubbing their backs and taking a breather, as the horse swung the cart round and faced the top of the field. May waited on the headland. Tom was proving who was boss and she wouldn't rise to his bait.

Sally called, 'We're nearly empty. Shall I go up for another load?'

'Chuck that off, all of you. We'll go up for dinner an' re-load.' Tom said. The two girls joined Sally on the cart and, between them, they forked the remaining manure into a heap at the edge of the field.

'You'd better get up,' Tom said to May, clambering on to the seat and taking up the reins.

She jumped up and sat next to him in silence as the girls chattered behind them. Was this the end of her time on the farm? What would she do? The munitions factory would close as soon as the war was over. Those that worked there would all be looking for work alongside the men coming out from the Forces. She stared into the fog.

When they reached the farmyard, Sally went to fetch Blossom's nosebag and the girls headed into the barn for their own food.

Tom led Blossom to the water trough. As the mare drew a long draught, he said, 'D'you reckon you'll be set up avore them pullets come?'

She tried to keep the relief out of her voice. 'As long as the weather isn't too bad, yes. I'll be able to bring the baby back with me in the afternoons.'

'My hens mussen' suffer, mind.'

'They won't. Thank you, Tom.' She touched his arm.

'You'd better get off for your dinner,' he said, pulling up Blossom's head and turning her to where Sally had the nosebag. 'Let me know avore the lad goes back to school.'

May collected her bike from the barn, keeping the smile off her face until she was out in the lane.

Chapter 19

Rose waved as she passed the window.

'Come in,' May called, rinsing out the washing-up bowl.

'How're things?' Rose slipped off her coat and blue felt hat. She placed the hat on the arm of the chair beside the range. 'The brim's drooped in the fog. Instead of a dinner plate, it looks like a soup bowl. I hate this hat – it seems like I've been wearing it all my life.'

May laughed. 'I feel like that about all my clothes and especially my shoes. I've had my navy courts repaired so often the patches have got patches.' She dried the crockery with a faded tea towel. 'Things aren't going too badly. I'm having a bit of trouble getting Spencer into a routine – it seems ridiculous to have to wake him up for a feed when he's sound asleep and so am I.'

'You'll get used ter it,' said Rose. 'You'll both adapt.'

'I hope so.' May said, propping the plates on the dresser and picking up two cups and saucers. She poured tea and they settled at the table.

Rose asked after Cliff. May told her he'd had been indoors all morning and made his own dinner. He'd left as soon as she'd got back from work. 'Now there aren't any more Yanks around to pester for sweets, he'll be poking about in the woods, I expect,' she said, 'building dens and things that boys do.' She sighed. 'He's been marvellous with the baby. He looks after him while I'm at work. It seems unfair, but he says he doesn't mind.'

It was good to talk. 'I'm worried that he got used to being

put on by his mother. I don't want him to think that's all coming round again, and I don't want him to resent me.'

'There's no fear of that,' said Rose, leaning forward to rest her elbows on the table. 'He worships you. And that little sweetie over there.' She nodded towards the pram.

May smiled as she remembered how Cliff, half out of the door, had come back, looked down at his sleeping brother and whispered goodbye.

'He does adore Spencer, you're right,' May said, hand poised over her cup. 'Tell me...' Did she want to know the answer? 'Have you heard any gossip about me?'

Rose put down her own cup. 'What's happened?'

May bit her lip. She had to tell someone. She took a deep breath and let the story of the clashes with Ephraim and Tom flood out.

'You knew Tom would be awkward, he hates change. I reckon he'll come round, given time. But Ephraim and Isabella? All they have ter talk about is other people's problems. It's their life's work. I haven't heard any gossip, but I've been at the factory all morning.'

Rose, lines of tiredness around her eyes, ran her fingers through her springy hair and May spotted a fleck of grey amongst the brown. She'd panicked a couple of days before, when she'd thought she'd spotted a silver strand in her own hair. It was a trick of the light, but how long before brunette became pepper and salt? If Cliff's adoption ever happened, she'd hoped – with her similar colouring – she might be taken for his natural mother. After six years of war, she felt middle-aged and if the adoption didn't happen soon, she'd look it.

She said, 'I have to go in to the village this afternoon. We need shopping and I've got to sort out Spencer's ration card and get milk powder at the clinic. I'll have to take the pram.

That'll give confirmation to all those wagging tongues that I'll have to pretend not to hear.'

Rose said, 'I can walk in with you. Victoria Potts won't say much faced with two of us, or I could stay here and look after the little one while you cycle up ter the village. You choose.'

Rose had been working since early morning. She couldn't impose.

'The twins are out. Like as not they'll meet up with Cliff and we won't see hide nor hair of them until dark. Why don't you give yourself a break and bike up there? Chances are a lot of them don't know yet anyway.' She drained her cup. 'You get ready. I'll pour myself more tea, and I might even join Spencer in a doze.' She stood up and lifted the yellow cosy from the teapot on the side of the range.

Why give herself more worry? May took a coat and hat from the hooks beside the door. Rose, nursing a cup and saucer, had sunk into the armchair beside the stove and closed her eyes. May hesitated.

'Go on,' said Rose, without opening her eyes.

'The nappies are in the chest in front of the window. He'll probably sleep 'til I get back, and he's not due for a feed until three o'clock,' she said.

'I'll cope. Have you got his ration card?'

'In my bag,' May said, picking up her scuffed brown handbag from the dresser.

The lane seemed ghostly in the fog. Before May reached the junction, her beret was as damp as Rose's hat. She listened carefully for traffic at the crossroads. Seth's old trench coat kept her dry, but the fawn-coloured fabric was invisible in fog.

The clinic was held on Wednesday afternoons in the village

hall. May leaned her bike against the wall. Was it only five days ago she was here running the Christmas Fair?

She pushed open one of the green double doors and went in. No noise and bustle today. Instead of the smell of home-baked biscuits and the warmth of a packed room, the place was chilly and reeked of disinfectant.

A nurse sat at a table spread with files, facing a row of empty canvas-seated metal chairs. Screens had been placed across the bottom part of the hall to provide a private area. A hand-written sign was pinned by the entrance: *Expectent and Nurseing Mothers.* May could hear the low rumble of conversation from the far side.

The nurse looked up. 'Can I help you?'

May explained about Spencer and handed over the documents that Lynette had sent. The nurse consulted with a woman in civvies stationed in the kitchen. After much discussion and form filling, she was able to leave, clutching two blue and white tins of dried milk, a sheaf of pamphlets and instructions to bring Spencer for examination the following week.

'Hello, Mrs Sheppard.'

Just when she'd thought she'd got away without being spotted. She slid the tins into the leatherette holdall that hung from the bike's handlebars.

Putting on a bright smile, she turned. 'Hello, Mrs Harris. How are you?'

Evelyn Harris had come with the first wave of evacuees. She'd been three months pregnant and had a small daughter in tow. The baby, now four, was wearing a tweed coat cut down from one much larger. The hem poked unevenly and May itched to take an iron to it.

'Hello, Valerie,' May said.

The child didn't answer.

'Just come to get 'er orange juice,' said Mrs Harris. 'They say it stops 'em getting colds. Don't seem to work; she's always got a runny nose.'

The nose problem was very evident and May looked away as the child ran her sleeve across her face. She must get Doreen to put another hygiene talk on the WI agenda, although much of it seemed to pass by the people who needed it most and the others grumbled about hearing the same message over and over again.

'It's the vitamin C, I think,' said May.

'Well, it don't work on 'er, but 'er big sister loves it. Better get me skates on. They'll shut soon. T.T.F.N. Mrs Sheppard.' She tugged Valerie through the green doors.

May rode out into the fog. Would Mrs Harris share Ephraim's view of Spencer? Would she look on him as a baby who should have his share of orange juice, or as an alien who didn't deserve a home in the village?

It may have been because she was expecting it, but the shop seemed to fall silent as she walked in the door. She stared straight ahead and made for the grocery side of the store. Her footsteps sounded loud on the uneven wooden boards. From the corner of her eye she saw several customers waiting at the post office counter where Victoria was holding court. With a bit of luck, they'd keep the old battleaxe busy for a while.

She stood in line behind three women she knew only by sight. She fixed her gaze on Fred, the elderly assistant who came from the next village, as he slowly wound the handle of the bacon slicer. Couldn't he get a move on? Someone she knew well was certain to come in soon. The machine made a shushing noise as it reeled off a small pile of rashers. Barely enough for a meal, let alone a week, she thought, remembering the huge breakfasts she'd cooked for Seth before he left for a day's harvesting. She closed her eyes for a second as a wave of loneliness swept over her.

'He should be at home with his feet up.' A whisper, close to May's ear, startled her. She turned to see Doreen grinning at her and nodding to the assistant. 'Fred, I mean.'

May said, 'I think he was, until he was called up for grocery service.'

Doreen laughed. 'Anything you want to put on the agenda for the meeting?'

May was telling her about the hygiene talk when she caught a glimpse of Victoria. She quickly turned away before the woman caught her eye.

'For goodness, sake get a move on,' she said aloud, forgetting herself.

'In a hurry, May?' Doreen said. 'You look a bit peaky.'

How was she to deal with this? She couldn't blurt out, 'I'm foster mother to a brown baby,' in the bacon queue, but if she hid it everyone would think the worse of her.

She shuffled forward. The woman in front turned in surprise as May's handbag hit her in the back. 'Sorry,' May mumbled.

Two more women joined the queue behind Doreen.

May said quietly, 'I'm looking after Cliff's brother at the moment. I'm not used to two children. It's a lot more work.'

Doreen's eyes widened, 'Is that why you had to leave the Christmas Fair in a hurry?'

'Yes. Thank you so much for stepping into the breach.'

May was second in the queue now. She heard Doreen draw breath to probe deeper just as the woman ahead moved off.

'Lard, flour and tea, please,' she said, shoving the ration books at Fred. She needed bacon, but she couldn't wait while he faffed about with it. Scrambled eggs on their own would have to do for tea. 'And marge,' she added, fumbling in her bag for her purse.

'Drat. I'm sure I put it in.' She fiddled about, rambling distractedly, not leaving Doreen a chance to question her.

Finally her purchases were ready.

'Ah, here it is.'

'So—' Doreen began.

'Sorry, Doreen, I've got to get back. I'll be in touch about the meeting.'

She swept the packets into her arms and headed for the door.

'Mrs Sheppard.' Victoria stood in the doorway like the SS.

'Good afternoon, Miss Potts. Sorry, I'm in a hurry.' May tried to step round the woman, but Victoria held her ground. Dumpy, with hair plaited into a grey rope wound tightly around her head, Victoria wore the same grey cord pinafore dress every day, only varying the sweater or blouse beneath.

The look in her eyes was pure malevolence. Rumour had it no man had ever shown interest in her, and she'd remained devoted to her brother all his life. Anyone who upset him upset her and usually lived to rue the day.

The shop was silent, and May sensed all eyes on her back. She wished Seth's old coat made her invisible indoors as well as out.

'Got to get back to that piccaninny, 'as 'ee?'

May's mouth was open, but no words came out. The quizzical silence of the other shoppers turned to mumbled speculation.

'Better get on then 'adn't 'ee?' Victoria's rictus grin belied the vindictiveness in her eyes.

Still mute, May moved to pass, but Doreen appeared at her side. 'Mrs Sheppard's just been telling me about Cliff's little brother. How wonderful to have an exotic child in the village, don't you think, Miss Potts?'

Chapter 20

'What's the matter?' said Rose. She looked concerned as May flung her coat on a chair.

Rose was feeding Spencer beside the range. It was a blissful domestic picture and the contrast with the scene with Victoria brought a lump to May's throat. She could still hear the hurt in Doreen's voice outside the shop asking why May hadn't confided in her about Spencer.

'Nothing's the matter,' she gulped. 'Nothing apart from being humiliated in public by Victoria Potts and offending Doreen, who is such a good friend she came to my aid nonetheless.'

She flopped down at the table and sank her head into her hands, sobbing. She was dimly aware of Rose, juggling Spencer and his feeding bottle, dragging out a chair next to her. She felt the comforting weight of Rose's arm wrapped around her shoulders.

'Tell me about it. You'll feel better if you do.'

May blew her nose. 'I never realised, when I took on this baby, how bad it would be.'

'You didn't take him on. That madam foisted him on you, knowing you wouldn't refuse. You don't have ter do this. He's been abandoned. You could turn him over ter the authorities; they'd find him somewhere ter go.'

May looked down at the tiny face. Eyes closed, dark lashes lying on his amber-coloured skin, his mouth worked the teat less vigorously as the bottle emptied and sleep overtook him.

'Could you let him go?' Rose said.

She looked at Rose, whose features softened as she too gazed at Spencer.

'It wouldn't be easy,' she said huskily, feeling she spoke for them both.

Spencer was asleep in his pram and Rose, insisting she didn't need to leave until the two of them had thrashed out "the Potts' problem", made tea. Still feeling the tightness of tears around her eyes, May put away the shopping and hung up her coat.

Sitting by the range, she let warmth seep into her and gradually sank back in the armchair.

'Cliff will be back soon. I don't want him to know what happened yet. He's bound to hear about it at school but that's not for a couple of weeks. He was so proud when he told Ephraim that Spencer was his brother, and he took it better than me when he was so vile.'

'Ephraim's always given him a rough time, so he probably expects it. I suspect he's had it all his life. It can't have been much fun having a tart for a mother – everyone knowing what she did. Even though he was too young to understand, he'd pick up on the atmosphere. Does he even know who his father is?'

'He thinks he was a sailor, but I doubt even Lynette knows. I've tried comparing their looks to get some idea of what the father may have looked like, but it's impossible. Under the peroxide, you can't tell the natural colour of her hair. It could be Cliff's tawny or it could be raven black. She's got blue eyes; his are hazel. Both have fair skin. It could be anyone.'

'What a way ter live,' said Rose.

'I'm pleased for her that she's got out of it, and I can't imagine why she got into it – unless she was forced to by poverty – but I'll never forgive her for the way she treated Cliff.

I could never let him go back to her,' May said. But could she let Spencer be sent somewhere else? Somewhere there might be children like himself. What were children like himself? Helpless babies abandoned by their mothers seeking a better life? Could she let herself take the easy way out? No snide comments from the Pottses. No sneaking to the clinic.

'It will get worse, May. They don't tolerate outsiders here,' said Rose. 'We have been more or less accepted because we married locals. Anyone else is just a "furriner".'

'D'you think I'd have been like that if I'd stayed in my parents' village on the east coast after they died?'

'You'd never have been like that, May. You'd have welcomed people.'

'But they welcomed the Americans here. Think about the tea parties and dances they ran, and the meals they gave them in their own homes.'

'Segregated tea parties and dances. Blacks in one place and whites in another.'

'That was the Yanks; they wouldn't mix.'

'Then, yes. And a lot of local people disagreed with it, but the Yanks were only here temporarily. They were helping us. Fighting for us. They can see Spencer is here ter stay, especially now they know Lynette's emigrated.'

'Ephraim seized on that. What do they think Spencer's going to do? Contaminate the air?'

'He's different. That's enough. I don't understand prejudice, but I know these people and some of the Yanks' attitude is bound to have rubbed off. Remember the way the black GIs were treated and given the ropiest jobs?'

'A lot of the whites considered the blacks were a lower class. For heaven's sake, they can't think that about Spencer. He's a *baby*.'

May's voice rose just as the door opened.

'Is Spence all right?' Cliff looked concerned.

'He's fine. Take off your muddy boots,' May said.

'I hadn't realised it was so late. I must go,' said Rose. 'Did you see the boys?' she asked Cliff, as she gathered her belongings.

'Yeah, we was in the wood. They've gone home now,' he said, kicking off his boots.

'They'll be starving. I'd better hurry.' She looked at May. 'I'll see you soon.'

There was just enough light from the glow of the range to see the baby lying in her lap. He was demanding his milk. Loudly. At 3 a.m. she wanted to encourage him to get back to sleep as soon as possible after his feed and had switched off the lights after she'd changed him.

'Ssh. You'll wake Cliff,' she said, settling him into the crook of her arm and offering him the bottle. He took it with a gulp.

Could she send him away? The best thing would be for him to go back to Lynette, but that wasn't possible and, thinking about how she'd treated Cliff, what would she do with a – what did Doreen call him? An exotic baby. On the other hand, Southampton was used to different races. Cliff spoke of seeing Chinese, Asian and Indian sailors as an everyday occurrence. But Lynette wasn't in Southampton now. No one knew where she was, but it must be somewhere that a black baby wouldn't be accepted. Like Crompton Parva.

Spencer fell asleep before taking the last half-ounce of milk. May laid him in the pram, hoping he would sleep through without it.

'Goodnight, little man,' she whispered.

***

She shook her head to relieve the muzziness. She'd been unable to get back to sleep after tending to the baby and fidgeted the rest of the night, mulling over the decisions ahead.

The farmyard was quiet when she arrived for work; the land girls already out somewhere on the farm with Blossom and the old gelding, Ben.

She quickly collected the few eggs and washed them in cold water. The job left her hands chapped and raw. She left the clean eggs in the dairy, ready to go to the packing station, and put a handful of cracked ones on the harness room table, in a nest of straw. Tom was generous to his staff. It was a quality she'd always admired in him. He could have sold the damaged eggs, but he preferred to let the girls have them to eke out their rations. She'd kept a couple for herself and, wrapping them in her scarf, laid them carefully in her bag.

She didn't pull into the cottage but cycled on, taking the fork into Chapel Lane. Halfway up the hill she gave in and walked. Doreen lived next to the old chapel and its adjoining meeting room, which the WI had used since the Local Defence Volunteers commandeered the village hall.

She went round to the back of the house and tapped on the door.

From inside, the opening tune from *Music While You Work* stopped abruptly and Doreen called, 'Come in.'

The kitchen was no tidier than usual. Every surface was cluttered. Doreen cooked, sewed and wrote letters to the troops, often simultaneously. Needles and reels of thread lay in baking tins and half-written letters were spread on the sideboard, weighed down by pairs of scissors and darning mushrooms. Doreen whisked a pair of men's trousers – one leg cut down to half its length – off a chair to let May sit down.

Was she pleased to see her, or was there a touch of coldness? 'Tea?'

'Lovely. Thanks,' May said. 'Sorry if I smell of the henhouse. I haven't changed yet.' She slipped off her coat. 'I brought you these.' She laid the two eggs on the table.

'That's kind. Thank you.'

'And I wanted to explain about yesterday. I owe you an apology, not to mention a thank you for dealing with Victoria.'

'Nothing I enjoy more than putting a Potts in their place, as you well know, hen.' Doreen smiled as she handed May a cracked cup and mismatched saucer. 'I must admit, I was a bit put out by what Victoria said, but when I looked at you and saw you'd been poleaxed by it, I knew I had to do something. Would you like a biscuit? I made some of my Crunchies earlier.'

She couldn't face the dripping-tainted biscuits and refused, saying Cliff would have a sandwich ready for her.

'By the time I got home,' Doreen went on. 'I realised, with Christmas and everything, you hadn't had time to tell me about this baby, and the shop queue wasn't the place. I don't s'pose you'd told anyone had you?' she looked straight at May, eyebrows raised.

Hell.

'The only person I had to speak to was Rose,' she said.

Doreen sniffed.

May rushed on, explaining about Spencer's unceremonious arrival. 'I needed baby clothes and such, and Rose was the only person who might have been able to help.'

She let the bike freewheel down the hill. Doreen's honour was satisfied. May had persuaded her that Rose was the obvious person to ask for baby equipment, and let her think she was in the know as much as Rose. She'd never be able to take Doreen into full confidence; she was too inclined to drop hints about other people's business – a trait that could also be quite useful. Today, she'd revealed a nugget that intrigued May: Isabella and Ephraim had officially refused to take an evacuee. By some means, they'd overcome the regulations even though they had two spare rooms in their house. Very puzzling.

As she turned into Elem Lane, a flash of white over the bushes on the village road caught her eye. Was that an ARP helmet? Ephraim seemed to consider it his right to wear his uniform even when he was off duty. The only other attire he wore was a tweed overcoat and black homburg. The whisper was that he modelled himself on Winston Churchill.

Chapter 21

There would be trouble. If Auntie May had given him the chance to explain the day the first pheasants arrived, he would have told her everything. Now, another one had been left on the step while he was at the farm. Why hadn't Auntie May answered the door? He picked up the hen bird by its cold scaly legs and went indoors, dreading the explosion.

She wasn't in the kitchen and he took the pheasant through to the scullery, laying it on the draining board where its buff-coloured head lolled into the sink.

'Auntie May?'

She wasn't upstairs and the sitting room was chilly and empty. No sign of Spence's pram either.

It was almost five. Why was she out so late? She'd told him she'd stopped working in the afternoons because she couldn't take Spence out in the cold.

He'd grabbed the chance to work with the chickens on Saturday and Sunday afternoons, overjoyed to have a job and be trusted to work for Mr Arrowsmith.

The cocoa tin, where he saved his wages, had a decent amount in it and soon he might have enough for food for a puppy. He dropped hints about having a dog every few days. So far, Auntie May hadn't said he definitely couldn't.

He wandered back to the scullery and poured himself some milk. What was for tea? He lifted the lid of a saucepan and found a stew of potatoes, onions and carrots in thick gravy. He took a deep sniff, carried the pan through to the kitchen and put it on the range.

He switched on the wireless. There was still a quarter of an hour before Children's Hour. It was the last episode of a Biggles story tonight. The set slowly warmed up and, after a few crackles, the sound of a man's voice came on. He was rabbiting on about growing onions, and Cliff turned down the volume.

The house was strange at this time of day. Without Auntie May and Spence it felt empty, like the shell after he'd finished a boiled egg. He went to the window, staring towards the dark lane before drawing the curtains. Should he walk up to the village to look for her?

He lifted the lid of the tin that had a picture of the King on it. One lonely jam tart. Should he? He'd be in trouble for the pheasant anyway, so what the heck.

The pastry was stale and the jam stuck round his teeth like treacle toffee.

He went up to his bedroom and put his wages in the cocoa tin. Mr Arrowsmith hadn't been very pleased when Cliff told him he hadn't found any eggs. Nora, the new land girl who did Auntie May's job when she was away, jumped in and said there had been quite a few that morning. Cliff felt Mr Arrowsmith eyeing him suspiciously, and he protested that he'd looked in all the places that Auntie May had shown him over the years.

'Auntie May says there ain't many in the winter,' he said.

A grunt was all the answer he got. He quickly mumbled goodnight and left, sure that the farmer didn't like him. As he wheeled Auntie May's bike through the gate, he heard the sound of laughter.

'Goodnight children, everywhere.' Uncle Mac signed off just as Auntie May arrived home.

'Where were you?' He helped lift the pram over the step, his head full of Biggles' derring-do.

'Sorry, Cliff. I went to take some papers to Mrs Douglas for the meeting. It took longer than I thought.'

Spence was crying and Auntie May was fussing around making his feed. She still had her coat on.

'Can you get Spencer out, please? I hope he's not cold.'

He took off the pram cover. Spence's face was dark with anger; his eyes screwed up as he yelled. His bonnet was lop-sided with the ribbon caught behind his ear. Cliff gently eased his fingers under the little body and carried him to the armchair.

'He's nice 'n warm. But he wants his tea,' he said. Poor little baby. He was starving, too. He untied the bonnet and smoothed the curly hair.

When Spence grew up, he wondered, would he be like some of the black GIs and have those tight curls that looked like the coat of a new-born lamb? He jogged the baby on his lap making shushing noises and whispering about the adventures they'd have together when they were older, but he couldn't stop him crying.

Auntie May brought the bottle. Cliff wriggled back in the chair and held the bottle to Spence's lips. He guzzled the milk as if he hadn't been fed in days.

Spence was back in his pram and they'd eaten the stew before Cliff remembered the pheasant in the scullery. Heck.

'Auntie May,' he began.

She looked at him, eyebrows raised.

'When I got back from the farm…'

'Yes.'

'There was a pheasant on the doorstep.'

He waited. Please don't let her flare up.

She sighed. 'Where have you put it?'

'In the scullery, but I ain't hung it up.'

'Haven't.'

'Right.'

'Well, go and do it and put something underneath to catch the blood.'

He went into the scullery. It was freezing after the warm kitchen. How come she hadn't gone off the deep end? Was she ill? She looked really tired. She'd been very quiet lately and hardly went out. Several times she'd asked him to call at the butcher's on the way back from school. It shut earlier than the grocer's, and she only dashed to them just before they closed.

At school, they'd told him about Spinster Potts in the grocer's. She called Spence a piccolo or something. He didn't know what that was, but it meant he was a darkie. Everyone had known about his brother when the new term started. Bob and Pete wouldn't have blabbed, but their mum said you couldn't blow your nose in Crompton Parva without everyone knowing. Other children asked him what Spence was like – as if he'd be different from a white baby. Cliff was glad Buster Johnson had left before Christmas; he'd have loved something else to taunt Cliff with.

In the playground, someone had said darkie babies were born with a tail. Bob threatened to punch out the lights of whoever said it, and no one dared repeat it.

He closed the scullery door quietly. Auntie May had fallen asleep in the armchair and he crept across the kitchen and pulled out a pack of cards from the table drawer. He began playing patience.

'What time is it?' Auntie May woke up with a yawn. 'Good Lord, it's almost nine. You should have woken me, Cliff. I've barely seen you all day. How was work?' She got up and set the milk pan ready to make their cocoa.

'It was all right, but Mr Arrowsmith wasn't happy when I told him there weren't any eggs this afternoon. He paid me though – for tomorrow as well.'

Auntie May poured milk into the pan, added some water and put it on the range. 'So I should hope; you're doing the work. But no eggs? I've never known that. Three or four maybe, but never none at all. I wonder whether Nora found any this morning.'

'She was there. She said she'd found a lot.'

Auntie May took two beakers from the dresser. 'She was there tonight? What for? She's only supposed to cover my shifts.'

'I dunno. She didn't come near the henhouses, but she and Mr Arrowsmith were laughing when I left.'

'Were they, indeed,' said Auntie May, banging the milk pan on the hob.

'I nearly bumped into Old P…, Mr Potts, as I came out the farm gate. I just spotted the white on his helmet. He didn't have a light on his bike,' said Cliff, packing up the cards.

May spooned cocoa powder into the beakers and added a little cold water. She dropped a saccharine tablet in each before pouring on the boiled milk and handing a steaming mug to Cliff.

'He probably wasn't on duty, but he says he wears the helmet to stop him hurting his head if he falls off his bike.'

Cliff gave a yelp of laughter. 'He wouldn't fall off if he 'ad a light!'

Chapter 22

'Your turn to be Jerry.'

As Pete shoved the parcel into Bob's hands, Cliff noticed the brown paper was torn along the edge and the string was loose. Where was the label that was on it when they left the Gale's house?

'Come on, Cliff, he's gettin' ahead. Chocks away.' Pete spread his arms and made revving noises as Bob plunged away up the slope into the trees, struggling to hold the fat parcel that was their aunt's birthday present.

Cliff and Pete raced up the runway, took off and raised their landing gear as they crashed through the undergrowth.

'Pincer movement,' yelled Pete, veering off as they spotted Bob, lit by a beam of sunlight, in a clearing at the top of the hill. Cliff spread his arms at quarter to three, steeply angled his body and took the opposite flank. The boy ahead, wearing a green balaclava, an outgrown jacket and flapping wellies became a silver Messerschmitt with a swastika on the wing and a pilot, wearing a flying helmet, in the cockpit.

'Nerr-ow.' He bounded on, straight into a bramble patch. A briar snagged his leg. Blood was dribbling from a cut beside his knee.

'Dog fight. Ert, ert, ert, ert,' shouted Pete, his arms stretched out, palms touching. 'Get him with your cannon, Cliff.'

Cliff aimed his arm-cannon, but the brambles had slowed him down and he watched Pete jump on Bob, yelling, 'The Spit's done it. Jerry's down.'

The twins wrestled on the ground like a pair of puppies.

Brushing off leaves and mud, Bob said, 'Cripes, look at the parcel.'

The package was squashed, torn and mud-splattered. Something knitted and yellow was poking out of the end.

'We'll be for it,' said Pete, using his muddy hand to stuff the material back in the paper. 'Aunt Hermione's a right tartar.'

Miserably, they trudged down the hill towards Crompton Magna. Cliff had only met the aunt once. She had whiskers and a loud voice and wanted to kiss him. Could he make an excuse to get away? Mrs Gale had asked the twins to take the present to her sister-in-law and they'd asked Cliff to come along. Games in the woods and a trek over the hill sounded a good lark, but he didn't want to be in bother with someone else's relations.

How could he get out of it? The houses came into view. Bigger than Crompton Parva, Crompton Magna thought it was better in other ways: more shops, a library and three pubs. Auntie May said Magna WI looked down on everything Parva did.

The path from the hill dipped down towards a farm. The owner, Bill Tyler, had been a friend of Seth's. Auntie May told him a story about the two men entering a ploughing match. They'd come equal first and decided to share the prize, a flagon of cider, as they drove their horses home. When Seth got back, he'd put both his horses in one stable and his stepfather, Mr Arrowsmith, had been furious.

From above, Magna Farm looked like a toy farmyard. It had a tractor in the yard and chickens pecking about. They kept their hens all year here because they had a hatchery and sold on the young birds. Mr Arrowsmith bought his new hens from them every year.

Cliff was in the lead as the muddy path wound behind the

farm buildings. His leg was stinging. The top of his boot had flapped against the cut and spread the trail of blood so it looked much worse than it was. How long before he could get long trousers? Buster Johnson had them when he was thirteen, a year before he left school, by then he'd looked ridiculous in shorts, like an elephant in swimming trunks. Auntie May kept saying Cliff was growing out of his clothes. Maybe they could get them when he was twelve, in September. Although, he was hoping to get a puppy for his birthday present. If she let him have it, he only had seven months to go before he got his own dog.

He peered between the sheds. Wizard. The tractor, an Allis-Chalmers – bright orange – looked magnificent. Why wouldn't Mr Arrowsmith get one? He craned in at the next gap and stopped short.

'Wha's up?' said Bob, just avoiding crashing in to him.

'I got a stone in me boot and me leg's sore. You go on and I'll wait here.'

'Coward,' said Pete, cuffing Cliff lightly round the head with the ragged parcel.

Aunt Hermione lived on the far side of the village, and the twins carried on along the path. Once they were out of sight, Cliff turned back to the gap where he could see into a corner of the yard. He heard people talking.

'That all you've got? Tidden' worth bikin' over that hill for them few,' a man said.

'Ssh.' A woman's voice. 'I'll get the sack if they find out. I d-didn't know when you were going to turn up. I was just told to w-watch out for the hat.'

'I'll tek 'em, but save them up for a few days in future. Here.' Cliff heard the jingle of coins. 'I'll be back by and by.'

Cliff ducked back as a woman in land army uniform crossed

the gap, putting something in her pocket. The man walked across the yard to where a bike leant on the gate. He put the box he carried on the back carrier and placed the ARP helmet on his head. What was Old Potty up to with eggs?

Cliff shuffled his backside around on the damp bank. It was cold, waiting for the twins. He was tired of squinting through the gap to look at the Allis-Chalmers, but he couldn't quite pluck up the courage to go into the yard and see it close up.

What was Old Potty's game with the eggs? The last three weekends he'd found no more than a couple of eggs at Elem Farm. Nora insisted she found more than him, and Mr Arrowsmith was getting ratty.

'Evenings is gettin' lighter and we should be gettin' more, not less. I never should a given Mrs Sheppard time off for that babby,' he'd grumbled, his face red and shiny.

Cliff kept his eyes down as the old farmer went on, 'Mebee Nora ought to do all the afternoons.'

Cliff stayed quiet. He didn't want Mr Arrowsmith to know that Nora was there in the afternoons even though she wasn't working and could easily do his job.

He heard Bob and Pete before he saw them. They were joking and larking around as they came in sight.

'Here, cowardy custard,' said Pete, handing Cliff a fluff-covered toffee out of his pocket. 'From Aunt Hermione.'

'What happened? Didn't she mind about the parcel?'

'Not when we told her what we suffered to get it there. How our pal was injured when we all slipped over on the hill path.'

The boys grinned at Cliff.

'You might have to make out your leg is as bad as it looks when you speak to Mum,' Bob said.

'You'll have to tell her,' Cliff said, 'I want to get to work early today.'

He inched Auntie May's bike down the side of the cart shed. The farm cart wasn't being used today and hopefully no one would notice the bike wasn't in the barn. Maybe he'd move it when it got to his usual starting time.

Auntie May hadn't seemed interested when he told her he'd passed by Mr Tyler's farm. He told her about the tractor, but she just smiled and nodded. What was the matter with her? She was so different; hardly going out, even missing her meetings. He didn't say he'd seen Old Potty. She'd probably say he was imagining a mystery where there wasn't one.

Instead of crossing the yard to the barn, he went around the edge, past the dung heap. Keeping flat against the wall, he put his head gingerly around the barn door. Good. No one was around apart from the Clydesdales. Blossom stopped eating her hay to look at him, hoping for a titbit. He rubbed her nose before picking up the egg basket and returning to the cart shed by the same route.

A few hens were pecking around the floor. The carts often carried sacks of seed and grain, and the birds were always on the lookout for any spills. He checked along the low beam that ran the length of the shed, like a belt around its middle. The corner was a favourite egg-laying place and, as he reached into the darkness, his hand felt warmth: two white eggs.

Following his usual trail through the farmyard, around the hayricks and along the hedges, he collected a total of fourteen eggs. There were a couple more in the hen houses, although most of the birds preferred to lay outside during the daytime.

He checked Seth's old watch, which Auntie May had lent to him for work. Five to three. Just time to move the bike. He put the egg basket under the back of the cart and wheeled the bike across to the barn. Nora was already in there searching for something.

'Hello,' Cliff said.

'Oh, hello. Are you early?' She scowled at him.

'It's just on free o'clock.' Was she angry with him? 'I'll get on,' he said, picking up the fork and shovel.

'Don't you need the egg basket?' she said in a sneering tone.

Damn. Cliff looked over his shoulder. 'Probably ain't any. I can carry 'em. If I find any.'

Nora glared at him.

It was dusk by the time the work was finished. He hoped Mr Arrowsmith would come down and he could show him the basket of eggs, but there was no sign of him.

He stood in the shadows of the cart shed. Should he take the eggs up to the dairy for safekeeping?

The gate squeaked and Nora stepped out of the barn. 'Come in here, quick,' she called, in the direction of the lane.

Old Potty, wearing his helmet, scuttled into the barn. Cliff picked up the basket of eggs and crept to the barn door.

'I haven't got any. The boy's up to something—'

'That little beggar? He's a bliddy menace. That May Sheppard's got a lot to answer for.'

How dare he. Old Potty and his family made life hell for Auntie May. No wonder she didn't want to go out. Without thinking, he shot round the door, held out the basket and said, 'Is this what yer 'ere for?'

Potty swore, Nora gasped and made a grab for the basket. In the next second, Mr Arrowsmith thundered through the barn door. 'What the devil's going on here?'

The trio froze, but Old Potty recovered first. 'I'd heard about black market eggs bein' sold in t'village, and I've been looking in to it. This young lady here,' he pointed to Nora as if he'd never met her before, 'was just telling me you'd had eggs go missin' when in marches me laddie here with a big basket. Reckon 'e thought we wus someone else.'

He couldn't believe his ears. He pointed at Old Potty. 'He was at Magna Farm this morning. He was buyin' eggs off a land girl.'

Old Potty blustered, 'I was checking to see whether they'd had eggs go missin'. The girl said they had and now we know why. This little bleeder's been up there, too.'

Mr Arrowsmith swung Cliff round by the shoulder. 'Did you see Mr Potts buy eggs?'

Cliff looked from Mr Arrowsmith to Old Potty and back. 'Well… no. But I 'eard 'im and I see the girl puttin' money in her pocket.'

'You saw the money?'

'No, but—'

'You *heard* it?' Old Potty sneered.

Nora giggled. Mr Arrowsmith glared at her.

Mr Arrowsmith looked at Cliff. He shook his head. 'I knew there were more eggs, an' I was set on finding out what you were doing. Who've you been selling them to?'

'I haven't. She has.' He pointed to Nora. 'To him.' He swung his arm to point at Old Potty who glared back, his eyes black holes beneath the brim of the helmet.

Why wouldn't Mr Arrowsmith believe him? He said, 'Don't you wonder why she's always here when she ain't working?'

Nora opened her eyes wide, feigning innocence, and simpered, 'I admit I've been hanging around here on the afternoons Cliff works. I knew you were worried and I was trying to catch him out. Like you,' she said, touching Mr

Arrowsmith's arm.

Mr Arrowsmith flinched away. He turned back to Cliff. 'You'd better go. When you decide to tell me who your buyer is, I'll decide whether to tell the authorities or not. You needn't bother to turn up tomorrow.'

'What about me money?'

'I think you owe me more than I owe you, young-fella-me-lad. Tell Mrs Sheppard I'll speak to her on Monday.'

Chapter 23

Putting Spencer in the garden for an hour had been a good idea. Quietly content, he'd watched the overcast sky and the fresh air helped him go to sleep straight after his feed.

The smell of the liver and onion casserole simmering in the oven reminded her she should be peeling potatoes. But Cliff wasn't due back from the farm for some time and she couldn't resist another ten minutes by the range. She had so little energy these days. It was an effort just to cycle to the farm and do her work. Getting up for Spencer's night feeds was exhausting and, night after night, she lay awake, her mind swirling with the possibility of letting him go. With only a month or so before the new hens arrived, she had to buck up and make a decision or she'd have no job.

The only other time she'd felt this drained was when Seth died. The news of his fall had been brought by a frantic farmworker hammering on the door. She had no recollection of riding her bike down the lane. Later she'd been told she'd almost ended up a casualty herself, skidding at the last minute to narrowly avoid colliding with the ambulance. It had barely stopped as she was hauled aboard to join Tom at Seth's side.

With her eyes closed, the impression of the hospital was as clear as if she'd just left it: a sea of starched white linen and waves of meaningless words crashing over her head. At the time, all she saw was Seth's face. His usual ruddy complexion was as pale as the dressing on his head. He never opened his eyes and the doctor pronounced him dead minutes after they arrived.

Apart from attending his funeral, she hadn't left the cottage for three weeks. Tom had hosted the sorry wake at the farmhouse and she'd crept away as soon as was decent. Rose and Doreen brought soups and fussy puddings to the cottage to tempt her to eat, but she'd had no appetite. She'd used safety pins to take pleats in her waistbands to keep her skirts from falling down.

Gradually, she'd come to terms with what had happened. When the war came the following year, and Cliff with it, her life had turned around. But now? Back in the Slough of Despond. She saw the worry on Cliff's face. She knew he realised why she rushed to the shop at the last minute; knew she couldn't cope with Victoria, Ephraim and anyone else who looked sideways and whispered as she passed. Doreen was shielding her from comments at the WI but that couldn't go on forever. Seth would have told her to get a grip but, at the moment, everyone else had a grip on her.

Spencer lay outside, oblivious. He wasn't the source of the problem. The source of the problem was probably sipping mint juleps, served by a black servant on a plantation in Mississippi.

In spite of herself, she chuckled. 'Too many films, May,' she said, getting to her feet and going into the scullery.

As she brought out a handful of potatoes, she discovered Cliff hanging up his coat.

'You're early,' she said, trying to sound bright.

Cliff mumbled something as he crossed the kitchen to go upstairs.

'Liver casserole for tea,' she said.

No response.

She stared after him. What was it now? A row with Tom? Again?

'Come down, the food is on the table,' she called. Cliff had been upstairs for half an hour.

He came down, feet dragging with every step like a prisoner on the way to his execution. She must give him some attention. She'd virtually ignored his attempts to chat for weeks.

'How was work?' she asked. 'Have you been paid?' He squirreled away his wages for some secret purpose.

He stopped pushing his food around the plate and said, 'I'm not gettin' paid and I ain't got a job no more.'

'What on earth...?' Having a family was just one problem on top of another. 'Tell me what's happened, Cliff, but first eat your tea before it gets cold.'

He finished his food as if she'd served up ashes. Gazing at the empty plate, he began the story.

'Why didn't you tell me about seeing Mr Potts at Magna Farm?' she asked when Cliff described the morning's scene. He looked up, meeting her eyes, saying nothing.

'All right, I know. I haven't been very talkative lately, have I? I'll try to do better. Tell me the rest.'

He continued and, at the end, he said, 'Mr Arrowsmith said I was to tell you he's goin' to talk to you on Monday.'

Ephraim was a bigot and a bully, but she'd never imagined he might be a black marketeer. The thought of the high and mighty Isabella associated with illegal goings-on was laughable.

Cliff was looking at her anxiously. 'You do believe me, don't you?'

'Of course I do, Cliff. I'm just astonished that Mr Potts would do such a thing. After all the lectures he's given you. The old hypocrite.'

'Yeah, but Nora's got my job, and Mr Arrowsmith says he'll report me.'

She wasn't going to let that happen. She felt something she hadn't felt in weeks: a surge of anger. 'Apart from him being completely blinkered where you're concerned, he hasn't got any evidence. No-one has seen you selling eggs, but someone has seen Mr Potts buying eggs.'

Cliff looked astonished. 'Who?'

'You,' she said. 'And he won't want you questioned by anyone. He'll have tried to stop Mr Arrowsmith doing anything, you mark my words.'

'D'you think so?' Cliff sat up.

'Certain of it,' she said. 'Can you finish up the casserole, there's a bit left?'

Cliff pushed his plate forward.

She timed her trip on Sunday to coincide with the break between the morning farm work and the afternoon work with the poultry. She had no intention of running into Nora.

A raw wind blew across the bare fields and her face was stinging by the time she turned off the lane and bumped along the track to the farmhouse.

'May. I told that lad I'd speak to you tomorrow,' Tom said, opening the back door. He was in his braces, and the remains of a meal lay on the only part of the kitchen table not covered in piles of letters, newspapers and farming catalogues. 'I was makin' meself a cup of tea. Will you take one?'

'Thanks.' May settled herself into one of the wooden carvers that would have comfortably accommodated Billy Bunter.

He handed her a cup and saucer that she recognised as being part of Seth's mother's best tea service. She was getting the royal treatment.

Tom sat at the opposite side of the table. ''e's told you what happened yesterday?'

'He's very upset, Tom. You can't seriously believe he's stealing your eggs?'

'Hmph. He brought in a big basket. Most I've seen for weeks in the arternoons.'

'That was to prove to you there were plenty. He saw Ephraim Potts buying eggs up at Bill Tyler's Farm.'

'So 'e says. Potts says the boy was pinchin' them up there too.' He pulled out a grey handkerchief and blew his nose.

'He was with the Gale twins. How could he be stealing eggs? He's usually at school and when he's not, he's working here. How would he get the time? It's two miles over the hill, and I wouldn't want to carry eggs down that slippery path.' May picked up her cup. The tea was weak. Gnat's pee, Seth would have called it.

Tom ran a hand over his pink scalp and stirred his few grey strands of hair. 'I can't take him back now. What about Nora, I've told her she can have his hours.'

'Yes, Tom, what about Nora? Ephraim aside, you must see she's in on whatever's going on. Since she took over the eggs, the output has dropped—'

Tom took a breath to speak.

'And don't say it's because I'm not here all the time. That's tosh and you know it.'

Tom's shoulders sagged and he shook his head. She sat back in the chair. She'd won. She felt alive again. Ready to fight for her family. Her two boys. Spencer was staying.

119

Chapter 24

'Mr Arrowsmith is deciding what to do about Nora,' she said.

Cliff was slouched in the armchair, flicking over the pages of an old *Beano*.

'He understands he jumped to conclusions and he's sorry about the way he treated you. He asked me to give you this.' She handed Cliff a florin.

His face lit up. 'Two bob? That's for two days and I'm not working today.'

'Take it as an apology. I suspect it's the only one you'll get. Come on. You lay the table – our Sunday dinner will be cinders if we don't eat it soon.'

It would have been better to wait until next day to visit Bill Tyler, but it was too far to walk Spencer in the cold when he'd have spent a morning at the farm.

Braking hard as the bike sped down the hill into Crompton Magna, she felt the first view of the village make its usual impressive impact on her. The broad main street was pristine as ever, and the set-back houses and orderly shops gave the illusion of a wealthy town – Bath or Leamington Spa – rather than a country village. Magna residents understandably took much pride in their village but, because they denigrated less auspicious villages, it was easy to see why they were disliked.

The street was deserted. It was like the set for a film – somewhere too good to be real. The legacy of a long ago impoverished aristocratic family, even the Luftwaffe seemed to have respected Magna's elevated status. No bombs had fallen anywhere near the village, although many Parva inhabitants would have enjoyed seeing a few fallen chimney pots or broken windows make a dent in the Magna pride.

She turned into the side road leading to Bill's farm and the elite impression evaporated. A terrace of tumbledown cottages and a couple of unkempt houses fronted the road. She looked across at a muddy garden where boys were kicking a ball around, just as they would in any other village.

Bill Tyler was renowned for hard work and was likely to be in a barn or shed. She checked several buildings in the main yard and, walking around the gleaming orange tractor that Cliff coveted, went through to the poultry yard. The sound of sweeping came from the hatchery and she called Bill's name.

A sliding wooden door trundled open and a wiry man appeared. He had strikingly blue eyes and strands of carroty hair escaped from under a flat cap. He was clutching a yard broom.

'May!' Bill grinned in the familiar way she'd known so well in the years he and Seth had been friends.

'It's good to see you,' he said, rolling the door shut and resting the broom against the wall. 'Nothing wrong is there?'

'No, no,' said May. 'I just wanted to have a word – if you've got time?'

'Of course. We'll go up to the house but, while you're here, take a look at your pullets. They'll be ready in a couple of weeks.'

She followed him across the yard to a huge black shed where a great clucking could be heard through the closed door.

In the foetid warmth, where feed and manure combined with the dust from hundreds of birds fluttering about on straw bedding, the atmosphere was as thick as soup. Light filtered through the wire-netting-covered windows, and she saw Bill had a handkerchief clutched over his nose and mouth. He'd always had chest problems and hadn't been able to enlist because of it.

'They look in fine condition, Bill,' she said. Anxious to get him away from the dust, she stepped outside. The pullets looked almost ready to lay. Clearly, they were going to arrive before she'd been expecting them. She'd have to find some way to cope with the extra work.

It wasn't Bill's problem; he'd produced strong healthy birds and she said, 'If you give me a week's notice, I'll get the houses ready.'

'Right you are.'

In the farmhouse, parts of which were said to date back to Tudor times, the kitchen was warm and snug.

Sitting over cups of tea and enjoying the treat of a slice of apple cake made by Bill's housekeeper, she told him what Cliff had seen that morning.

'I've never trusted Ephraim Potts,' Bill said. 'He used to be foreman up at the quarry. The men hated him. He was a real B to them.'

'Seth said something like that,' said May, 'but I don't remember any details.'

'I don't know if there was anything specific. Just the general impression. He rode roughshod over the men – stopping time off, docking wages on the slightest excuse, that kind of thing.'

'He left suddenly, around the time the war started, didn't he? I heard a bit of gossip, but I wasn't really taking notice of other people then.'

'I remember,' said Bill, ruefully. 'I don't think anyone found out why he left. They kept it pretty quiet. Doesn't look too good in light of what Cliff's discovered, though.'

They both sipped their tea.

'I'll look into this egg business,' he said. 'Most of my land girls live in the hostel. Gossip spreads like stink, there. There are a couple I can trust and if any are on the make, they may have heard about it. You can bet other farms are involved. Is Tom reporting it?'

'I don't want him to. I don't want Cliff involved.'

'Trouble is, we need evidence. I'll have a think.' He stood up and switched on the light. 'I'll run you back in the lorry.'

'But what about your petrol ration?'

'Farm business. Besides, you look all in. That baby keeping you up?'

Her private affairs had reached Magna. Did no one mind their own business anymore?

Bill must have seen her expression. 'I'm sorry, May. Didn't realise you didn't know it was common knowledge. It's the land girl grapevine. Don't look so upset.' He patted her arm. 'I think you're doing a wonderful job and so do the girls. They say women are getting lives of their own, making their own decisions. It's never going to be the same you know, after the war. I don't think it's a bad thing and nor would Seth. He had absolute confidence in your judgement. You're just a bit ahead of the locals. They'll catch up once the war's over.'

'I wish I thought so,' she said, but she wondered whether he might be right about Seth. Maybe he would have understood.

Chapter 25

The bike wobbled in the direction of the ditch. Cliff jerked the handlebars back towards the middle of the lane. Practising for a slow bicycle race with the twins, he struggled not to put his foot on the ground. They'd all be equally handicapped because Mrs Gale's bike was as big as Auntie May's and the ground was a long way down.

His first day back at work after three weeks. How would Mr Arrowsmith treat him face to face? What about Nora? Auntie May said she'd been transferred off poultry duties and was helping with other farm work. He crossed his fingers she would be out of the way before he arrived.

There was something white under the hedge. Snowdrops. He'd drawn one in Nature Study a couple of weeks ago and Mr Leavey, the teacher who took the top class, pinned the picture on the classroom wall. This term it was about all spring flowers. A bit further along, he spotted a clump of yellow flowers that he was pretty sure were primroses.

Auntie May loved flowers. He'd stop and pick some for her on his way back. In Southampton, the only flowers he'd seen were in the park. When he'd first arrived in Parva he'd stared at the houses; almost every one had roses growing up the walls and round the doors. He'd never realised houses could be pretty.

Rats. He was at the farm gate. Gingerly, he raised and lowered the rusty catch. He went towards the barn, placing his feet quietly, step by step. The bike's three speed made its ticking noise; in the quiet yard, it sounded like a machine gun.

Last time he'd been here he'd crept in the door and didn't get spotted. His crossed his fingers and rolled the bike forward.

'Get over, Blossom, you great lump.'

A woman's voice. Heck.

'Morning, Cliff.' Sally was grooming on an upturned bucket, using her fingers to separate a tangle of tail hair.

When the horses' tails were brushed out they looked like a lady's flowing hair. He tried to forget why some horses had really short tails. Auntie May told him they were 'docked': their tails cut off short when they were foals. People said it was to keep their tails from getting muddy or caught in the harness, but Auntie May told him it was just a fashion that had stuck.

Seth had persuaded his stepfather it was cruel and Mr Arrowsmith left his horses' tails to grow down to their hocks. If Cliff owned horses, that's what he would do.

Blossom whickered and he went over, pulling a crust of bread from his pocket. She took it gently from his hand. 'You haven't forgotten me have you, girl?' he said, stroking her neck and ending up with a fistful of loose hair.

'She's moulting now the weather's getting warmer,' Sally said, pointing to the mat of roan hair down the front of her sweater. 'Put that handful out on the wall. The birds'll take it to line their nests.'

He patted the hair into a little pancake and laid it on the end of the wall. There were birds singing nearby and they'd collect their present when no one was around. He went in to get the tools while Sally chatted on as if he'd never been away.

Maybe it wasn't going to be too awkward being back. He charged across the yard, careering the barrow over the bumps, making the fork and shovel leap a foot in the air.

Blossom's hair had gone from the wall by the time he'd

finished. Somewhere a little bird was snug in its horsey-smelling nest. He put the basket of eggs he'd collected on the harness room table and tore a scrap from an old gymkhana schedule. He scribbled a note saying, '23 eggs', just in case anybody pinched some before Mr Arrowsmith took them up to the dairy.

'Almost two dozen,' he told Auntie May, as she placed a blue china jug on the kitchen table, primroses spilling over the top.

'Well done,' she said. 'That'll please Mr Arrowsmith.'

She put a Spam sandwich in front of him. 'If we hurry up and eat, we'll have time to go to the village. We need shopping and I've got some letters to post. We'll be home in time for you to get back to work.'

He nodded as he bit into his sandwich. She'd been almost back to normal since she'd tackled Mr Arrowsmith about Old Potty and Nora, but she'd still avoided taking Spence out where they'd meet other people.

'Can we get *The Beano*?' he said.

'I'll take it now.'

He let Auntie May take the handle of the pram before they crossed the main road. As they reached the village street, he saw her looking around again and pretending not to.

At first of the houses, a man was cutting the hedge.

'Arternoon, Mrs Sheppard,' he said, touching his cap. Auntie May answered and they walked on. A few doors down, a lady was cleaning windows. Her little dog barked as they got near.

Cliff put his hand through the gate. 'Hello, Sammy.' The dog's coat was like hairy string. He rubbed its ears and the little creature squirmed in delight. Auntie May spoke to the lady, who asked her whether she'd be at the WI meeting on Tuesday. He waited for her answer. She hadn't been for ages.

'Probably,' she said, starting to walk on. 'If this little one goes to sleep.'

'His big brother will look after him, won't you, Cliff?'

'Course,' he said, nodding at Auntie May.

'We'll see,' she said. 'Goodbye, Mrs Wheaton.'

No one's said anything about Spence being black, he thought, after they'd spoken to a couple more people. They behaved as if he was any other baby. But we haven't met any Pottys yet. He crossed his fingers.

'We'll go to the post office, first,' Auntie May said, as they reached the village centre. 'I'm not leaving Spencer outside with the way things are. Can you carry him?'

Auntie May held the door open and Cliff went in with Spence in his arms. The baby was awake and looking around. He'll be smelling that funny mixture of soap-powder and bacon, Cliff thought. It seemed to get in his throat whenever he came into the shop.

There was nobody at the post office counter. He jiggled Spence and read out the dog-eared notices on the wall as they waited. 'Dig for Victory; Let Your Shopping Help Our Shipping; Save for the Brave. That's a rhyme, Spence. Save for the Brave.'

After a few minutes, Auntie May jingled the little bell, which was shaped like a lady in a long old-fashioned dress. He bit his lip.

The curtains at the back were jerked apart and Spinster Potty appeared. Like the dame in the Christmas pantomime, Cliff thought. He wanted to shout, 'Behind you.'

'Yes?' she said, her lizardy eyes sliding over them.

127

She saw Spence. Her scowl deepened and her pinched mouth turned down. It made her look like Blossom.

'Good afternoon, Miss Potts. Two stamps, please.' May placed her letters in front of the grille and, when she was silently handed the stamps, licked them and stuck them on. Victoria's eyes were fixed on the envelopes. She must be trying to read the addresses upside down.

Auntie May said, 'Will you put my *private* letters in the pillar box outside, please, Cliff.'

Victoria jerked her head back like she'd been poked in the eye. Cliff grinned as he went out to the postbox. Auntie May called after him, 'Put Spencer in the pram – you've got to get back to work before long.'

Victoria's snort reached him just before the door swung shut.

He was happy as they walked up the road away from the village; he would read *The Beano* as soon as he got back from the farm, and Auntie May was in a good mood because no one had said anything nasty about Spence, even when he'd started crying in the baker's.

They stopped at the main road. Auntie May muttered, 'Damn.'

He looked past her. The Pottys were walking towards them from the bus stop, carrying big shopping bags. Old Potty was wearing his black Churchill hat and the dragon was, as his mum would have said, done up like a dog's dinner. They scowled at the sight of Auntie May and Cliff.

One of the cars on the main road put out its trafficator to turn into the village. An Austin Ten. Dr Haskett. Cliff waved and watched the doctor manouvre his car round the corner. How smashing it must be to drive a car or, even better, a tractor.

Because a couple of lorries were coming along the road, they had to wait. The Pottys were going to pass within inches. He lowered his eyes – he didn't want to give Old Potty an excuse to say he was insolent. There was a strong flowery smell as Mrs Misery Guts passed him in the middle of the path, trying to make him step into the road. Auntie May seemed frozen to the ground and to avoid bashing into the pram, the Pottys had to squeeze into the hedge.

'Good afternoon,' Auntie May said.

Neither Potty answered although Old Potty half-raised his hat once his back was to them.

'Shall I see you at the meeting on Tuesday, Mrs Potts?'

The woman half-stopped, muttered something and went on without looking back.

He stole a look at Auntie May. She winked at him, a wide grin on her face.

Chapter 26

She couldn't use Spencer as an excuse to miss another meeting. The little soul was perfectly behaved and saying he wouldn't go to sleep was unfair. He was a dream baby. He took all his milk, rarely cried unless he needed a nappy change or was hungry and slept most of the night. Any mother – except his own – would be proud of him.

Saying she couldn't leave him would give the bigots more reasons to condemn him. She had to chair the meeting for his sake, if not her own.

She was early enough to avoid running into Isabella and her cronies walking up the hill, but she pushed herself to cycle to the top. It would marvellous to get the use of the village hall back when the war was over, but it might be difficult. The Home Guard had already been stood down, but they were slow to remove their kit and give other groups access.

Doreen had switched on the meeting room lights. It was still daylight, but the room was always gloomy despite the over-shadowing oaks having been felled early in the war. The sorry row of stumps, now overgrown by brambles, did nothing to raise the depressing atmosphere in the tiny churchyard as she parked her bike.

'It's good to see you back, hen,' Doreen said, with a warm smile.

They sat together on the makeshift dais and discussed the agenda.

'I think we should make a start on planning something for when the war ends,' said May. 'Everyone thinks it won't be long before it happens. A committee to prepare a village street party, do you think?'

'Definitely. And we must lay on something special for the bairns – a lot of the evacuees will be going back to their parents soon after,' said Doreen.

Not Cliff and Spencer, May thought. 'It must be a happy day. We need games, competitions and so on. Give them something to remember. We'll see what ideas the members come up with.'

Doreen went off to welcome the ladies. They trickled into the room, vying to get the least sagging canvas chairs, bustling around laying out refreshments and lighting the spirit stove under the huge kettle, which took half the meeting to come to the boil.

'Only spot-the-sultana scones, I'm afraid,' said a woman, placing tea-cloth-covered plates on the table.

May didn't want to make eye contact with anyone, keeping her head down as the room filled up. No one could be oblivious to Isabella's entry as she commandeered the second row, and May felt herself perspiring, despite the chill of the room.

She bit her lip and forced herself not to react when someone pointed out that she was back. Isabella's snort was clearly designed to reach the entire audience, along with her stage whisper, 'We *are* honoured that our President has left her waifs and strays to join us.'

Apart from one titter, there was an embarrassed silence followed by the clamour of voices as everyone spoke at once.

May's pencil hadn't stilled but, with relief, she checked her watch, fixed a smile on her face and raised her head.

'Good evening, ladies. How nice to see so many of you here tonight,' she began.

Isabella leaned over and whispered to her neighbour. They

131

both turned to May with fixed stares. She wouldn't look in their direction. Other members of the audience wore encouraging smiles as she thanked Doreen for covering for her absence whilst she coped with the arrival of a new foster child. Were there a few mutters of sympathetic approval? She refused to let her eyes stray to Isabella's row and announced the first item on the agenda.

She introduced the subject of the street party after the break for tea. 'After so many years, it is a real pleasure to propose that we begin making plans to celebrate the imminent end of the war.'

The audience burst into applause. Risking a glance at the second row, she saw Isabella glare at her applauding neighbour and jab her in the ribs. She looked away and asked for suggestions for activities to run alongside the street party.

'Madam President,' hissed Doreen, nodding towards the second row. May's heart sank. Isabella was on her feet.

'Yes, Mrs Potts?'

'Isn't it premature to plan to celebrate the end of the war? We have no idea when it will be. All the fuss and bother in the press is just guesswork. We should wait for Mr Churchill to tell us. We shouldn't tempt fate.'

If she allowed herself to be trampled again, she'd always be the underdog, always allow bullies to take the lead.

'Thank you for voicing your opinion, Mrs Potts. However, I don't believe the end of the war *is* speculation although the actual date is as yet unknown. The shops are selling bunting and Union Jacks, and I don't think Parva WI wants to present the village with a poorly-run street party, organised overnight, because it didn't give the matter enough forethought.'

There were murmurs of hear, hear and Doreen nodded

vigorously.

'As for tempting fate. Can you really see Herr Hitler mounting a last-ditch offensive because the Crompton Parva WI have made arrangements for a tea party?'

The room exploded into laughter. Isabella turned a violent shade of puce, grabbed her bag and, dragging her friend by the arm, stalked out.

Chapter 27

The end of the war! What would it be like? Would they be able to get sweets and bananas every day? He remembered some squishy sandwiches his mother had left for him, but he couldn't remember how the banana had tasted.

When Auntie May came back from her meeting, she'd swept in, hugged him and kissed Spence. She'd been humming songs ever since: *Bless 'em All, We'll Meet Again* and others Cliff didn't recognise. He couldn't think when he'd last seen her so happy.

She asked him to think of ideas for games and competitions for the street party. Everybody was going to bring their tables and chairs outside. The whole village was taking food and they would eat it together – in the street. He and Auntie May and Spence would take their table into the village as the lane was too far away to join in, and they'd look daft sitting outside the cottage on their own.

'We want a fancy dress competition. Pete, Bob and me are going as a gang of pirates,' he said. The carving knife was just right for a cutlass. He slashed it through the air. 'Heave-ho me hearties!'

'You'll cut someone's throat with that.' Auntie May said, putting it back in the drawer. 'You need to make a cutlass out of wood. Have a look in the shed.'

He mooched up the village street, kicking a stone. One of the most exciting things about THE END was that no one knew when it would be. It could be tomorrow and, if it was, they wouldn't have any cutlasses. Bob and Pete had no wood and there was nothing in the shed. Everything had been used for firewood or patching up something else.

He'd already asked at the butcher's, but they couldn't help. They probably knew he hated their shop. He'd once asked what kind of meat the dark red slab in the front the window was and the butcher, wearing a bloodstained apron, laughed and he said, ''Os meat, sonny. Os.'

He'd felt sick at the thought of Blossom or Ben ending up in a butcher's shop and didn't look in the window anymore.

In the baker's, they'd just taken some currant buns out of the oven. The smell made him hungry and he felt in his pockets. Nothing except his penknife and hanky. He asked about wood. No luck.

Outside, he tugged up his socks and walked on. Would he dare ask at Spinster Potty's? He kicked the stone on with a hefty whack. It skittered along the path and came to a stop at the open side gate of the post office.

He sidled up and peered in. Nobody in sight. If the post office was busy, Spinster Potty wouldn't be on the prowl and he could have a root around. They were bound to have something useful amongst the junk that littered the yard.

He tiptoed around some broken cardboard boxes and the rusted frame of a delivery bike, to a pile of bottle crates. Would these do? He lifted a hinged lid, but the crate was divided into squares for the bottles. He'd never be able to break them up.

He moved on and spotted something promising poking out from beneath a rotting sack. It was on the far side of mesh-covered window that overlooked the yard.

He bent double and crept below the windowsill. A sheriff raiding the outlaws' hideout.

The window above him was ajar. Voices. He froze.

'Not long now, Victoria. Once we get the armistice, those city brats will be back in their filthy hovels and we'll get our village back to ourselves.' It was Old Potty's missus.

Spinster Potty said, 'Yes... but 'ee do buy stamps and use the shop—'

'That's a small price to pay to get rid of them. Now Ephraim isn't in charge they do just what they like. The sooner they get back to their rat-holes the better.'

Cliff wished he was the sheriff. He'd stick his revolver through the window and make her put her hands up until she apologised.

'Some of 'em aren't that bad. A couple a little girls is quite polite. And clean.'

'None of them're clean. They live like pigs. Those slums. You wouldn't believe the conditions—'

'How do 'ee know, Isabella? Have 'ee bin there?'

Cliff held his breath. *Had* she been to his old streets?

'I just know,' she said. 'You'd best watch your windows – they'll put them out, running riot at this so-called *street party*.'

Spinster Potty said, 'But surely, they'll be kept an eye on—

Old Potty's missus snapped, 'Not if the foster mothers get drink in them. They'll soon forget the little savages.'

Cliff wanted to bash the windows in right then. He daren't move, even though he was getting cramp.

A bell jangled. 'I'll leave you to your customers, Victoria. You mind what I've said.'

A door closed. He moved on, stretching his cramped leg. Old witch. He clenched his fists. If he was a man he'd show her. Good job she'd didn't get any evacuees, they'd have been worse off than Jim and Susan. Their foster father made them eat slops and beat them with his belt. They'd run away back to Southampton – to their rat-hole. He remembered Susan cowering in the corner of the playground, too frightened to go back to their foster home. He hoped they'd made it through the bombings.

He lifted the sack and it fell apart, releasing the stink of rotten cabbage. He wrinkled his nose, but what was underneath the shredded hessian was just what he was looking for: an old vegetable crate with one side smashed in. Just right to break up and re-use.

He tipped out the slimy greens and checked over the box. He'd be able to break out the nails with a bit of force but it might make a noise. He couldn't ask whether he could take it – Spinster Potty would think he was planning to use it on her windows.

Could he hide it and come back? He'd hardly ever seen the gate open and they were sure to shut it again soon. He bit his lip, looking down at the crate and wondering how noisy it would be. Was it worth the risk?

A lorry was rumbling up the street. As it got nearer, he aimed a kick at the crate where the end and the side joined. With a bit of luck, the noise of the engine would cover the splintering wood. The lorry stopped with a squeal of brakes. It was delivering to the shop. That was why the gate was open.

The driver and his mate got out of the cab. Arguing loudly, they left the engine running. Cliff wrenched out three slats and chucked the reeking sack over the rest.

Nails sticking into his jersey, he stuffed the slats under his jacket and ran across the yard. He craned his neck around the gate. The lorry driver was lowering the tailgate and Spinster Potty, hands on hips, was moaning the delivery was late. She had her back to him and he shot out of the gate and up the street.

He'd foxed the outlaws. Yippee!

Chapter 28

'Can we take the table now?'

'Cliff, we haven't finished breakfast.' Auntie May spread marge on her toast. 'Mrs Gale's sending the twins to help when they've put out their own table.'

'Can we put it on Spence's pram?'

'No. You'll have to carry it. I need the pram for the food and your pirate costume. And Spencer.'

The baby banged his spoon on the tray of his highchair. Bits of rusk flew off and he gave one of his big grins.

'You've got a white moustache,' Cliff told him, picking up the piece of old towel they used as his flannel. He dabbed around Spencer's mouth. Dipping the chunky Bakelite spoon into the mashed-up rusk, he offered it to his brother.

Spence opened his mouth like a baby bird. Their mum must have fed him like this when he was a baby. Did she ever think about that? Did she ever think about what she was missing with Spence? Perhaps she hadn't liked it when he'd been a baby, so it put her off another one.

'Mum says you don't need your table – they've put a treadle out for you, Mrs Sheppard.'

'Treadle? Ah, trestle. I hope it's near the end,' said May.

'Dunno,' said Pete, going red.

He does know, Cliff thought, and it ain't.

'Can we go?' he said. His feet wouldn't keep still. He'd been looking forward to carrying the table. It would've been a Lanc. A big lumbering bomber. Now he just wanted to get to the party.

The two boys ran up the lane, dogfighting as they swerved around the potholes, Cliff lunging with his cutlass. Auntie May told him to carry his own costume now they hadn't got the table. He had to put it on their chairs when they got to the party.

They crossed the main road and he ran ahead, dying to see the village street. As they reached the pond, he stopped dead. Pete cannoned into him.

'Watch it.'

'Cor! It's—'

'Good, ain't it?' Pete said.

He stared. The street. It was completely different. Little pointed red, white and blue flags hung in long lines across the road. Union Jacks flew from the church tower, hung from windows and were draped over fences. And the people. He'd never seen so many in one place since he'd left Southampton.

As they got nearer, villagers called out. 'Where's Mrs Sheppard?' and 'Is your brother coming?' and 'What are 'ee dressin' up as?'

It was never like this. He felt part of the village. Other evacuees seemed as stunned, grinning nervously as people, who usually ignored them, patted them on the back and asked if they were looking forward to going home.

Buster Johnson walked towards them. The bottoms of his trousers swung six inches above his boots and he wore a tweed jacket with an elbow patch flapping like a wing. He had on the checked shirt he wore to work in the munitions factory. Pete's mum said the jobs in the factory were being cut down and would end completely once the Japs were beaten. What would Buster do then?

Cliff looked around but there was no time to hide and he cringed as Buster swaggered up. Pete ducked to the side, but

Buster put his big paw on Cliff's head and ruffled his hair.

'Soon be back home, won't yer, Erwin?'

Cliff wanted to say he *was* home, but people were listening, and Auntie May hadn't told them he was staying. None of their business, she said, but he wished he could just say it. And say he was going to be her son. But until his mother sent the letter, it wasn't certain. If it didn't come, he might have to go back to the city, alone.

'Yeah,' he muttered, trying to move aside. Buster punched him on the arm. It felt like a kick from a horse.

'See yer sonny-boy,' he said as he strode off.

'Where's ours?' They stood at the foot of the line of tables and chairs that wound up the street. Each one had plates and knives and forks on it. People were bringing out piles of food and big bowls covered with cloths.

Pete looked shame-faced. 'It's over there.' He pointed toward the place where a sort of stage sat. 'They wanted it to go up on it, but Mum made them put it on the ground. It's that one,' he said, nodding to an empty table facing the whole row.

It couldn't be. Not there. He said, 'I ain't sittin' there with everyone gawpin' at me.'

'They said it's for the Wimmins Institution. The leaders, like.'

He had a lump in his throat. He couldn't let Pete see him cry. He'd been looking forward to this party for so long. Now he had to sit with a load of women, being stared at by everyone.

He wiped his nose on his sleeve. 'Where's your mum?'

'There.' Pete pointed to a table back up the street. Cliff recognised the twins' grandad talking to Bob.

'C'n I put me stuff over there, for now?'

'Course.'

Chapter 29

When she arrived at the party, May stood with her back to the churchyard wall. She smiled as she looked at the patriotic red, white and blue bunting and Union Jacks fluttering in the breeze. There was an air of regatta in the village. Or was it freedom? Voices full of excitement, relief and anticipation jumbled together to produce an incomprehensible sound that was at once electric and contagious. Even Ephraim had a smile on his face.

Tables snaked up the street. The tapestry of coloured cloths, which had been so evident first thing this morning when she'd checked on the WI activity, was virtually invisible under mountains of food. Who would have guessed that every household had, at the back of their pantry, some delicacy squirreled away for a special occasion? Occasions didn't get more special than VE Day, as it was being called, and they'd risen to it. Tins of ham and tongue; jellies, in brilliant reds and greens, wobbling out of moulds disused for more than five years; great bowls of trifle and fruit cakes made with hoarded dried fruit, all graced the tables alongside the everyday fish paste sandwiches, sausage rolls, chocolate pin wheels and prune sponges. In pride of place, a huge box of Cadbury's chocolates; the once-bright ribbon bow now faded to flesh pink.

The bombed-out barn at the top of the hill opposite the church overlooked the celebratory scene. Its blackened rafters were a reminder of the danger they had faced until a few days ago, and she'd noticed Rose glance up at it. She was sure to be thinking of Len, still not safe, on a ship in the Far East.

She'd tried to conceal her dismay when she discovered their table was next to the dais the committee had erected for speeches and prize giving. It wasn't how she'd envisioned spending the first day of the new era: on show to everyone. Cliff's crestfallen face, when he pointed out where they were expected to sit, reflected her own feelings and she gratefully accepted Rose's invitation for him to join her and the twins.

'I'll take the little one, too, leave you free ter keep an eye on everything,' Rose said.

Thank goodness. She didn't want the baby on display like a zoo animal. They'd tucked the pram behind Rose's table where Spencer was at a distance from prying eyes and safe from poking fingers. She could see him sitting up, his black hair a mass of curly wool against the white pram hood.

She'd avoided contact with all three Potts. They had placed their table in the centre of the row. Their snowy white cloth and gleaming cutlery nudged cosily up to the creased damask and tarnished silverware Squire Mountjoy's family brought from The Lodge. Without servants, it seemed the Mountjoys were struggling.

The Squire was to present the prizes to the children. All suggestions that it should have been Ephraim's place, as village ARP warden, had been firmly rejected.

Over my dead body, May had thought. If she gave him preferential treatment, then what about the LDV, the WRVS, the firewatchers – almost everyone had taken a turn at that – and all the other bodies that had contributed to the welfare of the village over the duration.

Miffed by her response, Isabella refused to take any part in the arrangements and was still throwing her malevolent glances.

As she walked beside the row of tables, she caught a glimpse of Valerie Harris trying to snaffle a biscuit and earning herself a slap from her mother. Should she announce food was served? The early light rain had cleared and it was warm under the blue sky. She'd give it another ten minutes – Tom still hadn't arrived. She didn't want to start without him, especially as he'd donated the three chickens she'd boned and roasted. The thought of the tender white meat and the parsley and thyme stuffing she'd made whetted her appetite.

Other people weren't in a hurry to eat. Before the war there would have been impatience, but appetites were not what they had been. People were content to chat to one another. Safe, not straining their ears for sirens or engines that might cut out any second. They were laughing and relaxing in a way she hadn't seen for years.

Except for Rose. She looked pensive. The boys were off practicing the three-legged race – falling over more often than they stayed upright. Rose's in-laws were sitting with her, but they were engrossed in conversation with friends at the next table.

'Are you all right?'

'Yes,' said Rose, switching on a smile.

May sat down next to her. 'What is it?'

Rose shrugged. 'I'm just thinking about Len. I wish the war with the Japs was over, too. It's difficult to celebrate when he's still out there.'

'I wondered if you'd feel like that,' May said. 'If you don't want to stay—'

'No. The boys would never forgive me – all that work for the pirate costumes and I don't watch the parade. Never.' She laughed. 'I've got my Box Brownie, so I can show Len the photos when he gets home.' She patted the camera hanging on the back of her chair. 'I know. Before we eat, let's get a picture of the two of us.'

She leaned over and asked her father-in-law to take a snap. As Mr Gale focussed on the two of them, Rose whispered, 'Any truth in the rumour Ephraim's in for a knighthood?'

'Wha—?'

The two of them threw their heads back, roaring with laughter, just as the shutter clicked.

Chapter 30

'I'm starvin'. How soon can we eat?' Cliff asked.

Auntie May had got it straight away. He didn't have to ask if he could sit with Pete and Bob. She'd rather sit with them, too, but she was stuck at the front. At least Old Potty's missus wasn't with them. She was with old Misery Guts. They were sucking up to the Squire.

Cliff's stomach was rumbling by the time Auntie May said they could eat. They had to wait for the vicar to say grace. Cliff saw a boy at the next table sneak a hand out and grab a sandwich when they should have had their eyes shut. Could he get one too? Mrs Gale fixed him and the twins with one of her looks. He waited.

After the prayer, like a conjurer, she flicked off the tea cloths to reveal the food.

Blimey. Plates of ham and chicken, meat pies, huge slices of bread, big jammy cakes; bigger than he'd ever seen. And jelly. He laughed as it wobbled about in the dish until Bob got a ticking off for jogging the table.

His belly hurt. Could he be ill?

He saw Pete clasp his hands across his own middle. 'I'm so-o full,' he said.

That was it. He was full-up. He couldn't eat another thing. What a smashing feeling. It was wizard, now the war was over.

Chapter 31

The meal was perfect. Meat, jelly and cakes all vanished in minutes. The few leftovers wouldn't be around for long, either. Tom had arrived, breathless and sweating, just in time to join in the grace. He been deep in conversation with another farmer, but May had noticed when he pushed back his Sunday-best cap, his face had a purplish tinge. She must persuade him to take some time off.

A crowd gathered around the games area and there was a sense of friendly rivalry: parents exaggerating the prowess of their foster children as proudly as their own. Squire Mountjoy's surprise gift of a barrel of cider was probably responsible.

Doreen marshalled the children at the start and the races began along the wide roadside verge opposite the church.

'That lad of yours is doing well,' said Mr Mountjoy.

She stood next to the Squire, noting down the results ready for the prize giving.

'Yes,' she said, 'he's a good boy.'

Was this leading up to something? She remembered the conversation she'd overheard months ago between him and the Potts, mentioning Cliff's name.

'I hope you enjoyed the pheasants?'

Her hand jerked and a line of pencil streaked across the pad. Not today. Not when everyone was so happy. He couldn't accuse Cliff of poaching now.

'Did you get that one? Mrs Sheppard?'

'What? Oh, sorry. Yes, Buster Johnson first in the egg and spoon.'

'And this time he didn't trip anyone up.'

'Perhaps we should have sorted them by size, not age,' May said. 'Um, about the pheasants—'

'Yes, I'm always sorry when the seasons ends – the birds come in useful to top-up the rations, don't you find?'

Was this sarcasm? Was she going to incriminate Cliff if she agreed?

There was a roar from the crowd. A pile-up in the wheelbarrow race. Cliff, quick off the mark, tugged Bob's legs to one side and, managing to stay on his hands, Bob veered past the chaos to bring the pair home in first place.

May cheered. Rose whooped from beside Spencer's pram, startling the baby for a second, before he gave one of his trademark grins. Cliff ran up and hugged his brother. May saw Isabella whisper something to Ephraim. They looked as if they'd bitten on wasps.

The Squire must've followed her gaze. He said, 'It can't be easy for you. People here are the salt of the earth, but they don't welcome change. You're lucky to have Clifford. Such a responsible boy. I'm very fond of my son, but he hasn't got half Clifford's common sense.'

What *was* this about? He wasn't upset about Cliff. Quite the opposite. Her mind reeled, but the three-legged race was in uproar – too many legs and more children on the ground than on the course. The Squire went to assist and the moment was lost.

'There'll be carnage if we don't get it judged soon, hen,' Doreen said, as they watched the costumed children parading in a circle around Mr Mountjoy.

Cliff, Peter and Bob looked the part in their homemade pirate costumes, complete with eye patches and bright scarves wrapped round their heads. They were strutting ahead of a pair of local boys from an outlying farm who wore chicken-feather headdresses and smudges of paint on their cheeks.

Things were getting heated. The farm boys clearly thought the pirates were their biggest rivals. They began dashing forward to perform a war dance in between the pirates and the judge every time they passed him.

Both sets of boys carried weapons: cutlasses and war-axes (May thought the drips of red paint on the cutlasses a step too far, but Cliff had insisted). Things could get out of hand.

As they watched, the pirates came round again. Cliff whispered something to Peter and Bob and, just as the Red Indians began to move between them and the judge, the three lifted their cutlasses.

'Oh Lord,' she passed her clipboard to Doreen, ready to wade in.

But the pirates stopped dead, bringing the circle to a halt. The Red Indians didn't notice and moved on to do their war dance in the judge's eyeline. They finished, grinning at each other and then saw they were standing alone, leaving the pirates in clear view. Taking the advantage, the three boys sang out, '*Fifteen men on a dead man's chest. Yo ho ho and a bottle of rum.*' Linking arms and spinning, they waved their cutlasses and a bottle that had been mysteriously acquired and bore the word 'Rum' in dribbled white paint.

The crowd cheered and waved their Union Jacks.

She felt an aching tiredness. The work of preparing for today with little sleep was overtaking her. The night before, excitement had been running wild. Church bells rang out (Cliff had run inside asking if it was the invasion), cars and Jeeps drove up and down the lanes, hooting at every house they

148

passed. Most people already believed the war had ended before the official announcement finally came on the wireless just after seven thirty. Some said a German broadcast had announced it earlier in the day. According to the wireless, crowds had been at Buckingham Palace from the early morning. Exciting. Joyful. An historic moment. Nevertheless, the two days had sapped her energy.

Just the speeches and prize giving, then she could go home and put her feet up. It didn't look as if the party was going to break up anytime soon but they could manage without her. She stood on the dais, conscious that her cotton dress was creased and her hair dishevelled, but she didn't care. She waited until the noise hushed.

'Ladies, gentlemen, boys and girls,' she began. 'I'd like to thank you all for making our VE Day party so successful—'

She was drowned out by the cheers. She stepped back, extended her arm to the Squire and gave him the stand.

More applause. He talked about how they'd all pulled together during the hostilities and that shouldn't be forgotten, although they needed to look to the future. Those who were no longer with them would always be remembered for their sacrifice and he saluted those still fighting. She saw Rose wipe her eyes.

'Now, we get to the important part of the day,' he said. 'The prizes for the children's races and fancy dress competition.'

The children nudged each other and launched into cries of hooray as May stepped forward with her list of names.

The three highest placed children were presented with red, white and blue rosettes and were allowed first pick from the box of chocolates.

'I hope there's enough to go round,' Doreen said.

'I just hope they don't get food poisoning,' said May.

'Heaven knows how old they are.'

'The bairns won't know they aren't meant to be this colour,' said Doreen looking at the white rimed chocolates. 'I expect the centres will be fine.'

Cliff and Bob took first place rosettes for the wheelbarrow race. Cliff had come second in the sack race and third in the egg and spoon.

The tension mounted as everyone waited for the results of the fancy dress. Cliff, Peter and Bob had moved to the other side of the crowd from the Red Indians. She had agreed with Rose they would step in if feelings ran too high.

'First prize for the girls' fancy dress goes to Miranda Wheaton for her clever red, white and blue costume. I especially like the hat,' said the Squire.

The child stepped up. Her jacket and skirt were made from newspapers, painted in the patriotic colours, topped off with a matching Robin Hood style hat. May pinned the rosette to her paper lapel.

'And last, but not least, the boys' fancy dress.'

Clowns, toy soldiers, chimney sweeps and cowboys craned forward in anticipation. The pirates and Red Indians glared at each other.

'Squire'll give it to 'ee Da'set boys,' Ephraim declared loudly.

Rose gave him one of her looks. He turned away.

'It was a close-run thing,' said Mr Mountjoy, 'but, in the end, I decided to award first prize to the competitors who showed initiative, as well excellent costumes. First place goes to the pirates.'

The audience bellowed approval.

Cliff, Peter and Bob took their rosettes and shook Mr Mountjoy's hand. He said something to Cliff and patted him on the back. Cliff glowed. May hugged him. Rose had taken Spencer out of his pram. She waved his little hand at his brother.

May's heart lifted, thrilled the lad had done so well. She looked to where Ephraim and Isabella had been standing. They weren't there. She spotted them heading off to their table, turning their backs on the boys.

Chapter 32

She gently closed the stairs door. Spencer was still asleep in the box room – *his* room she should call it, now they'd installed the cot Rose had lent her.

The pile of washing-up on the draining board half-covered the window. Last night, after the street party, she'd been too tired to tackle it. She'd unloaded the pram – Spencer squeezed in amongst crocks, cutlery and pirate costumes – put him to bed and dozed in the armchair. Cliff had stayed out with the twins to see the bonfire. He'd arrived home, after eleven, and said the party was still going on. The sound of music had drifted on the breeze when she went out to the lavatory before bed.

School was closed for another day's holiday and Cliff offered to do her work at the farm. You can have a rest, he'd said. Some rest with all those dishes. But it was a kind thought.

She'd need plenty of hot water. If she lit the copper, the water should stretch to washing the tablecloths and Spencer's laundry, too. She laid kindling on scrunched newspaper in the grate under the copper and struck a match. Cliff had liked doing this when he first arrived. He'd had a young boy's fascination with matches, but she'd been scared he'd burn the house down; his mother had never given him any safety instruction.

He'd looked at her pleadingly yesterday when there was talk about the evacuees going home. She had to let it be known he and Spencer were staying in Parva, but the party wasn't the right time to risk a bad reaction. It was only when she got home that she realised Ephraim couldn't have told everyone Lynette was in America after their showdown about Spencer – the gossips would have made capital out of that juicy material. Perhaps he was hoping the boys would be shipped out to join her and he could forget all about them.

She slipped the first plate into the warm soapy water and gazed through the window at the wide blue sky, which no longer held a threat. She couldn't truly believe they didn't have to worry about air raids and invasions, gas masks and shelters. No fire-watching duties. There would still be lists of casualties from the Far East, and Rose and the twins would worry about Len on his ship, but the danger for the village, for the country, had passed.

She began to sing, 'There'll always be an England...'

Her shoulders ached. The dishes were put away, the laundry was fluttering on the line and Spencer was content outside in his pram. He was playing with a saucepan lid and a wooden spoon. The tinny banging was audible through the open door but far away enough for her to ignore it. Time to strip the chicken carcasses for a stew. Cliff would be ravenous when he got home. There were a lot more hens at the farm now and it was hard work caring for them.

'Auntie May?'

'Cliff?' She dashed to the door. Cliff was running up the path, shirt hanging out. 'Mr Arrowsmith. 'e's gone to 'ospital. The doctor's comin' ter get yer.'

A clammy hand seemed to clutch May's insides. She must be calm for Cliff.

'Wait until you can speak.' He was panting, bent over, hands on knees, gasping for breath. His boots were caked with muck. May dragged a chair over to the door. 'Sit down and tell me what's happened.'

'Mr Arrowsmith was hitchin' up Blossom and he fell down. Collapsed. Holding 'is chest.'

'Were you there?'

'I was emptyin' the barrer on the muck heap; Sally was with Mr Arrowsmith. She got me to bike to the house up the lane and ask them to phone for the doctor.' Cliff's eyes were wide, his face flushed.

'What about Mr Arrowsmith?'

'When I got back, he was sat up next to the cart with an old horse blanket round 'im. He looked awful, kind of grey. His cap had come off and he was shakin'.'

She should've made him see the doctor weeks ago. 'He looked ill yesterday, but he insisted on going back to do the animals at teatime,' she said. I don't suppose all that cider helped, she thought. 'What happened when Dr Haskett arrived?'

'He looked at his chest and used them earphone things. Then the ambulance turned up and they put him on a stretcher and took him away. The bell was ringin' an' everything.'

Déjà vu. In a month's time, it would be the seventh anniversary of Seth being taken from the farm by ambulance. His last ever journey.

'What did you say about the doctor coming to get me?' she asked.

'He's going to pick you up in a minute and take you to the hospital. I can look after Spence. Sally said to tell you she'll sort out the hens tonight.'

Worries spread like ink on blotting paper. How seriously ill was Tom? How long would she have to leave Cliff? What if the doctor couldn't bring her back and she had to get a bus from Dorchester?

She ran upstairs, telling Cliff to get his boots off and keep an eye on the baby. She stepped out of her old patched skirt and flung it on the bed. She pulled on her charcoal costume. It was warm; she wouldn't need a coat. But what if it rained, or if she was on the bus late in the evening? She left the skirt on and swapped her blouse and jacket for a twinset the colour of ripe apples. She'd take her coat and an umbrella.

As she came back into the kitchen, she could hear Cliff playing with Spencer. She called him in. Looking around the kitchen she wondered whether Tom would need anything. There was a new toothbrush in the scullery cupboard. She collected it, a tin of tooth powder, soap and a flannel and put them in a bag.

'Would Mr Arrowsmith like a book?' Cliff asked.

'I've only ever seen him read the Farmer's Weekly,' May said, but glimpsing Cliff's hurt expression, added, 'But it's a good idea. What were you thinking of?'

He fetched *Biggles Sees it Through* from the shelf beside the range. It was one of his favourites and she added it to the bag.

'I'll tell him it was your idea to loan it to him,' she said.

'Will he… will he be all right?' Cliff asked.

She should have realised how shocking the experience was for him. 'I hope so. You got the doctor there quickly and that's sure to have helped. Will you be all right? Use the chicken to make a sandwich for yourself. Spencer's got some purée in the larder.' she said. 'I could get Dr Haskett to stop at Mrs Gale's and ask her to come round if you're worried?'

'We'll be all right. When will you be back?'

A car horn sounded in the lane.

'I must go. I'll be back as soon as I can. If you're worried about anything, put Spencer in the pram and go to Mrs Gale.' She grabbed her coat and umbrella, landed a quick kiss on

Cliff's cheek and dashed out of the door.

As the doctor's black Austin pulled away, she saw Cliff standing beside the pram. He looked forlorn.

Chapter 33

Beds were ranked on both sides of the ward. She squinted into the sunlight slanting through the large window that dominated the end wall; added to the volume of white linen in the room, the scene was dazzling and picking out one individual, impossible.

The stale smell of cooked food pervaded the ward where men of various ages were lying or sitting on the cream-painted, metal-framed beds. Some had visitors at their side, others looked eagerly towards her as she as she made her way down the centre aisle to a desk.

'Excuse me, I'm looking for Thomas Arrowsmith.'

The nurse finished writing on a form and put it in a folder before looking up. 'Are you a relative?' she asked.

'His daughter-in-law. How is he?'

'As well as can be expected.' She opened another folder. 'Sister will be able to tell you more. She's not on the ward right now.'

'Mr Arrowsmith's doctor is in the hospital. I'm sure he can update me if you can't.'

The nurse stiffened. 'The bed in the corner. He's very tired. You'll only be able to stay for a couple of minutes.' She pointed to the furthest bed, below the window.

She would never have recognised him. He was gazing up at the window where the branches of an oak tree, framed by blue sky, were swaying gently. He must be longing for the outdoors.

'Hello, Tom. How are you feeling?'

He turned his head and she was shocked at the pallor of his

weather-beaten face. His usually broad shoulders looked as if they'd shrunk and he seemed to have aged a decade since the day before.

'Not too clever, gel.' His voice was weak. Nothing like the cantankerous old devil she knew.

'They'll soon have you up and about,' She pulled out a chair and sat beside the bed. 'I've brought you some washing kit. I should have thought: you'll need a razor. I'll bring one next time. And Cliff's sent you a book.' She placed it on the bedside table. 'Biggles. It's one of his favourites. He's really worried about you.'

''e's not a bad lad.'

How sad that it took something like this to happen before he could be kind about Cliff.

He was speaking again, his voice so muffled she could barely make out his words. She bent towards him.

'It's down to you, gel. The farm. It'll be yours if I don't make it.'

She hadn't expected confusion. The attack must have affected his mind. What should she say? Eventually she stuttered, 'Tom, I—'

'Mr Arrowsmith is tired. He needs his rest.' The nurse was beside May, her starched apron rustling as she moved to plump up Tom's pillows.

'Can I just say goodbye?' May said.

'One minute,' she replied, and rustled away.

'Tom, I'll take care of the farm until you come home, but it won't be long until you're back running things.'

'Mebee. But you mind what I've said, gel. It'll be yours avore too long.'

The nurse was back at her elbow.

'I'll come tomorrow. You just concentrate on getting well.

The farm will be fine.' She touched his gnarled hand before picking up her bag and surreptitiously wiping a tear.

As Dr Haskett drove home, her mind churned with the logistics of keeping the farm going. Seth used to talk about his farming plans but Tom always had the final say. That was why they'd never had a tractor. Would a tractor have lightened Tom's load, put less strain on his heart?

May's only hands-on experience of farm work, other than working in the poultry yard, was helping with haymaking. Most of the village turned out to help, and she had little more experience than any other local woman. Her major resource was the land girls. They worked hard and Sally was experienced and a good leader. Nevertheless, they needed direction from someone who knew what they were doing.

Dr Haskett dropped her at the cottage gate. He'd warned her that Tom would need complete rest once he was allowed home. I'll try to persuade him to stay with his sister, she'd told him. In reality she knew that was unlikely. Tom loved the farm too much.

'What's that smell?' Cliff sniffed the air as she walked into the kitchen. 'Fish and chips!'

'I knew I couldn't keep them a surprise from you.' She laughed. 'Dr Haskett stopped to let me to buy them on the way back.'

May quickly served up the food.

'Mum used to bring fish 'n chips home a lot,' Cliff said, tucking into his heaped plateful. 'We ate 'em out of the paper.'

'Hmm.' May picked at her own food, almost too tired to eat.

Her mind was revolving like her old mangle; the list of tasks entering fully formed, but decisions coming out shapeless. She needed someone to talk to. Rose was the obvious choice. How much she owed that woman. She couldn't leave Cliff again, and Spencer needed bathing and putting to bed.

'Would you mind popping up to Mrs Gale and asking whether she can spare half an hour to come and see me?'

'You want to tell her about Mr Arrowsmith?' Cliff polished his plate with his bread.

'He was very grateful for the book you sent. He said you're a good lad.' May ruffled his hair. 'And you are. Very good. I couldn't manage without you.'

Cliff smoothed his hair and grinned. 'Can I use your bike?'

'Be careful crossing the main road. I don't mind you spending some time with the twins but be back by half past eight. School tomorrow.'

Cliff groaned.

'Do you think he'll ever work again?' Rose asked.

'I really don't know. I can't imagine what will happen if he doesn't,' she said, elbows on the kitchen table, nursing a thick tumbler. 'I suppose I could keep the farm ticking over until the men come home and then Tom could take on some kind of foreman.'

She topped up their glasses of rhubarb wine. She'd intended to take it to the street party but hadn't been able to fit it in the pram.

'What about caring for Tom? If he won't go ter his sister's, he won't be able ter manage that big house on his own. Has it even got a bathroom?'

'It's practically medieval, but there is one. It's upstairs. There's another lavatory downstairs, so he could cope if he couldn't get up the stairs. Parts of the house haven't been touched since Seth's mother died. It's a bit Miss Havisham.'

'You won't have time ter deal with that. You'll have your hands full with the farm. Maybe the sister would move in for a while?' Rose took a biscuit from the plate that May had put out. More party surplus.

'I doubt it. She's very much a townie. Dr Haskett spoke to her on her neighbour's telephone. She didn't suggest helping out.'

'It could fall on you. Have you got a plan for the farm work?'

'Sally. She's my lynchpin. I'm going to speak to her in the morning. For the moment, I won't be able to manage the hens, so we'll need another land girl, maybe two, until I can take over again.' She'd pushed Tom's comment that the farm would be hers to the back of her mind. 'I don't know whether Tom can afford more workers. I've no idea how well off he is. Seth used to joke he was a skinflint, but I don't think he had much idea of the figures.'

The wireless was playing quietly in the corner. The tones of Vera Lynn singing *A Nightingale Sang in Berkeley Square* drifted across to them.

'It's going to be strange, not having to listen out for the news every day, isn't it?' she said. 'Sorry. I know you'll be listening for the latest from the Far East.'

'I feel a bit cheated ter be honest,' said Rose. 'Everyone's celebrating that it's all over, but we're still in limbo not knowing whether we'll get Len back safe and sound.'

'When he's back, and I mean *when*, what will he do?'

'I don't know, but I reckon he's had his fill of the sea. His letters are more and more about opportunities here. He says big changes are coming and his engineering skills will be in demand.' She drained her glass and sighed. 'I hope he's right.'

May changed the subject. 'I've made one decision. I'm having a phone put in at the farm.'

Rose brightened. 'That's a good idea. It'll be there if Tom's taken bad again and he'll be able ter keep in touch with his sister.'

'If he'll use it. You know how stubborn he is.'

'I think you'll find him altered,' Rose said as she got to her feet to leave. 'He'll have ter accept help now.'

Chapter 34

'We're goin' to live here?' May watched Cliff look around the farmhouse kitchen, doubt etched on his face.

What was the problem? The house was enormous – old-fashioned, inconvenient and cleaning it was a marathon task, but that wouldn't affect a boy like him.

'Just until Mr Arrowsmith's out of hospital and on his feet again. I can't walk Spencer backwards and forwards from the cottage several times a day and someone needs to be here overnight,' she told him. 'It'll be fun being farmers and there's a lot more room here than at the cottage.'

He didn't answer, just seemed to shrink into himself, his face expressionless.

Was he worried about leaving the cottage? Was that it? She was under pressure with everything going on and needed his co-operation. They had to bring things over from the cottage and she was relying on his help.

'Would you like to choose bedrooms for you and Spencer?'

He glanced at the door leading to the stairs but didn't move.

'Buck up, Cliff. I need your help.'

He was rooted to the spot. It was as if he was scared.

She was about to snap at him when it struck her; this was the largest house he'd ever been in. The boy was over-awed.

'Tell you what, we'll bring the baby and all look round together,' she said.

Cliff's face relaxed into a smile. 'I'll get Spence.'

She was seated at the kitchen table. A pine monstrosity with three drawers on each of the long sides, it would comfortably have sat a dozen. At present, over half its length was heaped with teetering piles of paperwork, seed catalogues and farming magazines. She was sifting through them, looking for the information she needed to determine exactly what regulations she had to comply with to satisfy the County War Agricultural Executive Committee – the War Ag as it was known. The wastepaper basket beside her chair was overflowing and she had yet to make any noticeable impact on the stacked table.

Cliff had helped her bring their essential items from the cottage, tirelessly wheeling the pram piled with clothes and possessions up the lane. Most were dumped in the three bedrooms they were using. Spencer's cot looked lost in a room big enough for a party.

Cliff had hung a couple of model airplanes in his room and she noticed he'd removed the pictures of brooding mountains that had deadened the dreary decor. They'd left patches of bright flowery wallpaper behind. The flowers brought a touch of lightness but they wouldn't be the first choice of an eleven-year-old boy.

She wanted him to feel settled in the house, but he was worried about being separated from his friends. Peter and Bob will love coming here, she told him. He could take them round the fields, Mr Arrowsmith wouldn't mind, as long as they kept to the headlands and respected the crops, like proper farmers.

Immediately, he'd said, 'Can I have a dog? All farmers have a dog.'

The dog again. She'd worked her stock answer around their new situation. 'I don't know how long we'll be here and dogs need food. We can't stretch our rations to another mouth.' Then, seeing his disappointment, added, 'Tell you what, now he's a bit brighter I was going to ask Mr Arrowsmith, but instead I'll decide myself. Would you like to take on my job with the hens on the weekday afternoons? I'll pay you, of course. There's another land girl coming for the mornings, so it would only be collecting the eggs and shutting the birds in.'

Dog apparently forgotten, he'd beamed. 'A job? Every day? Wizard!'

An hour later, she'd produced some sort of order. A box piled with magazines was put aside for Tom; many unread, they were filled with pictures of tractors and new machinery, so perhaps he'd be inspired to get the farm mechanised and make work easier.

In another box was a pile of assorted documents, including forms partially completed in Tom's looping hand, which needed her attention. There must be a deadline for returning some of these things – Tom was always moaning about the War Ag getting on his back over late paperwork. She hadn't a clue and would have to get help.

Bill Tyler would know what she was supposed to do and he could advise her on the routine she should be following for the crops. Sally was carrying on with the work already in the pipeline, but the hay would need cutting within a month or so and the flax and potato harvests were on the horizon.

Large as the kitchen was, even with the back door open she began to feel claustrophobic. She couldn't spare the time to walk into the village with Spencer. He was in his pram under the pear tree in the garden, but Cliff could park him by the poultry yard gate while he was working and the baby could watch the comings and goings. She'd cycle to the village. She had several letters to send and provisions were running low. Tom's larder could have been used as a museum exhibit and most of the contents had already been consigned to the compost heap.

She stood up and stretched. As an afterthought, she took a postcard from the drawer under the table she'd earmarked for stationery and addressed it to Bill Tyler. She wrote a message asking if he could pop in when he was passing the farm.

As she entered the village shop, she saw Ephraim in the queue at the counter. Hell. She wanted to avoid him.

'On your own, Mrs Sheppard?' he said, lifting his hat. A cloth cap, May noted.

'Cliff's looking after his brother,' she said, aware the background chatter from the half dozen other customers had ceased. Her public battles with Ephraim were becoming regular entertainment. 'Mrs Potts not with you?'

''er's sufferin' with a cold.'

'Oh dear. I've just popped along from the farm. You've heard Tom Arrowsmith's in hospital?'

'Ow's 'e farin'?' Fred, the shop assistant, asked as mutters of sympathy came from other customers.

'Improving, thank you. They think he'll be home in a couple of weeks,' May said. Fred was so slow. He spent more time gossiping than he did serving. She wanted to get her shopping and leave.

Ephraim paid for his purchases and slowly picked up the packages. He turned back to May.

'Reckon 'ee'll be getting in a man for the farm 'til Mr Arrowsmith's back on 'is feet?' he said.

'What can I get 'ee?' Fred asked.

May said, 'Here's my list and the ration books.'

She turned to Ephraim, and the shop at large, since everyone was agog, 'There aren't any experienced men around. Most of those that know farming are running their own places, and the others are in the Forces. I've got the land girls and Cliff. I'll be able to cope.'

'A bunch a wimmin runnin' a farm? I 'ent never 'eard the like,' Ephraim said.

May's heart pounded. She didn't want another public scene. If she ignored Ephraim, perhaps he would just go. She didn't look in his direction although the other shoppers were agog for her reaction.

Fred was winding the bacon slicer even slower than usual. She wanted to fetch a knife to speed up the job. From the corner of her eye, she saw Ephraim take a step towards the door.

'Your bacon, Mrs Sheppard.' Fred held out a greaseproof-wrapped package. 'I'll jest get the rest.'

Halfway to the door, Ephraim said loudly, ''ee won't have time for young un's will 'ee? Hev to send that black cuckoo back.'

May's stomach clenched. She turned very deliberately and glared at Ephraim. A pin dropped would have been deafening. She caught a glimpse of Victoria at the post office counter, franking stamp suspended.

'As you were told weeks ago, Ephraim, Cliff and Spencer's mother is currently overseas. The children will be living with me for the foreseeable future.' She stared him down.

As he turned away she switched her gaze to the gawping audience. They quickly collected themselves and broke into rapid chatter.

A cough behind her announced Fred with a query about her list. The paper trembled as she consulted it.

Chapter 35

Was that Old Potty looking over the wall? Cliff put down the egg basket and clambered through the bushes to look into the lane. Someone was cycling away. A man. He couldn't be sure who. Just like Potty to spy on them. One of the boys at school told him Auntie May had another run-in with the old misery guts in the shop. About him and Spence staying in the village. Auntie May hadn't said anything about it, but she told him she'd asked Mrs Douglas to take over all the meeting stuff until Mr Arrowsmith was well again. She wasn't going to hide away again, was she?

He picked up the basket and began searching under the hedge for eggs. There weren't many at the moment. He'd looked in all the usual places: the barn, behind the cart shed and in the rickyard, yet he still had barely half what Auntie May used to get. He remembered what had happened when Nora had been working there. Thankfully, she gave up farm work soon after the scene with Mr Arrowsmith. It might be the new hens. Perhaps they weren't as good as the old lot.

He carried the basket to the barn and put it on the harness room table. He'd take the eggs up to the dairy when he went home. Home. The farmhouse didn't seem like that. What would it be like, living with Mr Arrowsmith, when he came back? Would he speak to him indoors? Since he'd taken him back on, he'd barely spoken to him at work.

'You must be C-Cliff?'

He jumped. A girl in a green land army sweater was leaning in the doorway.

'You the new girl?' he asked. He wished she'd move; he couldn't get out and didn't want to push past.

'Yeah. Ivy.' She stayed where she was, staring at him. The harness room was dim and she had her back to the light. He couldn't see her face.

'I gotta finish the birds,' he said, moving toward her. She was small, not like Buster Johnson when he blocked your path, but she was stocky and had his same manner. Threatening.

'Not m-many are there?' She nodded to the basket.

'No. Not this afternoon. You?' Usually he liked the smell of this room: leather and saddle soap, but it began to feel airless. He wanted to get out.

'Na. Reckon them p-pullets ain't any good. Want to get by?' She stepped back at last, and he caught the same sneering expression Buster had when he bullied you.

'They was good birds. Auntie May said so,' he said, glaring at her, and not willing to admit to the same thought.

'P'raps she got it wrong?'

Flippin' cheek. He squeezed past, angling round her chest. He thought about the dresses his mother wore when she went to work. Mounds of white skin bulging out of the front.

He looked straight at the girl's face, willing himself not to blush. 'Bye.'

She sniggered. 'Bye, s-sonny.'

He hurried across the farmyard. Where had Auntie May got that girl? Her stutter. He'd heard one like it before.

'Did she say why she was there so late?' Auntie May said, shifting a big pile of papers so they could eat at the kitchen table. Cliff was laying out cutlery. He put a little blue Bakelite spoon in front of Spence's highchair.

'No,' said Cliff. Had Auntie May forgotten that Nora had

169

hung around late, too? 'She ain't very friendly, either.'

'She *isn't* very friendly,' said Auntie May. 'I expect it's because she's new. A lot of the girls are thinking about going home now the war's over. We have to take who we can get and, with the hay cutting and harvesting coming up, we need as many hands as possible. Try to get on with her, Cliff.'

'Come on, Spence, into your chair.' He lifted the baby from his playpen and eased him into the highchair. 'Someone was looking through the hedge by the henhouses,' he said.

'Who?'

'I'm not—'

'Hello. May?' a voice called.

Mr Tyler was at the back door. 'Sorry to interrupt your meal,' he said, 'but you wanted me to pop in?'

'Yes, thank you, Bill. Come on in,' Auntie May said.

He ducked his head as he came through the doorway and took off his cap. Cliff had never seen him without a hat. He had thick ginger hair. A lot of men looked older without their hats, but Mr Tyler looked younger. Auntie May looked twice as he sat down, and patted her own hair as she went to get him a glass of the gooseberry wine they'd found at the back of the larder.

'How are you, Cliff? Looking after my hens, I hear?' he said.

Should he say there weren't many eggs? Could Ivy be right and the pullets he'd sold them weren't good layers? Auntie May would be cross if he said the wrong thing. 'Yes,' he said.

'Spencer's grown,' Mr Tyler said.

Spence waved his fist and said, 'Der, der.'

'That means he wants his dinner,' said Cliff. He had a meaning for all of his little brother's noises.

'Can you feed him, Cliff, while I talk to Mr Tyler?' Auntie May asked, picking up a pile of papers.

As he spooned Spence his mushy food, he wondered

whether Seth would have been like Mr Tyler. Maybe, unlike his friend, Seth would have joined up. Perhaps he'd have been killed in the war, and Auntie May would still have been a widow and wanted to adopt him. Or perhaps he'd have come back and wanted them to have their own baby.

Mr Tyler wasn't married. Someone looked after his house, and Cliff had seen the land girls using the orange tractor in his fields. That was it. That stutter – in the yard at Magna Farm.

'Cliff, don't let him do that,' said Auntie May. Spence was blowing bubbles and spattering food over his chin.

Cliff mopped him up. 'He's finished,' he said, moving the bowl before Spence could put it on his head. It made Cliff laugh, but Auntie May had to wash his hair every time.

'How's Tom?' said Mr Tyler, downing his wine and getting to his feet.

'Coming home at the weekend,' Auntie May said, standing up.

At the weekend. Two days' time. Just when he'd got used to living here, it was all going to be different. Again.

Mr Tyler patted Spence on the head.

'Um, Mr Tyler,' Cliff said.

'What is it, Cliff?'

'Did you have a land girl working at Magna Farm, called Ivy?'

'Cliff—' began Auntie May.

'I did, but I got rid of her after that egg business you spotted. Why?' asked Mr Tyler.

'Don't say it's the same one.' Auntie May sank on to the chair. 'That's all I need.'

Chapter 36

Mr Arrowsmith slept a lot. When he'd stayed in his room, it hadn't made much difference to them – except Auntie May had to keep going upstairs to take him things.

Today though, when Cliff got home from school, he was in the kitchen in a big armchair brought through from the sitting room. He had a blanket over his legs and he looked really small. His hair stuck out like Worzel Gummidge, and he was nothing like the frightening farmer who yelled at you if you did things wrong.

'Have 'ee seen that contraption, boy?'

Cliff jumped. He was tiptoeing across the room.

'Hello, Mr Arrowsmith, I thought you were asleep. What contraption?'

Mr Arrowsmith pointed to the hall doorway. Cliff couldn't see anything, other than the stairs and the dark passageway that led to the front door that nobody used.

'On the table.'

A couple of feet into the passageway was a shiny cane table. It usually held a lacy mat and an old picture of a lady with a behind like a shelf. Now, a black object squatted there.

'A telephone! Wizard.' He picked up the chunky handset and placed it to his ear. A purring sound began and then a posh voice said, 'Number please?'

Heck.

Mr Arrowsmith called out, 'Don't you go messin' with it, boy.'

'Caller are you there? What number do you require?' the

voice went on.

'Sorry. Mistake,' Cliff whispered, and gently laid the handset back on its rest.

He ran upstairs. 'We got a phone, we got a phone.'

Banging open the door of his room, he stopped short. He didn't know anyone to ring.

In the farmyard, Cliff checked there was no sign of Ivy. All clear. On the evening Mr Tyler had dropped in, he'd ended up staying to eat with them. It was fun because it just happened and there was no fuss about the best china or proper table manners, he just fitted in.

They'd talked about what Cliff had seen, what they should do about Ivy, Old Potty – they all thought it likely it was him Cliff had seen peeping through the hedge – and the shortage of eggs. They listened to what he said and he felt as if he was one of the grown-ups, taking part in the plans.

'I'm sure the pullets aren't the problem,' said Mr Tyler. 'I've kept some of that batch myself and they are laying well.'

Auntie May said she'd check everything was all right with the feed and the hen houses, and they decided Cliff would let her know immediately if Ivy turned up, or if he saw Old Potty poking around again. Meantime, she'd speak to Ivy to let her know the poor egg numbers had been noticed. It might be enough to frighten her into stopping it for a while or, at least, until they got the hay crop off.

It seemed to have worked because he'd hadn't run into Ivy again and they'd been getting more eggs.

He'd checked all the nest boxes and got quite a good haul, so it was just the yards and barn to go. He slid his hand around the bole of one of the elms. His fingers touched a chalky shell. Three warm eggs. He was always wary here because you couldn't see if a hen was sitting, and he'd had a few nasty pecks. He picked up two of the eggs, leaving one to tempt the hen to come back and lay more. The tree was always a good bet, Auntie May said. Even when the hens had only just arrived, they found it and made it a favourite spot.

As he worked his way along the wall, searching under the trees and bushes, he heard yells coming from the lane. He jumped up to lean across the top of the wall, wriggling on his belly until he could see past the trees.

He began to laugh and called out, 'Over here,' waving an arm.

Pete and Bob skidded to a lopsided stop beside him. Pete was on the pedals of their mother's bike and Bob, both arms around his twin's waist, on the seat.

'Can yer come for a bike ride with us?' Bob asked.

'I'll have to ask. I've gotta finish the hens. Come and help.'

The boys dumped their bike at the gate and went into the barn with Cliff.

'Careful you don't stand on any eggs,' he told them. 'The hay's nearly all gone. It's more fun when it's up to the roof.'

Cliff and Pete were checking in the dark corners when Bob let out a shriek from Blossom's loosebox. He ran out, clutching a pecked hand, a furious hen on his heels. 'She was in the manger,' he said, 'I didn't see her in the dark.'

His face! Like Mrs Parrot when someone made a bad smell in class. Cliff and Pete rolled in the hay in hysterics, only to start all over again when Bob plucked up the courage to go back in and came out with only one egg.

'Thought you'd found a dozen at least,' Pete teased.

The sound of hooves in the yard sobered them and, quickly brushing off some of the hay stuck to their clothes, they went outside to see Auntie May and Sally unloading Spence's pram from the cart.

'Hello, Spence. Been for a ride?' Cliff asked.

Auntie May picked a bit of hay out of Cliff's hair. 'He's had a lovely time watching us working. How're you doing?' She looked at Pete and Bob, who were patting Blossom and fending off her nose as she snuffled at their pockets. 'You've got some help, I see.'

'Can I use your bike to go for a ride with the twins, please? I've almost finished the hens.'

'Ah, about my bike…'

Heck, she wasn't going to say he couldn't use it was she? What a nit he'd look in front of the twins.

Pete and Bob had helped Sally unhitch Blossom and Bob was leading the mare to the water trough.

'Just a little drink,' Sally called as she and Pete backed the cart into the shed. Cliff hoped they couldn't overhear what he and Auntie May were saying.

'Have you ever been in that shed in the corner over here?' She pointed to a ramshackle lean-to under the elms.

Cliff shook his head. What was he supposed to have done now.

'Mr Arrowsmith's bike is in there. He says he's never going to use it again and you can have the use of it on cond—'

'A bike of my own?'

'On condition... that you clear out the junk that's in the shed. You'll have to clean up the bike, it hasn't been used for years.'

'Yes. Yes. That's no bother.' He ran towards Pete and Bob, then stopped and looked back. 'Thanks.'

'You need to thank Mr Arrowsmith,' Auntie May said, smiling and shaking her head. 'Finish the hens before you go looking for the bike.'

***

175

Cliff's heart sank. The bike must be buried under the junk that filled the shed. It would take days to clear. 'Go without me,' he told the twins. 'Maybe I'll come out on Saturday – if I've dug it out by then.'

Pete peered over his shoulder. 'It won't take that long with three of us. C'mon, let's get stuck in.'

The sun was sinking by the time they reached the bike. The shed was the dumping ground for anything that got broken. They had uncovered toothless hay rakes, spades with snapped handles and yards of frayed rope. Cliff had begun to think the bike wasn't there, but at last they found it, wrapped in an oily tarpaulin.

They dragged the bundled machine into the fading light, 'I bet it's an old boneshaker,' Bob said.

'Bound to be,' said Pete.

Cliff said nothing and tugged off the sheet. 'Cor. Look at that,' he said.

The twins were silent as Cliff held it at arm's length.

'It's a corker,' said Bob, eventually. Cliff caught a hint of envy in his voice.

It was a corker: a full size man's bike with a three-speed, a light and a bell. He wiped a spitted finger over the green paintwork, and the words *The All Steel Bicycle* in gold lettering glinted in the last of the light.

'It's a *Raleigh*,' said Pete, rubbing dirt from the fancy gold badge below the handlebars. The same make as Auntie May's bike.

'You boys have got to stop now.' Auntie May came into the yard. 'It's almost dark. Your mother will be wondering where you are,' she said to the twins.

'It's a wizard bike,' Cliff said.

'Put it back in the shed. You can carry on with it tomorrow.

You've done wonderfully well getting all that junk out. We'll see what can be re-used and put the rest on the bonfire.'

They walked to the gate with the twins, who climbed on their bike in the lane and switched on the light. Before they could move off, another bicycle swept past making them all jump.

'No lights,' Auntie May called out as the cyclist vanished into the gloom. 'Mind how you go,' she said, as Pete and Bob wobbled away.

Auntie May checked round the poultry yard and Cliff went to the barn. It had lost its sweet horsey smell now that Blossom and Ben were out in the paddock for the summer. He slid the doors shut and swung the heavy metal bar across.

As they made their way along the track to the house, he said, 'Did you see who that was on the other bike?'

'Yes,' said Auntie May. 'Ephraim Potts.'

Chapter 37

He was in his Spit. The Japs were behind and they couldn't catch him. He dived fast. Faster. He thought his lungs would burst. Then, all too soon, he was at the farm gate. He braked furiously. The brakes he'd adjusted pulled him up sharp and the loose stones at the side of the lane scattered like bullets.

The seat was at its lowest position, but his feet didn't reach the ground and he lurched sideways, saving himself with a foot before swinging the other leg over the angled crossbar. He had the gate open by the time the twins arrived. Bob's face was beetroot red from pedalling and Pete, on pillion, hoarse with egging him on.

He'd let them each have a go on his bike. A short one. All the time they were on it he wanted to shout out, 'Be careful.' He loved it. It was the best thing he'd ever had. The only thing he'd ever had that people were jealous of.

Pete and Bob swapped places before they carried on home for their tea. 'See you tomorrow,' they called.

He'd be late for the hens, but it was a warm evening and they were happily clucking round the yard. He put the bike in the shed, gave the polished leather saddle a pat and ran up the track to the house. The muscles in his legs ached from the afternoon's pedalling. He'd need to do more to get really fit.

If he changed his clothes quickly and got back down to the yard straight away, he wouldn't be too far behind time.

'Auntie May?' he called, dashing into the kitchen. Silence. Spencer's pram wasn't in the back-kitchen, so he guessed she'd gone to see the twins' mum.

He was halfway up the stairs when he remembered Mr Arrowsmith. He went back to the kitchen. In his armchair, the blanket was pushed aside as if he'd just got up. Strange. Mr Arrowsmith used the lav off the back-kitchen, but the door had been open when Cliff came in.

He'd better try to find him. 'Mr Arrowsmith?' he called. Nothing. He went upstairs. Perhaps he was asleep in his bedroom. He tapped on the chocolate-coloured door. 'Mr Arrowsmith, are you there?'

No reply. The gloomy passageway was creepy and he longed for the lightness of the cottage landing.

Should he go in? Ill or not, the old man was still capable of snapping his head off. Gingerly, he turned the brass doorknob. He'd never been in this room, and the smell of worn clothes and old socks made him wrinkle his nose as he stuck his head round the door.

The curtains were closed and he crept further in. He could just make out the shape of a body on the bed, but it was lying crossways – the head furthest from the door and the feet dangling on Cliff's side. One slipper had fallen off revealing a holey sock.

'Mr Arrowsmith?' Cliff was terrified. He daren't go near the bed. But he must. He must see if he was breathing. They'd done first aid at school because of the air raids, but he'd never had to use it. He ran to the window and wrenched back the curtains. The room was at the front of the house, overlooking the lane. He could have cried when he saw Auntie May and Spence in the road, almost below him. He tried to lift the sash, but it was stuck. He banged on the glass. She couldn't hear. In a second she'd have passed, heading for the farm gate. He banged again and she looked around.

'Up here. Auntie May, up here.' He banged frantically.

She looked up, startled. 'What's the matter?' she shouted. He read her lips.

'Mr Arrowsmith,' he mouthed. 'Hurry.'

She began shoving the old gate in the wall. Cliff shook his head and pointed down the lane to the farm gate. The house gate was useless. He'd tried to open it once, but plants had grown over it and it wouldn't budge. Auntie May began to run. Spence was bounced around in the pram. Cliff saw his mouth open and imagined his frightened yell.

She would take a few minutes to get up the track. He had to look at Mr Arrowsmith. He went towards the bed, took a deep breath and looked into the grey face. The lips were blue, but he thought he detected a slight rise in the man's chest. He wasn't dead. Not yet.

He pounded down the stairs and grabbed the telephone. Auntie May had shown him how to use it. In case of emergency, she'd said. She'd pinned a list of numbers to the wall.

'What number do you require?'

'Crompton Parva 85,' he said.

'Putting you through, caller.' He waited and a ringing noise came on the line.

'Haskettt.'

The back door crashed open. '*Cliff?*' Auntie May's voice was almost a shriek.

'This is Clifford Erwin from Elem Farm,' he said into the receiver. Auntie May burst into the hall.

He spoke into the telephone. 'It's Mr Arrowsmith. He's collapsed. His lips are blue, but he's breathing. A bit.'

Auntie May flung herself up the stairs. Spence was wailing in the kitchen.

The voice on the telephone said, 'I'll call an ambulance.

Look out for it, Cliff. You'll need to tell them to go through the farmyard. I'll be on my way as soon as I've got them.' The doctor hung up.

Cliff ran upstairs. Auntie May was bending over Mr Arrowsmith, feeling his pulse.

'The doctor's on his way and so's the ambulance. I've got to look out for it.'

'Before you go, help me swing him round. You lift his feet.' Her face was as white as the sheets.

Mr Arrowsmith gave a low groan as they manhandled him round and rested his head on the pillows. Cliff pulled off the other slipper and laid the feet gently on the eiderdown.

'Well done, Cliff. You go and wait in the lane,' Auntie May said. He moved towards the door. 'Can you take Spencer with you?'

He didn't want to go back to the house. It was the second time he'd seen Mr Arrowsmith taken away in an ambulance. This time he looked worse than before and the doctor had spoken to Auntie May in a quiet voice as she got in the ambulance alongside the stretcher. As she waved to him before they shut the doors, he saw she was crying.

He'd just begun to like Mr Arrowsmith. The old farmer had spoken kindly to him a few times, especially when he'd thanked him for lending him the Biggles book. Cliff had thanked him for the bike and promised to look after it. He gave his word he'd finish clearing out the shed.

If Mr Arrowsmith died, what would happen? Who would the farm belong to? If Auntie May didn't have a job she wouldn't be able to look after him and Spence.

He wheeled the pram across the yard. The hens were fed and the poultry yard gate locked. The horses were happily grazing in the orchard, fenced-off from the fruit trees, their bulky shapes just visible in the dusk.

Spence had allowed himself to be cheered up while they'd waited by the gate. Dr Haskett had arrived just as they'd heard the bell of the ambulance. Spence hadn't liked the noise, but then he'd been fascinated by the big cream-coloured ambulance backing across the yard. The men in their dark uniforms had climbed out, scattering the hens as they'd grabbed the stretcher and run up the track with the doctor.

They'd quickly returned with the loaded stretcher, Auntie May alongside calling out instructions about feeding Spence and closing gates. They'd all driven away, leaving Cliff and Spence alone with a flock of hungry chickens.

He must give Spence some food. The little boy had been very good, babbling happily as Cliff went to and fro with eggs, wheelbarrow and feed. He wondered how Mr Arrowsmith was and when Auntie May would get back. They'd just have to wait. He closed up the barn. The farm felt very big and empty. He felt very alone, despite Spence gurgling beside him. A dog would make all the difference.

He looked towards the hills, dreaming of running with his dog. 'Look Spence,' he said, unclipping the straps and lifting the boy from the pram. His little body felt warm and reassuring. He held him up to face the sky. Rows of white clouds, flushed pink in the distance, were set against darkening blue.

'A mackerel sky,' he told Spence.

The sun, a glowing crimson ball on the horizon, sank as they watched. Spence stretched out his arm. He pointed his tiny finger towards the sunset. 'Der, der,' he said.

Cliff laughed. 'Right-o, dinner.' He grabbed the pram and, towing it behind them, carried Spence up the track.

***

The back-kitchen was dark. Cliff fumbled for the light switch. What was that noise? He couldn't place the sound and it was going on and on. This house. Why had they left the cottage? As he carried Spence through to the main kitchen, the sound got louder. 'What is it Spence?' He was getting scared. It was like a bell. A bell! He ran into the hall and snatched up the telephone receiver.

'Hello?'

'Cliff. I was getting worried. Where were you?'

Auntie May. It was Auntie May. She sounded different, kind of posher, but it was definitely her.

'Are you all right? How's Spencer? Say something, Cliff.'

'Sorry. Yeah, we're all right. I'm just doing Spence's food. I'm sorry it's so late—'

'Don't worry about that. I'm sorry you've had so much to do. I'm still at the hospital but I'll get back as soon as I can.'

'How's Mr Arrowsmith?'

There was a pause. Spence tugged at the phone lead and Cliff pulled his hand away.

Auntie May sounded very sad when she said. 'He's not very well, Cliff. Not very well at all.'

'Tell him Spence and I hope he's soon better,' he said.

She said hoarsely, 'I will. I'll see you as soon as I can. Bye, Cliff.'

'Bye,' he said, putting down the receiver.

Chapter 38

She felt more wrung-out than she had in months. Until last week she'd thought she was fairly fit again, but all her stamina had ebbed away. Her mind was wrapped in a sense of unreality and she just wanted to get back to normal life.

They'd all left. She'd given them the best spread she could, which wasn't much. Everyone had used the food they'd been hoarding on VE Day, and rations didn't give much leeway to cater for a funeral tea.

She'd be forever in Doreen's debt. She'd rallied the WI, and half a dozen members had helped with the catering. They'd made sandwiches and cakes beforehand and then served and washed up on the day. It had left May free to make the best she could of clearing the cluttered sitting room – battling the cobwebs and dust of the duration – and making herself presentable as hostess and grieving daughter-in-law. There'd been no time for real grief. She'd functioned entirely on form, rather than emotion. All things considered, they'd done Tom proud. His sister, Dorothy, had thanked her over and over before a friend with a car had run her back to Dorchester. Black market petrol, May suspected.

'Go on, I'll follow,' she called to Cliff, who was fidgeting at the back door. He jumped on the bike and bumped down the track towards the yard. That bike was a blessing. It had taken his mind off Tom's death and given him something positive to remember the old man by. Sad they'd only just begun to get along.

She closed the back door quietly. Spencer was flat out in his cot. Now he was sleeping through the night, she might get a good rest herself. If she could stop worrying about the farm.

Tom's will had been in a deed box under the old roll-top desk in the study. She'd searched every pigeonhole and drawer twice over before finally coming across the box when she caught her ankle on a sharp corner.

Convinced Tom had been hallucinating when he'd told her she was his heir, she'd scanned the document for the name of the true beneficiary, only to discover that she was, indeed, the owner of the hundreds of acres of farmland, the farmhouse and outbuildings, and the business known as Elem Farm. The enormity of it – the bequest, and the responsibility it brought – was incomprehensible and she'd made no plans beyond getting through the funeral.

She walked down the track. The ruts had dried concrete-hard and it was easy to turn an ankle. Passing the orchard, she heard the rip of grass as Ben and Blossom grazed next to the fence. Crushed under their hooves, the white and yellow mayflowers released their glorious scent that lingered in the still evening air. Her favourite summer smell. It was heavenly, and she felt the strain of the last week lifting. Perhaps she'd have a bath before bed. Throw in a handful of lavender and luxuriate in the fragrant steam. Bliss.

What was that racket? Cliff, shouting? She quickened her pace and rounded the corner.

He stood facing the barn, tearfully clinging on to his bike while Ephraim Potts jabbed a finger at him. 'Tom Arrowsmith 'int even cold in 'ee's grave afore 'ee laid claim to 'ee's bike. That were 'ee's pride and joy a few years back—'

'What's going on here?' May surprised herself at force of her own voice.

Ephraim's head snapped round. Something moved in the

shadowy barn doorway. Ivy. A basket of eggs on her arm. The girl started to slink backwards.

May threw her a glare. 'Stay there.' Ivy froze. May turned to Ephraim. 'What are you doing here?'

'I jest came to pay me respects to old Tom. Mrs Potts and I weren't invited to the funeral and—'

'You weren't invited because I don't like you and Mr Arrowsmith didn't like you either. And you were suspected of stealing from the farm. I repeat, what are you doing here and why is that girl bringing you eggs?'

'I don't know the gel. T'issen none a my business what 'er's doin' with eggs. You needs a man to run this place. All sorts goes on without proper supervision.'

Before May could speak, Ivy dumped the eggs on the ground and flew towards Ephraim.

She stabbed a finger into his chest, screaming, 'You lyin' old swine. You told me to be here. Eight o'clock you said, when Mrs Sheppard would 'ave her feet up after the funeral. With all that going on, you said, she'd never notice eggs goin' missin'.'

Ephraim lurched away, muttering, ''er's mad, 'ee can see that. Barkin' mad.'

May stepped up close to Ivy. Staring into her belligerent face, she said, 'I will be reporting you first thing in the morning. Get out, and don't you dare come here again.'

'I'm going. I wouldn't stay in this place anyway. Run by women and kids. It's a joke.' She turned on her heel and stalked out of gate, leaving it swinging.

Thank goodness she'd gone. May had no idea what she would have done if she'd refused to leave. Cliff was looking more composed, although he still held the bike between himself and Ephraim.

Ephraim's cap had been knocked askew and, in another situation, May would have laughed, but his moustache was bristling, his eyes glinting with malice. A twinge of fear crept through her. Had she done the wrong thing getting rid of a witness?

She tried a new approach. 'You owe Cliff an apology. About the bike.'

'That little beggar? 'e'd take the shirt off 'ee's back soon as look at 'ee.'

She was tired. So tired. A sad beautiful evening turned into battleground of words. Was this what it would be like, being the boss?

'Tom gave Cliff the bike a week before he died. He was glad to do it because he knew he'd been wrong about the boy. Like you are.'

'Pah! 'e'll never change. None of 'em do, them from the slums. Allers in 'em. Allers thieves. When the new owner takes over, 'ee'll make sure that guttersnipe's out. 'ee an' all, May Sheppard. And that black cuckoo.'

Cliff clutched the bike closer, knuckles white on the handlebars. She'd like to dash this sanctimonious little twerp to the ground.

'What new owner?' she said.

'Dorothy Arrowsmith won' keep the farm on. 'er'll drop it like a hot tater. The new man'll sort 'ee out right enough.'

'Get off this farm. If I ever have reason to suspect you of stealing from me again, I won't hesitate to call the police.'

'Stealing from you? You're no better than that tripe hound.' He nodded to Cliff and closed in on May, the mousy moustache raised in a sneer. 'Tom's estate belongs to Dorothy, not 'ee. Although,' his horrid little eyes lit up and May could smell tobacco on his breath, 'mebee there's enough fer all on us?'

'Get off my farm, you grubby little parasite.' Her voice was a growl. She'd throw him out if necessary. She thrust a pointing finger towards the lane and then did a double take. A man was limping across the yard.

Ephraim hadn't seen him, and when a voice close to his ear said, 'I suggest you do as the lady asks.' May had the satisfaction of seeing him spin round, craning his neck to look up at the man's face. One glance and he backed away.

'Don' 'ee tell me what to do,' he said.

How ridiculous he looked, sticking out his chest and clenching his fists. Next to this suave stranger he was just a mangy windbag. How could she have felt threatened by him?

'Ephraim, please leave and don't come back,' she said.

''ee might want to think again. Is 'ee sure 'ee wants to be left alone?' He threw a malevolent glare at the man, who hadn't taken his eyes off him.

'I'm sure we'll be fine. Now will you just go?'

'I forgot 'ee's nigger-lovers here aren't 'ee?'

Cliff gasped. May said to the man in the spotless green uniform, 'I am so sorry—'

'Mam,' he said. 'Please don't apologise. I've been insulted by experts. This creep ain't in the runnin'.'

Cliff guffawed. May tried to work out what the man was taking about. Ephraim blenched.

'I suggest you take the hint and leave this lady's property right now,' the man went on.

'It 'issen 'er...' It was like a light had gone on. Ephraim's jaw dropped. ''ee? Tom's left this lot to 'ee?'

'Goodbye, Ephraim.'

May put her arm around Cliff's shoulders as the man followed Ephraim into the lane and waited until he cycled off. He came back, carrying a holdall, his right leg dragging.

'Who is he?' Cliff whispered.

'No idea,' she said, 'but I'm glad he turned up when he did.'

'He's got wings on his uniform.'

'American pilot, then,' she whispered. She'd never seen a black pilot before.

The airman stretched his hand out to May. 'Lieutenant Jesson Cobb, Mam, and I apologise for walking in like that.'

'May Sheppard. Thank you, Lieutenant Cobb, I'm so glad you were here. For a minute there it was getting nasty.'

'I think you could have handled him, all right.' Jesson smiled. Under the peak of his cap, eyes the colour of ripe conkers sparkled in a warm-brown face.

She felt heat in her own face. She quickly turned to Cliff, 'This is my foster-son, Cliff.'

'Pleased to meet you, Cliff.' Jesson held out his hand. Cliff, apparently awestruck, shook his hand mutely. 'That's a fine machine you've got there.' Cliff just nodded.

May said, 'Put the bike in the shed, Cliff. And then could you check the poultry yard, while I speak to Lieutenant Cobb.'

Cliff pushed the bike across the yard, looking over his shoulder to stare at Jesson.

Jesson was gazing around. 'This is just beautiful.'

She tried to see it through his eyes – the hills, steep, green, too difficult to plough despite the War Ag's demands; a lot of trees gone, but a few left in the most inaccessible places; the evening sun softening the old buildings. Idyllic to an outsider.

'It must seem so. Where are you from?'

'Houston County, Texas, Mam,' he said, then went on, 'Mam, this isn't the right time of night to come visiting, but I'm not used to transport in these parts. I'd expected to be here much earlier. If you could tell me where I could get a bed for the night, I'll come back tomorrow.'

'You look exhausted. Your leg…'

'My ticket home, Mam.'

She frowned.

'Sorry, Mam. Shrapnel in the thigh. Got away with it but it's the end of the line for me and the Army. I'm headin' home.'

It didn't explain what he was doing in her farmyard, but he wasn't in any fit state to walk over a mile to the village.

'Come up to the house and have something to eat. I'll try to think of something.'

'Mam. I can't—'

'Of course you can. Without your intervention I don't know what would have happened here tonight. Come into the barn and sit down while I lock up.'

She left him sitting in the harness room. The way he'd sunk on to the chair confirmed how exhausted he must feel. What was she going to do with him? He couldn't stay in the house; the gossip would never die down. Even now, Ephraim would be spreading poison about her entertaining men before Tom was barely in his grave. Tom. What would he have made of all this? She shouldn't have said he hadn't liked Ephraim. But he hadn't, and he'd have been incensed about the egg business.

Cliff was padlocking the poultry yard gate. Even more important after this evening, although she doubted Ephraim would have the nerve to rob the henhouses direct. He always needed someone else for his dirty work.

Chapter 39

May cracked three eggs into Tom's blackened frying pan.

'You deserve these – certainly more than Ephraim Potts and his black market friends,' she said. And, she added silently, you look as if you need it.

Jesson was sitting at the kitchen table, his right leg stretched out to the side. If it weren't for the pigment of his skin, he'd look very unwell indeed. We're so used to judging people's health by the colour of their skin, she thought flicking fat over the eggs. And not just their health. Hell. Didn't Americans have peculiar ways of cooking eggs – sunny side, or something?

'Um, Lieutenant Cobb, do you have a preference for the way your eggs are cooked?'

He jumped, caught unawares. Had he nodded off?

'No, Mam. Anyway you like. I'm just grateful for food,' he said, rubbing a hand over his face. Without his hat he looked different, less assured, more a lost soul. May guessed he was in his late twenties.

He needed a good night's rest after the harrowing journey he'd told them about – trains and buses from Southampton, ending up by mistake in Crompton Magna and walking two miles over the hill to the farm.

Dorothy had brought a piece of gammon as a contribution to the funeral tea. She had to have black market connections – strange, because Tom was as straight as they came. Of course, there were pig clubs, but she couldn't see the straight-laced Dorothy keeping a porker in the back garden of her townhouse.

They'd used most of the ham in the sandwiches, but May sliced the last of it, slid the eggs alongside and placed it in front of Jesson.

Once she'd assured him that she and Cliff had eaten more than enough at the wake, he tucked in. She sat and watched him eat. He was wiping bread around his plate when he looked up, abashed. 'I'm sorry, Mam,' he said, 'too much army living.'

'It's perfectly all right. It's good to see someone other than Cliff with a hearty appetite.'

Cliff was sitting silently at the end of the table. Why was he being so reticent? He'd been first in the queue for the candy the Americans had given the village children before they left for the landings.

'Cliff, could you pour Lieutenant Cobb more tea, please?'

He got to his feet and fetched milk from the larder before taking the cup from beside Jesson.

'Thank you, Cliff,' Jesson said, as the boy handed him the brimming cup.

Cliff returned to his seat. May had to find out why the man was here. He'd been fed and watered and, grateful as she was for his help with Ephraim, she was entertaining a stranger in an isolated house with darkness coming on.

'Lieut—'

'Mam—'

'Sorry, please carry on,' May said.

'Mam, I hope you won't think this impertinent, but,' he turned to Cliff, 'are you Lynette Erwin's son?'

Lynette? Was this the fiancé? Had he come to take Cliff back to her? Maybe she and Rose had got it all wrong about Lynette hiding her associations from her prospective in-laws.

Cliff looked poleaxed. 'You know my mum?' He sat rigid.

'I did, yeah. Sometime ago. I was on my way to join my unit

in Italy – I'd missed the convoy and had to get a ship that berthed at Southampton. I was only there a couple a days, but I… I happened to meet your Ma.' He glanced at May and dropped his gaze.

Thank heavens he'd watered it down for Cliff. He must know she'd realise what "met" meant. He was one of Lynette's clients. How did he have the audacity to admit it here, in her kitchen?

'That doesn't explain why you are here, now,' she said. 'We have no idea where Mrs Erwin is. We are waiting for a letter from her.'

'Auntie May's going to adopt me,' Cliff said. He stared at Jesson, defiance in his eyes. He thinks the same, thought May. That he's been sent to take him back.

'You don't know where she is?' Jesson looked stricken. 'Mrs Wallbanks said she'd told Lynette you'd been looking for her and—'

'You've spoken to Mrs Wallbanks about us?' What was going on here?

Jesson ran a hand over his close-cropped hair. Cliff had shrunk down in his chair, gaze darting round the room as if he was searching for somewhere to hide. May looked from one to the other.

'Lieutenant, I think you are far too tired to continue this tonight. I can't put you up here, but my cottage is half a mile up the lane. Do you think you can make it that far? There's electricity, but only cold water. The beds are made up. Perhaps you could take Cliff's room – the one on the right at the top of the stairs?'

Cliff jerked upright. 'But—'

May gave him a look. He pursed his lips and began scratching at the table with a fingernail.

'I'd be happy to take a room at a pub, if there's one in town,' Jesson said, despondently.

'The village is a mile from here and I'm certain you're not up to that walk. Would you like me to accompany you to the cottage, or do you think you can make it? It's the only one in the lane.'

He struggled to his feet and rubbed his thigh. 'I guess you're right. I appreciate it, Mam. I'll be okay to get there, now I've had some food.' He shook his leg 'Need to get some life back into it,' he said. 'Sometimes I wonder if it would've been better if I'd lost it altogether.'

There was no answer for that. She unhooked the cottage keys from the rack beside the back door.

'The smaller key's for the farm gate. It's the only way out to the lane at the moment,' she said. 'Here's a torch – flashlight. Come back in the morning and we'll talk then.'

He was still thanking her as she closed the door.

As she came through from the back kitchen, Cliff was framed in the doorway, sitting at the end of the enormous table, be-dwarfed and distant.

'Cliff, what on earth is the matter with you? I've never known you so rude.' She began clearing the crocks. He was still working his nail on the table. 'Stop scratching the table, it's not ours—'

He looked up at her, blank-faced.

She sighed, dragged out a chair and sat next to him. 'It is ours, isn't it? I keep forgetting. Everything has happened so fast and now, with this Yank turning up…'

'He's come to get me, hasn't he? He's goin' to take me away. To America, to her. Me mum.' A tear slid down his cheek and he wiped it away with his sleeve.

Just as she'd feared, he was terrified he was going to be uprooted. Who could blame him for feeling overwhelmed with everything that had happened over the last couple of months? She was so tired she could have fallen asleep right there, but she reached out and hugged him. He clung to her, sobbing into her shoulder. 'I don't want to go. I want to go back to the cottage with you and Spence and stay there. For ever.'

What happened to the end of the war being a new start? Since then their lives had turned upside down.

She sat back and gently pushed Cliff upright. He wiped his eyes. She took both his hands and faced him. 'At first, I wondered whether Lieutenant Cobb had come for that reason—'

'I knew—'

'But think about it. He was shocked that we don't know where your mother is. I don't know why he wants to find her, but he does, and it can't be because she's asked him to find you can it? He wouldn't be looking for her, then.'

She watched his blotched face as he digested her words.

'Maybe,' he said. 'So, why's he here?'

'We'll find out tomorrow. Now it's late and we both need to get some sleep.' She stood up. 'I'll make us some cocoa. Go and get into your pyjamas and I'll bring it upstairs.'

She missed hearing his feet on the stairs. This house was so big, they were lost in it.

Chapter 40

Cliff crept into the kitchen, still in his pyjamas. His hands were clutched across his middle. 'Auntie May, I've got a stomach ache.'

She should have expected it, the way he was last night. He wouldn't want to go to school leaving the reason for Jesson Cobb's visit unresolved.

Spencer was yelling in his highchair, waving his arms at his out-of-reach breakfast bowl.

'Keep your hair on, Spencer.' She picked up his spoon and dipped it in his scrambled egg.

'Cliff, you had yesterday off school for the funeral. You must go in today. Get dressed, please. You'll feel better once you get there.' He didn't respond, just stuck out his bottom lip. 'Shall I cook you an egg? I got up early and collected the eggs. I found half a dozen with cracked shells, so we've got plenty to eat up.'

A weak light had been filtering through the curtains when she'd woken. Her thoughts immediately turned to the farm. She'd sacked Ivy. Hell. There was no one to do the poultry this morning.

She clambered out of bed, pulled on the dungarees she'd adopted for the heavier work, and went down to the kitchen to make tea. She had to admit, an electric stove had advantages over a range – mainly that it came on at the turn of a switch. She poured her tea into a china beaker and carried it with her. Drinking outside. What would Tom have said?

The sky turned from rose to baby-pink as she walked down

the track. The promise of a beautiful day. Blossom whickered over the orchard fence and May stroked the mare's velvet muzzle. Ben pushed his head in, wanting his share of fuss. She gently pulled the old horse's soft ears and he drooped his head in pleasure. 'You two enjoy another couple of hours' peace,' she told them. Cliff would no doubt bring them a crust of bread on his way to school.

In the barn, May piled baskets and tools in the barrow, took the key from the harness room and went across to the poultry yard. She collected a sack of feed and made for the furthest corner. She hadn't seen Gracie in weeks, although Cliff kept a special eye on her. She opened the hatch and threw down some feed. Gracie appeared, but with none of her usual strut.

'You're becoming an old lady,' May told her. The bird cocked an eye before beginning to peck at her breakfast. 'I don't have to justify keeping you now,' May said. 'You can just live in peace.' Gracie ignored her, happily pecking away.

She'd let the hen have the odd brood or two to keep her company, but she'd earned her retirement.

Retirement. Just when other women were leaving the factories and wartime jobs, she was embarking on a lifetime of labour. If she wanted it. She could sell up; live in comfort on the proceeds. And do what? Cliff would leave school in a couple of years and be out at work all day. Spencer? Who knew; Lynette could turn up at any moment and reclaim him.

'Morning, May.'

'Sally! You're early.'

May was pleased to see the girl. Always cheerful, she was an indispensable part of the farm.

'I guessed you'd need help. Ivy stormed into the hostel last night saying she was leaving,' Sally said. 'She was up and gone before I left this morning. On the milk train, I reckon.' She held the shovel for May as she swept.

They closed the wire door of Gracie's enclosure. 'Between you and me, I told her to leave,' May said.

Sally carried the tools and May pushed the barrow, as they walked.

'She's been in cahoots with Ephraim Potts, the ex-ARP warden, selling our eggs on the black market.'

'Stealing, you mean?' Sally didn't sound as surprised as May had expected.

They stopped outside the hen house where May had left the egg baskets. Insistent clucking could be heard inside as the hens waited impatiently to be let out.

'It looks that way, although I don't actually have any proof.'

'Pity. There was some talk a few months ago when she worked at Magna Farm. I'd hoped that's all it was, but apparently not.'

May unlatched the wooden door and the squawking hens marched out.

Sally heaved the feed sack from the barrow, scooped some out and scattered it across the ground. The birds raced in a frenzied swarm to get to their breakfast.

'She's gone, anyway,' said May. 'And I hope we've put a stop to Potts as well.' She had a sudden picture of Jesson upstaging Ephraim. Well mannered, he'd treated her with respect as a landowner and as a woman. What kind of picture would she cut today in gumboots and dungarees, her hair hidden under a ragged turban?

Sally was heading to the next hen house, clutching the bulging sack of feed, feet shuffling at ten to two.

May sped after her and took hold of a corner of the sack. 'We need to talk about the work. The hay's nearly ready for cutting.'

'I was going to get the mower out today and give it the once-over,' Sally said.

May hadn't thought of that. How much she had to learn. Another girl might have taken advantage of May's ignorance, but she trusted Sally and happily deferred to her experience.

'What about hands? We're another worker short without Ivy.' They stopped at the next henhouse and released the clamouring birds.

Sally threw the feed in an arc and said, 'I reckon we'll be okay as long as the weather stays fine. We can cut it in a day, turn it on another and then row up on another. The worst bit will be the carting and stacking – we'll already be tired, and it's heavy work.'

They moved the sack on between them. 'I'll help, of course, and Cliff – he's mad keen to get involved. I might ask if he and the Dale twins could have the afternoons off school to help. The school is usually happy about it, although I don't really approve. We might get a bit of help from the village, too.'

They continued the discussion as they fed the rest of the birds and cleaned out the houses, before collecting the eggs from the nest boxes.

'A good load,' said Sally.

Now they're not being pinched, May thought.

When they'd carried the baskets of eggs to the dairy, Sally went back to give instructions to the other girls. They'd been arriving as May and Sally crossed the yard. How good it was to hear their cheerful teasing as they cycled in. They greeted her like a friend, and her worry that she'd be excluded and seen as the boss, was ill-founded. After yesterday's horrible scene, it was reassuring to know they were on her side.

Cliff, still clutching his stomach, was kicking at the corner of the rug with his bare foot. May was getting cross. If she had to ask for him to be off school again in the next few days, he must go in today or he'd miss too much.

She tried not to raise her voice. 'Cliff, you wanted to take your bike to school. You can do that and I promise I won't agree anything with Lieutenant Cobb that affects you. If there is anything to discuss, you will be included. Now please get ready for school.'

He took his hands off his stomach. 'You promise?'

'Promise.'

May had washed more than half the morning's eggs by the time Jesson arrived in the dairy.

'You must be starving. I'll make you some breakfast in a moment,' she told him, as he watched her rinse muck and feathers from the shells and place the eggs in big wooden crates, ready for Bill Tyler to pick up on his way to the packing station.

Jesson looked rested, his eyes were bright and his leg didn't seem to be paining him, although he took up May's offer to perch on the wobbly stool in the corner.

'I hope you slept well,' she said, her back to him as she lifted out the last of the clean eggs.

'Like a log, Mam,' he said. 'Didn't know where I was when I woke and fancied I was back home.'

'I'm sure your home is much more comfortable than my old cottage with no hot water,' she said. All she knew of America was what she'd seen in films, but she drew a mental picture of a pretty black wife in a stylish print dress, waiting for him in a spotless home.

'My folks' place ain't so bad. Not very large, but enough rooms for me and my two sisters. We do have hot water, though.' He grinned. May watched him spin his cap on the marble slab. 'But it *is* out of town. The family business is growing fruit. Plums, mostly.'

No wife then. May looked at him. In his smart uniform, she'd taken him for a town boy. 'Sounds like you'll be glad to get back,' May said.

'I do miss my family. But what I'll do for a living now my flying days are over…'

Jesson was finishing his breakfast. He hadn't mentioned the reason for his visit, and May had had enough of the game. This had to be sorted out before Cliff came home, and she still had a day's work to get through.

'Why are you here, Lieutenant?'

He sighed before setting down his knife and fork.

'I realise what you thought when I mentioned Lynette's name last night, and I apologise for talking about it in front of Cliff.'

'Cliff understands something about his mother's occupation, but we don't talk about it.'

He wouldn't meet her eye as he went on, 'As I told you, my ship docked at Southampton, but the forward transport to Italy, where my unit was stationed, wasn't leaving for a couple a days. The guys I was with… they were a bit lively after being at sea…'

May raised her eyebrows.

He went on, 'Anyway, they invited me to go out one night.' He swallowed. 'I got drunk. Very drunk. I didn't know until later that they'd spiked my drinks – for a joke. Anyways, we were in a bar and I got talkin' to this woman and I bought her a drink. She seemed kinda free an' easy for someone who said she was engaged and had promised her boyfriend, when he got posted overseas, she'd stay faithful. The other boys were older than I was and they were joshin' me about her. When I went out to the men's room, they discovered,' he lowered his voice to a mumble, 'she'd go with a black – for the right price – if you know what I mean?'

'It's pretty clear,' May said.

Jesson glanced at her, biting his lip, 'I said I wasn't interested, but they'd all chipped in and it was kinda difficult to refuse her.'

May snorted.

'I know, Mam, it's no excuse.'

May stared unseeingly at the dirty crocks on the table.

Jesson went on, his voice barely audible, 'I offered to back out of the… arrangement.'

But she saw what a dish you were and couldn't resist, May thought. She wanted to ask him to leave but her throat seemed to have sealed up.

'Next thing I remember, I was being woken up in my bunk and told there was a boat. We were supposed to wait for segregated transport, but someone swung it and we were headin' out. They said it was all round the base I'd fraternised with a girl who was engaged to some lieutenant – son of a Southern colonel.'

A colonel's son. Provider of expensive coats and leather bags?

Did she believe this? Was it the cleaned up version of a man embarrassed to admit he visited prostitutes? On the other hand, the coat, the bag, the fiancé. It did add up. And Lynette being tempted by a handsome face and money. That certainly added up.

She needed to check on Spencer. He was in his pram in the garden. She stood up.

'It's a good story and it fits with what I know of Lynette Erwin. But it doesn't explain why you've come here. I have to check on the baby. If you want more tea, help yourself.'

Spencer was burbling to himself as he played with his toys. He stretched out his hand and pointed as a blackbird flew off at May's approach.

'It's a blackbird, Spencer. Blackbird.'

Spencer gurgled an incomprehensible reply. If Cliff was here he'd make out he knew what it meant. She found herself studying Spencer's features. They were finer than those of many of the black soldiers who'd been stationed near the village. Likewise, his skin was paler – the colour of light brown sugar. Lynette's influence, of course. A touch of Cliff about the nose, perhaps? She jiggled a knitted teddy. The baby chortled and tried to catch hold of it.

Lieutenant Cobb's features were not heavy, the lips broader than Spencer's, his complexion more dark brown sugar than demerara. He hadn't mentioned the baby, but why else was he here? He hadn't said when he met Lynette, but it must have been in '44. How to play it? She couldn't walk in carrying the baby and say, 'Is he yours?'

'Mrs Sheppard?'

May tucked the teddy down beside Spencer, touched him on the cheek and went back across the garden to Jesson. He was looking towards the pram. The pear tree hid the baby from view.

'Did you pour me one?' she asked, seeing the cup in his hand. She walked on. What I really need, she thought, are answers.

They'd just sat down when there was a rap on the open door.

'Just come for the eggs, May. Sorry – didn't know you had a visitor.' Bill Tyler stood in the kitchen doorway, looking curious.

'Hello, Bill. Come in.'

Damn, May thought. She should be out on the farm, not interrogating a pilot in the kitchen. You couldn't keep anything private around here.

'This is Lieutenant Cobb.'

Jesson stood up and put out his hand. Bill shook it without hesitation as May introduced him. He looked at her for elaboration.

'The eggs are in the dairy, Bill,' she said. 'We've had another episode of stealing. I'll tell you about it when I've got more time, but I hope I've put a stop to it – with the Lieutenant's help.'

Bill's desire for more information was clearly vying with his good manners and only when it was clear nothing more was going to be said, did he reluctantly take his leave.

'Lieutenant, I really don't have time to mess about.' He'd been prevaricating about joining his unit in Italy and flying reconnaissance missions, but he'd mentioned nothing more about Lynette. 'I need to know why you are here and I need to get on with my work. We've acres of hay to cut tomorrow and I've workers to find for turning and carting it later in the week.'

'Sorry, Mam. As I was telling you, these flying missions weren't exactly combat—'

'Do you realise Cliff thinks you've come to take him away?'

'Take him away? Where?'

'He thinks you've been sent by his mother. I've told him you don't seem to know where she is, but the boy's worried sick.'

'I had no idea he'd… Okay, I'll cut to the chase, but please hear me out. Flying is exciting, but it's also frightening. We lost guys. We were strafing targets at first, but then we got to escorting bombers and going into combat. When you see your buddies getting shot down you start wondering what'll happen to you. How you can protect yourself. Some guys have lucky charms; some pray. I kept thinking about the good and bad things I'd done in my life and how they might weigh up. I missed my sailing because I testified in court when I saw someone stabbed in a street fight, but I could've messed up Lynette's chance of a good life with this colonel's son as a result. Maybe those things wouldn't balance out and the Lord would think I deserved to be punished.'

Despite herself, May was intrigued. Surely, a man who was used to going with prostitutes wouldn't suffer this kind of guilt about one drunken night? Perhaps his story was genuine.

'In March, we were escorting a photographic reconnaissance mission and my plane got shot up. I got a shrapnel wound in my leg. I was losing a lotta blood and I thought I wouldn't make it back. Anyhow, I promised the Lord if I got through, I'd make it up to Lynette – if I'd messed up her life.'

He stretched his leg and rubbed his thigh. 'When I was shipped back here to hospital and then had to wait for my ship back in Southampton, I saw it as a sign. I'd made it and I was meant to keep my side of the bargain. I had no memory of where we went that night, so I asked around. All I found was someone in a pub who said Lynette was bombed out in '40.' He shrugged. 'I figured I had the time to track her on from there and I found Mrs Wallbanks. She'd seen Lynette looking pretty good, but didn't know where she'd been living. The thing she did know was where her son was: in Crompton, near Dorchester, with a Mrs Sheppard.'

May tried to piece it together. She had told Mrs Wallbanks she was fostering Cliff and where she lived. She stared out of the window. The garden was a wilderness, but nothing like that decimated street. Those ruined homes. He could have found Mrs Wallbanks, as she had, and easily ended up in Magna, not Parva. She was well known, and, with Tom's death so recent, anyone could have told him where to find her.

Jesson broke in on her thoughts. 'Your baby. It's crying.'

'My—? Ah. I think you'd better come with me.'

She led him to the pram. Spencer reached out for her. She unclipped the harness, lifted him out and turned to Jesson. She said, 'This is Spencer.'

He blinked in surprise before taking hold of Spencer's hand. He said, 'Hello, little fella.' Spencer pulled at his finger. 'I had no idea your husband was a man of colour, Mam,' he said.

She said, 'I was widowed before the war, Lieutenant. Spencer is not my baby. He's Cliff's half-brother.'

Chapter 41

All the boys wanted a ride on his bike after school, but he said he had to get back to the farm.

The pilot would be there. Auntie May liked him – she'd given him food and let him sleep in his bed. *His* bed. This afternoon he'd be there. Waiting to take him to his mother.

A lot of evacuees were back in Southampton and the class was only half as big, which meant the teacher picked on you more. Today he'd been told off twice for daydreaming. Except he wasn't daydreaming. He was thinking about living in America. Would it be so bad? Hot dogs and hamburgers, cowboys and campfires; it could be wonderful. But he didn't know his mother. She was just someone who he used to live with and who didn't seem to like him very much. Auntie May was his mum and he didn't want to leave her, or Spence, or this place.

His satchel bumped on his back as he swerved around potholes and took off on the bumps in the lane. He passed the cottage without turning his head. The faster he rode, the more he could forget about the pilot. One more bend, along the wall and skid into the farm entrance.

Bugger. Someone was in the road. It was him. By the farmhouse gate. He braked hard as the pilot, jacketless and hatless, stepped into the road.

'Cliff, you sure had a tailwind there!' he said.

'I like going fast,' he said. 'What's happened to the gate?'

It was like a different place. The arched gate was wide open and the jungle beyond it had disappeared, revealing a brick path leading to the front door. A wheelbarrow was piled high with weeds and brambles.

'I thought I'd surprise Mrs Sheppard. She's been very welcoming. D'you think she'll be pleased?'

She would be, he knew. She was always moaning about having to go all the way round. But why did this man have to do it – he could have done it himself. If he'd thought of it.

'Suppose, so,' he said.

The pilot looked a bit disappointed. 'Give it a try – you can get around back now.'

'I keep the bike in the yard,' Cliff said, but he couldn't resist pushing it up the path.

'Mrs Sheppard said there's some *ginger beer*? You gonna join me?'

He didn't want to be alone with this man. Didn't want him to have a chance to tell him he was taking him away. Auntie May promised they'd all talk together – unless they'd arranged something while he was at school.

'I've got to do the hens,' he said, dumping the bike by the back door and running indoors to get changed.

When he came downstairs, the pilot was tugging at the front door trying to get it to open. Dirt and dead things fell out on to the rug.

'Happen to know where there's any oil?' the pilot asked. The door made a noise like it was in a ghost story.

'Back-kitchen?' Cliff walked on, hearing the pilot sigh.

He was almost outside when the pilot said, 'I haven't come to take you away.'

'What?'

'I'm not here to take you away, buddy.' He raised his hands like a cowboy nabbed by the sheriff. 'Not guilty.'

Cliff didn't know what to say.

The pilot said, 'Can we try some of that weird sounding drink and maybe talk a little?'

Still wary, Cliff said, 'Okay.'

'So, you're Spence's dad.'

'We don't know. That's the God's honest truth. But it seems on the cards,' Jesson said.

They could hear Auntie May and the girls laughing as they made their way up the track from the fields. Cliff and Jesson were leaning over the fence feeding Ben and Blossom with the carrot tops Cliff had pinched from the vegetable rack.

He didn't really understand why they didn't know for sure. He'd seen the bull at the other end of the village climbing on the cows. Mating. But what about humans. If that's what his mum did with those men, why didn't she have loads of babies; not just him and Spence? Sometimes, in the playground, they joked about what men and women did, and Buster once showed them some creased photographs. All Cliff could make out were some bare bosoms, but he'd laughed along with the rest.

He wasn't going to be taken away. Jesson – Auntie May would never let him call the pilot that – wasn't so bad. He made him laugh and his voices of Popeye the Sailor Man and Donald Duck were wizard.

'Cliff, I reckon we'd better keep mum about me 'n Spence in front of the land girls. Your Aunt May'll have our hides if her business gets all over town.'

Cliff gave Blossom a final pat and jumped off the bottom rail of the fence. 'Yeah, there's a lot of gossip round here and she hates it.'

The chatter stopped as the girls caught sight of Jesson. They'd be thinking how scruffy he looked: shirt open, sleeves rolled up, bits of twig in his hair. Funny though, they all pulled off their turbans and scarves and fluffed up their hair. Even Auntie May.

The girls swarmed round Jesson, all talking at once. Cliff went to see Spence and Auntie May followed him. 'Shall we take Spencer to see the horses?' she asked.

They pushed the pram to the fence. Blossom plodded over and pushed her big head towards the child, who cooed and touched her nose. Auntie May bent down and picked up something from the ground.

'Looks like a carrot top,' she said.

Cliff said nothing as Blossom took it in her whiskery lips.

'How have you got on with Lieutenant Cobb?'

'All right. He doesn't like ginger beer, though.' He climbed on the fence rail.

'Is that all?'

'He told me he might be Spence's father.'

'And that he hasn't come for you?'

'Yeah.'

The girls were moving off, and Jesson was walking across to the fence.

'Are you happy that he's not going to take you to America?'

'Yeah, I want to stay here.' He jumped down.

Auntie May smiled and touched his arm. 'I want you to as well.'

It was going to be all right.

'If you're sure it's okay for me to bunk down at the cottage again?' Jesson said.

'Of course. But we'd better ask Cliff – you're staying in his room after all,' Auntie May said.

Cliff had done his jobs for the day. They'd had tea and he was finishing his homework at the kitchen table. He was usually good at maths, but he'd got stuck on a geometry question and when he'd asked for help, Jesson explained how to do it. He made it sound interesting. Cliff had never thought that a pilot would have to be good at maths to be able to navigate.

'I don't mind about the room,' he said. He might need more homework help tomorrow.

'That's mighty decent of you, pardner,' Jesson said, in a cowboy accent.

Cliff laughed. He loved hearing Americans speak; it was like being at the pictures.

'I've thought about the hot water problem,' said May. 'If you look in the scullery, under the sink there's a primus stove. You could use that to heat a pan of water. You'll probably want to wash after all that gardening.'

Auntie May had thanked Jesson for the work he'd done on front door and the gate. She said it wasn't necessary and all that, but Cliff could see how happy she was someone had done something she hadn't had to ask for. Maybe that's why she asked him to stay at the cottage again.

Jesson was confused. 'Is that some kinda camping stove?'

'The language problem again. Yes, it is. There's some meths – lighting fuel – and paraffin. I'm sure you'll get the hang of it,' Auntie May said, before turning to Cliff. 'I'll be out on the farm early tomorrow morning. We're hay cutting and I need to make sure everything's ready so we can start as soon as the dew is off the grass. I'll leave you a note to take to your teacher, asking if you and the twins can have Thursday and Friday afternoons off school to help. We'll need the boys again on Saturday to help with carting. Can you ask them to tell their mother, please? She's going to come as well. And some others from the village, I hope.'

'Can I ride Blossom?' It was his favourite bit of haymaking, riding the horse on the way back to the yard.

'We'll see.'

'Mam, I can see you need all the help you can get. I'm just kicking my heels until my ship sails, so I'd be willin' to join the party. If you think I could help. I'm pretty good at driving a tractor.'

Auntie May and Cliff looked at each other.

'Have I overstepped... Ah, you folks don't have a tractor, do you?'

'Mr Arrowsmith was very set in his ways,' said Auntie May. 'I am thinking of getting a tractor, if I can find one—'

'A tractor? An orange one like Mr Tyler's?' Cliff jumped off his chair. This was news. A tractor! He could drive it.

'Cliff, it's only an idea. They are very difficult to find and I certainly couldn't pick one for the colour. Anyway, Lieutenant, thank you for the offer. If you'd like to stay, that would be very helpful. I'm not sure you're up to walking round the fields using a hay rake, but I'm sure we can find something that won't over-tax your leg.'

A tractor, afternoons off school and homework help on hand. Things were looking up. Maybe that's why Auntie May was smiling.

Chapter 42

May lay back in the shade of the elms, eyes closed. She listened to the girls' chatter and the sound of munching as the horses enjoyed their nosebags. The smell of newly mown grass overlaid with the honey scent of mayweed lay on the sultry air. This was her version of heaven.

'Ooff!' Spencer flopped on to her stomach. The girls laughed as she struggled to sit up and grasp the wriggling child. She chuckled and tickled his toes before sitting him back on his rug.

'Look.' One of the girls pointed.

Jesson came towards them, dressed in a pair of Seth's old dungarees. The glasses on the tray he carried clinked with his uneven gait. He'd found a huge earthenware jug May hadn't seen before. One day she'd find time to explore all the cavernous kitchen cupboards.

'Thanks, Lieutenant,' she said, pouring ginger beer into the glasses. 'Won't you have some?'

'No thank you, Mam. Tastes like fiery dishwater to me,' he said.

The girls began ribbing him about getting a supply of Coca Cola instead. He responded in kind, joking about British food and warm beer.

How long would it be before they asked her outright why Jesson was here? Heavy hints had been dropped and they must be guessing there was a connection between him and Spencer.

Sally got to her feet. The other girls drained their glasses and began packing away the picnic debris.

'It should only take an hour or so to finish the cutting,' Sally said. 'Then I'll turn out the horses and lend a hand here.'

They'd hoped to get the cutting finished the day before, but it was a surprisingly heavy crop. Tom would have been impressed by the difference the new fertilizer he'd been so reluctant to use had made.

So much learning to fit in, May thought. The account books hadn't been touched since the second time Tom had been taken ill, and the paperwork was piling up. She'd been asking Bill's advice, but he'd been stand-offish when he'd returned the egg crates earlier in the week, apologising if he'd interrupted May's "entertaining".

She strapped Spencer in his pram and parked it under the trees where he could watch the work.

The girls, Jesson in their midst, spread out across the field. They looked up, as one, at a rumpus on the track. Cliff, with his precious bike, alongside Bob and Pete were joking and larking around. Rose brought up the rear, looking serene in a slim button-through dress. As she strode, it split open at the knee revealing several inches of slender tanned thigh. May saw Jesson take a long look. Rose had elegance; flapping wellies notwithstanding.

Sally climbed on to the mower seat and clicked her tongue. The horses moved off, towing the mower on to the track. They turned into Little Hill Field on the opposite side of the lane, which had the last of the standing grass.

May handed each of the three boys a wooden hay rake. She'd reserved the smallest for them, but they still seemed swamped by the long handles. She placed the boys abreast of the work gang with instructions to turn over the cut hay that lay on the ground. Mown the day before, it was now dry on top, but underneath it was still moist grass. Once exposed, it would dry out in the baking sun.

The boys set to work. May hid a smile. Wearing an assortment of the largest straw hats from Tom's dusty collection, they looked like a row of giant mushrooms.

She returned to Rose. 'I am so glad to see you,' she said, handing her a rake and leading her to a strip of grass alongside the stream. Because of the curve of the bank, this section was shorter than the rest of the field, like a railway siding, and was left until last. It gave the two of them privacy to chat as they worked side by side.

'So that's him, is it? The one all the gossip's about,' said Rose, nodding at Jesson, who was working on the far side of the field.

'I knew it would be all round the village. Don't they have anything else to talk about?'

'You know how tongues wag, and when a good-looking man turns up out of the blue...'

'I suppose they've decided he's Spencer's father? We don't know ourselves, but when did the facts ever get in the way of gossip in this village?'

'It's not Ephraim this time. He's staying surprisingly quiet. It's everyone else.'

They worked in unison, flicking over swathes of hay as May updated Rose with the events of Monday evening.

'So it wasn't the boyfriend – sorry, fiancé – who brought her here that day?'

'Can't have been. The colonel's son was somewhere in Europe. You know Lynette, she'd have any number of connections. I reckon she covered up her pregnancy though. I didn't spot it under that huge coat, and she nipped into the sports car like a debutante, not a woman in the last weeks of pregnancy.'

'You have ter admire her gall,' said Rose.

'Goes with the territory. Or the occupation,' May said.

'Where does all this leave Spencer?' Rose asked, as they reached the end and began working their way back up the strip.

'Exactly the same as before. Nothing's changed. Lynette has all but disappeared, so I carry on. I have promised to contact Jesson if we hear from her. To be honest, I'm more concerned about Cliff's future; I can't adopt as things stand. I've got to see Tom's solicitor about the farm and I may ask his advice.'

'And what about the dusky lieutenant? He's staying in your cottage, I hear,' Rose grinned at her.

May sighed. 'They aren't yacking on about that, are they?' she said. 'I had to put him somewhere. He wasn't up to walking to the pub, and after the showdown with Ephraim I didn't have the energy to harness Blossom and drive him there. It seemed logical. And then, well, he's just stayed there. I need all the help I can get on the farm. Even a lame airman!'

'I quite under— What's that?' Rose stared up the hill, where Sally had been mowing.

One of the land girls shouted, 'Runaway' and pointed up the hill.

'*Sally?*' May shouted, dropping her rake and running.

Everyone ran towards the track as Blossom and Ben, tails high, dragged the clanking mower crazily around the hill at full pelt. The cutting bar, its unsheathed metal teeth glinting in the sun, flailed around as the mower hurtled over bumps.

'The gate,' yelled May. 'Shut the gate.'

With the bar down, the mower couldn't pass through the gap. If the horses attempted it, a crash was inevitable. One, or both, horses was certain to be injured.

Rose, at May's side, shouted, 'Boys, get out of the way.'

The boys were leading the rush on to the track. Rose's

breathless voice wasn't carrying. If one of the panicking horses got through and bolted for the yard, the children would be right in their path.

Jesson was running lopsidedly at the edge of the pack. May caught a glimpse of him angling away from the field exit, across to where the stream passed under a sleeper-bridge next to Little Hill Field gate. Realising he was cutting the corner, she followed. He was already clambering up the far bank as she splashed through the ankle-deep water. She joined him at the gate, tugging to get it free from the years of brambles and honeysuckle that entwined it. The horses had slowed to a canter, but the bar still clanged with every bump in the ground. Instinctively feeling home was the safest place to escape the devil behind them, they headed straight for the gate.

She thought her chest would burst. 'Pull,' she screamed at Jesson.

Together they gave a superhuman heave. The briars ripped away and the gate broke free and swung closed. The momentum landed them in a sprawling heap in the lane. Cliff panted up, climbed on the gate and spread out his arms. Like the crucifixion, Rose said later. Seeing him, Blossom rammed her shoulder into Ben, turning them to the side. As they slowed, so did the noise behind them and they stopped, heads down, flanks heaving, lather foaming like soap suds along their necks and shoulders.

Surrounded by feet and worried voices, May tried to regain her dignity as she clambered to her feet. 'Where's Sally?'

One of the land girls was at the horses' heads. 'She's over there,' she shouted.

Scrambling through the throng, May saw Sally running down the hill, skidding on the cut grass, ashen faced.

'Was anyone hurt?' she shouted, racing to the horses.

'Unhitch the mower,' she instructed, and two more girls went to help.

'No – at least,' May realised she'd left Jesson there on the ground. She looked around. He was on the bridge, gripping the rail, his leg stretched out in front. 'Jesson, are you hurt?'

'No, Mrs Sheppard, I'm okay. Leg's a little sore, that's all.'

Hell. She'd called him Jesson. She hoped no one had noticed. She had intended keeping everything formal.

May went to Sally, who was running a hand down each of the horses' legs.

'I can't see any damage, but it'll be tomorrow that we'll know for sure. I reckon Ben might have a bruised shoulder.' She rubbed the horses' heads. 'You silly old fools, you're too old to behave like that.'

'What about you,' May said. 'What happened?'

'I'm fine,' Sally said. 'A bit bruised, I expect. Something spooked them up by the top bank. We'd finished and I'd just got down to secure the cutting bar.'

She turned to the girl holding Ben's bridle. 'Can you walk him up to the yard?' she asked. 'I'll be right behind with Blossom. We'll sponge them down and walk them 'til they're cool.' The girl began to lead Ben away. 'And no water,' Sally called. Adding quietly to May, as she took Blossom's reins, 'The last thing we need is colic.'

May went over to the gate where the haymakers were milling around. 'As far as we can see the horses aren't hurt,' she announced. 'Thank you all for helping. If everyone is all right, could you get back to the hay turning, please? We've lost a lot of time. Lieutenant, you'd better go and rest. I can see you're in pain.'

The group began walking away, Jesson limping beside them.

'Blossom is all right, isn't she?' Cliff asked, eyes huge.

'She and Ben are fine. You were very brave. Seeing you made Blossom swerve, otherwise there could have been a nasty accident. But don't you ever do anything like that again.'

Chapter 43

May tapped on the cottage door. Strange to be knocking at your own door. Already it didn't seem like home; some of the familiarity had been lost. It would always be the place she and Seth had shared, but she seemed to have moved on more in the last six weeks than she had in the previous six years.

'Mrs Sheppard. Please come in – you don't have to knock.' Jesson was buttoning his uniform jacket.

'I've left Spencer by the gate. Are you ready?'

'Sure am.'

He picked up his cap and stepped out, pulling the door closed behind him, but not before May glimpsed shaving gear set out on the kitchen table. Her heart gave a leap; Seth used to shave there every morning.

As they walked to the gate, she realised that although she'd hoped most people wouldn't notice Jesson was living there, the underpants hanging on the washing line left no room for doubt.

They walked up the lane and she asked about his leg. She'd been concerned he'd done real damage yesterday afternoon. He'd been unable to work again in the hayfield but had insisted on collecting the eggs, leaving Cliff free for haymaking. May doubted he'd found them all but when Cliff went to bed early, tired out, she was left with only the feeding and shutting in of the hens to finish before dark.

The new poultry girl seemed competent. She'd collected a decent number of eggs from the nest-boxes that morning as well as scouting around for places Jesson had missed.

'Leg's a bit sore. I don't reckon I'll be doing any dancing today! Sorry I'm a bit slow.'

May usually strode out and it was a little frustrating slowing her pace to Jesson's halting gait. She couldn't complain; his help had averted a disaster.

'I've written to my folks,' he said. 'I need to get a stamp to mail it.'

'The post office is part of the shop,' she said. 'We can get everything there.'

She had been dreading coming shopping since Jesson had suggested joining her the evening before. Impossible to refuse, but the tongues would be wagging in double time when they left the village.

They'd got as far as the church with no more than a few askance looks and questioning good mornings from people. As the shop came into sight, she said, 'You'd better know, the postmistress is Ephraim's sister and she's just as bigoted as her brother.'

'Mam, I've heard everything before. It's water off a duck's back.'

Why should anyone have to accept that? He was a kind, hard-working man who had been injured in the service of his country. He should be welcomed, not reviled.

She parked the pram under the shop awning, making sure Spencer couldn't reach the vegetables piled in front of the window.

'May.' Bill Tyler's lorry was parked opposite. He crossed the road, then hesitated as he saw Jesson waiting by the shop door.

'Lieutenant, you go in. I'll be with you in a minute.' She smiled at Bill.

'I was going to call in,' he said, 'I heard you had a bit of trouble yesterday.'

Bush telegraph again. 'It was a bit hair-raising at the time, but nobody got hurt and the horses are all right. I didn't know old Ben could move that fast.' She laughed. 'Sally trotted them up this morning and there are no ill-effects. We don't need them today, so they're having a day off.'

'You've been lucky with the weather. Chose the right week.'

'I take no credit whatsoever; Sally is the one with the farming knowledge.'

'She's a natural with horses, too. They don't usually get the better of her. Do you know what spooked them?'

He seemed to know Sally quite well. She said, 'Something by the edge of the wood at the top of Little Hill Feld. Sally had just got off the mower. A good thing, or she could have been thrown.'

'I seem to remember Tom had an incident up there before the war. Same time of year, I recall. You ought to look in the farm diaries. Old Tom wrote everything down.'

May thought of the pile of dog-eared ledgers on a top shelf in the back-kitchen. She barely had time to open the post, much less to dig into farm history.

'Bill, I am a bit swamped with the paperwork again. I know you're as busy as me, but could I bring some of the most difficult forms over one evening and beg a bit of help?' He usually came to her, but with Jesson around it was more difficult. The two men had barely acknowledged each other just now.

'You're always welcome May, you know that. Give me a ring and we'll agree a time.'

'Thanks. I'd better go. I've been too long already.'

'Yes,' Bill said. 'You don't want to keep your friend waiting.'

She'd meant she needed to get back to the farm.

Jesson was being served at the post office counter as May went into the shop. She should have asked him to get her some stamps. She excused herself to the woman behind him in the queue but, when she went to speak to him, realized he'd already paid Victoria for his stamp and was holding out his hand for the change. Victoria, with an expression like she was emptying a chamber pot, placed the money on the counter. Jesson reached to pick it up but May stayed his hand.

'Hand him the change.'

Victoria glared at May. 'It's there,' she said, shoving the pile of coppers forward with her index finger.

'I've shopped here for ten years and you've always put the change in my hand, Victoria. Do the same with Lieutenant Cobb.'

'You're white. I don't touch darkies.'

There was a buzz of muttering in the queue and, again, May sensed the customers at the grocery counter craning to see what was happening. She ought to charge for entertainment.

'Mam, it's okay,' Jesson said, reaching for the money.

'No.' May pushed his hand back.

Victoria's eyes glinted. She called over her shoulder, 'Ephraim, could you come out a moment, please?'

Damn.

The rear curtain was drawn back and Ephraim appeared like a magician from a disappearing box. 'What's goin' 'ere?' he said.

'Mrs Sheppard has jumped the queue and is trying to make me touch the darkie.'

Conniving old bat. May said, 'I've asked her put the change in the Lieutenant's hand. It's common courtesy.'

'It might be if 'ee were a lootenant. But 'e int.'

'What—'

'Sir, I—'

Calling Ephraim, sir. May cringed.

'Where did 'ee pinch 'em wings?' He pointed to the twin badges on Jesson's lapels. 'All on us know Yanks don't put niggers in airplanes. 'ee's only fit to work a broom.'

May was at flashpoint but before she could speak, Jesson's deep voice cut in. 'Sir, I think you've been misinformed. I graduated from the Tuskegee Institute and I'm a fully qualified pilot with the 301st Squadron – The Red Tails. We're are a unit of black airmen. I flew nine missions in Italy before I was shot up by anti-aircraft fire.'

There were murmurs of respect from the listeners and May felt pride swelling in her chest.

Everyone waited.

'Whatever 'ee *may* have done in the war 'issen' worth two hoots here. The GPO isn't forced to serve 'ee.'

Jesson opened his mouth, but May was quicker. 'I didn't know you were employed to represent the GPO, Ephraim. Strange, I'd have imagined all their employees had to be above reproach.'

His mouth worked but no words came out. He looked murderously at May, but under the scrutiny of every person in the place, he eventually took a defensive line. ''ee've held up the queue long enough. Give 'ee the change, Victoria.' He turned on his heel and stalked back behind the curtain.

To May's surprise, a smattering of applause followed his exit, but one Medusa look from Victoria, handing over the change with the tips of her fingers, silenced it.

May heard Spencer's cry. She asked Jesson if he could go and see to the child while she did her shopping.

'Did you want stamps?' Mrs Harris, at the back of the queue with the ever-present runny-nosed child beside her, asked in a hushed tone.

'Oh Lord, I forgot,' said May.

'I'll get them,' Mrs Harris said, 'How many?'

May told her and joined the queue at the grocery counter. She felt she'd done a day's work and there were still fields of hay to turn.

As they walked back along the lane, May apologised for the behaviour Jesson had experienced. 'Many of the locals are friendly open-minded people, but others, like Ephraim and Victoria, were born here and want to protect their way of life. They feel threatened by change and believe that if they reject anything new, life will revert to the way it was before the war. It won't, of course, but it'll take them time to learn that and adjust. I hope you won't be offended, but I'd say it was the white Americans who brought this black prejudice. I never encountered anything like it before the US troops came over.'

They stopped at the cottage gate. Jesson said, 'Mam, thank you for taking on old Ephraim and his sister, but, as you've just said, that type of behaviour is normal in The States. I've dealt with it my whole life. As long as there are people like you – who see us as human beings – things will change.' He smiled his big warm smile and May felt herself blush like a schoolgirl.

Chapter 44

The plan to cart and stack the hay on Saturday was a good one because the children didn't have to miss school. Even so, with many of the evacuees having returned home, the number who were able to come was far fewer than in previous years. Doreen had marshalled them, their mothers and anyone else she deemed physically fit and able to lend a hand, even for a couple of hours.

'Look at that!' May said, as a skein of pitchfork-bearing folk trooped along the track. Most carried bags bulging with enough food and cold tea, or water, to keep them going through the day.

She spotted Mrs Harris, both children scampering around her. 'Thank you for rescuing me yesterday,' she said. 'I couldn't have faced Victoria again for a king's ransom, let alone stamps.'

'That woman and 'er brother needed knockin' down a peg or two. They've treated us like dirt ever since we come 'ere in '39. Lucky they didn't get any kiddies billeted with them. I'd pity any who had to live there.'

One day May would try to find out how the Potts had avoided having evacuees. Some WAAFs had been billeted there once and came under the lash of Isabella's tongue when they arrived home, rowdy after a dance. They'd left the next day. After that, they'd only had military personnel, much like Tom. He'd had an evacuee family at the beginning. They'd returned to the city after a few months, saying they missed cinemas and fish and chips. They'd been willing to risk the bombs to escape the boredom of the countryside. May suspected they'd complained how unwelcoming Tom had been. A succession of military people had used the farmhouse bedrooms over the years, but Tom had barely set eyes on them. They came and went at odd hours and ate their meals at camp or in the pub.

'I'm surprised you haven't gone back home,' she said to Mrs Harris.

'Nuffin' there. Bombed flat. The old man's still overseas and we like it 'ere, in spite of the Pottys. If 'e can get a job when 'e's demobbed, I'm all for stayin'.'

'The land girls are leaving the service in droves, so all the farms will be looking for workers – if he wanted to work on the land.'

''s worth thinking about. Ta.' Valerie tugged at her mother's skirt and Mrs Harris moved on.

Sally was organising workers into groups. Some for Little Hill Field, the last to be turned, where she wanted the hay raked into piles at the foot of the hill for easy collection; others in the remaining fields, piling up the hay ready to be loaded on to the carts. One of the land girls would drive Ben, taking the laden carts to the rickyard where Sally would be in charge of rick building.

Jesson had been delegated to drive Blossom's cart. He assured them he'd driven horses and mules since he was a boy. So far, he'd proved himself competent in harnessing up the animals and negotiating the narrow gateways.

May stood up straight and eased her back. The field she was working in was almost cleared. Jesson was edging a swaying hay cart gingerly into the lane. She held her breath as the overhanging hay skimmed the gateposts. A miscalculation could rip the load off.

They were through. Phew. She ought to trust him – he'd flown fighters and shot down enemy planes. He said driving a hay cart would be like taking candy from a baby.

'Last load, then we'll stop for elevenses,' she called to the workers pitching the last of the field's hay into heaps, as she headed to check on Spencer.

The land girl driving Ben eased a cart into the field. 'Sally says could you check on Little Hill Field, please? See how they're getting on.'

'Will do,' May said. She'd take Spencer. Everyone was used to him and he attracted no more attention than any of the other young children. He'd like to see the boys, they'd asked to work on the hill, loving the idea of trying to roll the hay downhill.

The haymakers were sitting in a group under the hedge by the stream enjoying drinks and mid-morning snacks.

'Brought us cold drinks, Missus? Allus the farmer's wife's job, that.'

Wilf Kettle. May looked at the old man: back permanently hunched; face like old leather under the tweed cap no one had ever seen him without; his once-white collarless shirt with the sleeves rolled-up.

'I think you know, Mr Kettle, I'm no longer a farmer's wife,' she said. Voices murmured for him to shush. May carried on, 'However, although I am now a *farmer*, my kitchen is open if you'd like to go up there and fetch us all a cold drink.'

In the ensuing laughter, the old man dropped his gaze and concentrated on his doorstep bread and dripping.

Cliff pointed to a huge stack of hay that would half-fill a cart. 'We've made that pile.'

'Well done, you must have been working hard,' she said.

'Can you look after Spencer for a few minutes?'

She unclipped the little boy's straps and sat him next to Cliff. 'Here's his bottle of orange juice.' Spencer reached for it with both hands.

May spent a few minutes discussing the work and then set off up the hill.

'Hang on, May.'

Rose had started up the slope behind her. The heat was already intense and both women had patches of perspiration under their arms. Rose tugged off her hat and flapped it in front of her face.

'Where're you off ter?'

'Something triggered the horses' panic the other day. Bill thinks it may have happened before and I'm just going to take a look. Have your break. Rose. Don't overdo it.'

'I may as well tire myself out today – I'm going ter have enough relaxation soon. The munitions factory's laying me off in two weeks.'

They slogged on up the slope, the sun beating on their bent backs. The woodland that bordered the field trapped the heat and the temperature soared as they reached the sandy bank along the boundary.

May turned left, Rose right, as they looked for any indication of what caused the horses to bolt.

May bent down to examine a trampled area. Deep hoof prints and, a few feet further on, a long scrape in the ground. This must be where the cutter bar crashed down. It would have dragged here before it began bouncing manically over the rough ground, scaring the horses witless.

Seth had told her that if something rustles in a hedge, a dog will go and investigate in the hope that it is prey, but a horse's instinct is to run because it could be something that wants to prey on it.

She couldn't see anything that could have scared the team. Ben was the older animal, but he was also the more nervous of the pair. He was harnessed on the offside, nearest the wood. She guessed something spooked him and that had then been exacerbated by the flailing cutting bar, causing the usually unflappable Blossom to bolt with him.

She walked to the end of the narrow field and was about to call to Rose when she saw her friend dead still, finger to her lips. May began to run but Rose gently flagged her hand. May slowed and moved out in an arc to arrive at Rose's back.

She crept forward and looked at the place Rose pointed out. On the bank, lying on a patch of bare earth, was a fawn S shape, like a piece of old rope. She clutched Rose's arm as it moved.

The snake regarded them with a cold eye before slithering away into the dry grass. The dark zigzag along its back generated memories of the warnings May had been given as a child.

The two women looked at each other. 'I think we know what scared the horses,' Rose said.

'Adders,' said May.

They walked back down the hill where the workers were picking up their rakes and pitchforks, ready to start again. May called them around her.

'We've discovered there are adders up on the top bank.'

'Adders? Wowee.' As one, the three boys raced towards the slope.

'NO,' May and Rose shouted in unison.

The boys mooched back again.

May faced everybody. 'No one, and I mean no one,' she looked at the boys, 'is to go anywhere near the top bank. If there is any hay there, just leave it. Start raking a few yards down. Boys, that is not up for debate. Do you understand?'

The boys shrugged and nodded.

'I'll head orf and fetch me snake stick,' said Wilf Kettle. 'Champion snake catcher I wus. Soon deal with them varmints.' He stabbed his pitchfork into the ground and reached for his haversack.

'Thank you, Mr Kettle, but I'm not making any decisions about the adders until I've had time to think.'

Wilf snorted and mumbled something about soft women farmers. May would have let it go, but there was a break in the chatter just as he added, 'Savin' 'em fer the darkie. 'e prob'ly eats 'em.'

Cliff rounded on him. 'Jesson don't eat snakes. He eats food like us and hamburgers in America. I bet you don't even know what a hamburger is.'

'Cliff—' Not again, was there no end to these rows.

'I eats my ham as nature intended. Straight off the pig,' sneered Wilf.

Everyone roared with laughter. May watched the old man wrench up his pitchfork as he tried to work out whether they laughed with him, or at him.

It was nine-thirty by the time May, Jesson, Cliff and Spencer returned to the farmhouse. Spencer had been tucked up in his pram for hours. May had fed him during a brief respite from the fields – making sandwiches for them all – at six o'clock.

The ricks were built and the last of the hay was stacked on the two carts, with tarpaulins thrown over, ready to be unloaded into the barn next day.

Jesson and Cliff lifted respective glasses of rhubarb wine and ginger beer to toast May's first successful haymaking.

'It's the workers we should be toasting,' May said. 'Without everyone's help, it would still be grass in the fields.'

Doreen had been wonderful. She'd organised paying the helpers – sitting herself in the rickyard with pencil and paper, calculating what everybody was owed and handing out the money May had drawn the previous week. Many people refused to accept anything, saying they were pleased to help. Predictably, Wilf Kettle was at the head of the pay queue.

'You let me know about 'em vipers, Missus,' he said to May as he left. 'We'll soon get rid o' they cropy divils.'

Cliff's eyes were closing as he sat in his chair, and May sent him to bed.

She said to Jesson, 'Thank you so much for your help today. You must be exhausted. I hope your leg hasn't suffered too much?'

'Driving the cart was a piece of cake,' he said, although she could see dark rings around his eyes. He'd been dragging his leg as they'd walked back from the farmyard.

'I'll make tracks in a second, Mam. Leave you to turn in.'

'Please call me May', she said. Where did that come from? Too much rhubarb wine, she suspected.

'If you're sure? And I'd be obliged if you'd call me Jesson.'

They smiled at each other and suddenly the kitchen felt very small and airless. May stood up, 'I'll just rinse out the glasses,' she said, ignoring the pile of crocks waiting to be washed.

Jesson put his glass on the draining board next to her. He smelt of hay and horse and something with a woody undertone. She concentrated fiercely on the glass she held, sweat seemed to be leaking from her every pore.

He moved away and said, 'Goodnight, May.'

She cleared her throat. 'Goodnight… Jesson.'

Chapter 45

'What's that?'

'Surprise for your aunt.'

Cliff looked at the newspaper-wrapped parcel under Jesson's arm. He'd gone home late last night and it was Sunday today, so he couldn't have got something from the shop. Cliff doubted he'd want to go in the shop anyway; Bob said Spinster Potty and old Misery Guts made a scene over giving Jesson change in the shop, until Auntie May made them shut up.

He stood his bike by the wall. He'd see what was in the parcel before going for a ride. Auntie May had given everyone, apart from the poultry girl, the day off. He had to see to the hens in the evening, but until then he was free.

Blossom and Ben were standing half-asleep, nose to tail, in the shade. Last night, riding on Blossom's back – as wide as a sideboard – with Auntie May, Spence and Jesson on top of the hay cart was a wizard end to the day. He'd been tired – couldn't even remember going to bed – but everyone had seemed so happy, especially Auntie May. Mrs Gale had brought along her camera and she'd snapped a photo of them on the cart. She promised him one of the prints, just for himself, if they came out.

Jesson was unwrapping the parcel on the table. Auntie May dried her hands and watched. 'I thought we could have these today, May. I'd be pleased to cook them.' He flicked back the last sheet of paper and revealed three golden fish spotted with red and brown.

'Trout? Where did you—?'

'One of the haymakers offered 'em to me yesterday. He dropped them off this morning. You do like fish, don't you?'

'We love it, don't we, Cliff? Thank you, Jesson.'

'It's a pleasure.'

Jesson? May? Maybe she'd let him—

'Thank the Lieutenant, Cliff.'

They were going to eat outside. In the garden. And Jesson was going to cook *outside*. The only times Cliff had eaten outdoors was when they were working or on a picnic. There was VE Day, of course, but that was special.

Jesson told Auntie May to leave it to him, but she kept fussing. She asked Cliff to bike up to the cottage. 'Some of the lettuces are ready for cutting,' she said. 'Can you get two and also some of the mint from the pot by the back door?'

Some day off. 'You can go up and see the twins first, but be back by half past twelve.'

It was funny going into the cottage garden, like it was someone else's house. He took out his penknife and sliced off the two largest lettuces in the row. He wiped the milky sap from the blade on to his shorts and folded the knife.

How much mint? He didn't know. He crushed a leaf and sniffed the peppermint scent. She'd asked Jesson to dig some potatoes from the field. Mr Arrowsmith would have had a fit – you weren't allowed to touch anything when he was still around.

He ran his hand over the mint plant. Why leave it here, she needed it at home. He stuffed the lettuces in between the leaves and picked up the heavy pot. He had a bit of string; he'd tie it on his carrier.

***

234

There was a sack in the barn. He grabbed it and ran back up the lane, clawing at the bumpy rash on his leg. It felt like millions of little needles sticking in. He had some on his arm as well. That stupid driver hadn't slowed down at all. The bike had seemed to take over. It wouldn't do what he wanted, and the swerve had carried him into the ditch.

He laid the pieces of broken pot in the bottom of the sack, then the mint plant – only a few stems were broken – and the lettuces on top. He'd shaken off most of the soil and she'd wash them anyway.

Scratching his leg, he walked back down the lane. He'd better go in the house gate, face the music and get some stuff for his arm and leg.

He heard voices as he followed the path around the house. As he turned the corner he stared at the garden. A fire was burning in the centre of a pile of bricks and a bit of iron railing was laid across on top. The table from the back kitchen was laid out under the pear tree with plates and glasses. Sitting next to each other, in some deckchairs he'd never seen before, were Auntie May and Jesson. Spence was in front of them on a blanket, chewing a rusk. Auntie May was holding a glass and laughing at something Jesson said. She looked like a different person. She was wearing her best dress and Jesson had on a checked shirt and blue trousers; Seth's he guessed. They looked so happy; like a family.

Tears came into his eyes. Spence would know his father, and Auntie May was his mum, not his real one, but the only one he'd know. Spence had a family. A whole family. Not like him. He didn't even know who his father was and probably his mother didn't either.

He sniffed and wiped his eyes on his arm. Jesson and Auntie May looked round.

'Cliff. What's happened?' Auntie May jumped up.

'I came off me bike. I fell into the nettles in the ditch and broke your mint pot.'

'Oh dear,' she said giving him a hug. 'Are you hurt?'

He looked down at his leg. Bloody wheals now ran down the bumps.

'Right. Let's bathe that with some Dettol. Is that the mint?' she pointed to the sack.

'Yeah. And the lettuce.'

'Jesson, could you take this?' She took the sack from Cliff.

'You okay, fella? Your bike?'

'It's in the barn. It's all right. Just a couple of scratches.'

Jesson ruffled his hair. 'You've won your spurs now, pardner. Not a true rider 'til you've taken a fall.'

He smiled. He liked Jesson but he would only ever be his friend. He wasn't his father, not like Spence. And Spence was only his half-brother. Auntie May put her arm round him and led him to the kitchen.

Auntie May wasn't anything. Not really. Not even his adopted mum.

Chapter 46

She couldn't remember a happier day, not since before Seth died. Jesson had refused to allow her to do anything and, joy, she'd sat in the deckchair almost all morning.

He did something magical with the trout; she'd never tasted fish like that. Something to do with cooking in the open air, or the apple branches he'd burnt, perhaps. Either way, she felt well-fed, refreshed, and perhaps a little bit tiddly. Nearly all of Tom's homemade wine had gone. She must make some more this year, if she could get the sugar.

Sugar. The thought meandered to jam making and the WI. She must write her resignation. She'd finally told Doreen that she would be resigning as President and insisted that Doreen, as Secretary, read out her letter at the next meeting. She would recommend that Doreen step into her shoes until the AGM. There was no guarantee she'd then be elected President but, if she proved herself in the next few months, she might just stave off Isabella.

Jesson was taking Spencer for a walk. He seemed truly fond of the little boy and she was certain he believed he was his son. He'd asked Cliff to go with them, but he'd refused. The lad had been very quiet since he got back from the cottage. Should she ask again whether he was hurt? Maybe it was the shock of coming off the bike. He loved the thing. It was big for him, but he seemed competent and he'd ridden her old boneshaker for years. She'd refused to let him go out again, saying he needed to stay quiet after his accident. He didn't argue, which was a sign he wasn't himself.

She got up and went indoors. Cliff was slouching in the armchair, reading *The Beano*.

'It's lovely in the garden. Why don't you come and read out there?'

'I'm all right.'

'Are you sure you aren't hurt anywhere?'

'Only the stings, and they're wearing off.' He didn't lift his gaze from the comic.

Why was he being like this? They were having a wonderful day.

She pulled out a chair and sat down. The kitchen was cool and quiet. 'I could do the hens tonight if you don't feel well.'

'No. You deserve a rest. I'm okay. You and Spence and Jes… *The Lieutenant* enjoy it. I'll do the hens later. Go back to your deckchair.'

May didn't move. What had caused this? He'd been happy when he left this morning. If it wasn't the accident, was it the cottage? Going back to it? He'd been happy there, loved their life from what she saw. He never let things like problems at school or Ephraim's stupid remarks affect him. He always came to her and they faced it together.

She ran back through her mind to when he'd got home with the broken pot. She hadn't been cross, just pleased he was all right. The lettuces were a bit bruised, but they'd had plenty of leaves for the salad.

There was something. The look on his face when she'd first spotted him: tearful, but something else. Sadness? Yes, he'd seemed really sad.

What had he seen? Herself and Jesson drinking, talking, laughing. And Spencer. At their feet, included in the family gathering. A family. Not a family, of course, but to a boy with no parents…? And the way he said "Lieutenant". She'd done this; excluded him. She called Jesson by his name and Spencer could be his son, but she shut Cliff out by insisting he remain formal. An outsider.

'I've been saving this for you,' she said, lifting a toffee tin from a top shelf. 'It's to thank you for all your help and the way you've adapted to living here. You do know I couldn't run the farm without you, don't you?'

He looked wary but interested as she pulled the lid off the tin. 'I know it's not much but I thought, as you're not feeling quite right…' She brought out a bar of Cadbury's Dairy Milk.

Cliff sat up straight as she handed it to him. 'Enjoy it. You don't have to share it. It's just for you.'

'Thank you,' he said, a small frown on his face.

Had that been too clumsy, too obvious she was trying to ingratiate herself?

They heard Jesson's voice. He was telling Spencer about the birds and butterflies in Houston County. All apparently bigger than in England.

'Bet ours are prettier though, don't you?' May said with a wink.

'And friendlier. Specially the robins,' said Cliff, ripping the purple wrapper off the chocolate.

Jesson called from the back door. 'Did you want Spence to stay outdoors?'

'What do you think, Cliff, shall we bring your brother indoors?'

'Nar. I'll come out,' he said.

'Shall I make some tea?' May had been dozing and woke up realising it was late afternoon.

'I'd be happy to.' Jesson put down the book he was reading.

'It's fine,' said May. 'You've done so much. I'll do the tea.

239

Can you help, Cliff?'

He put down the toy car he was pushing around the rug to entertain Spencer. When he came out into the garden, he'd been quite perky; offering pieces of chocolate to Jesson and herself and giving a tiny piece to Spencer, who dribbled it down his romper suit.

She'd tried to give him her attention and hoped he felt included. So silly. Without him there was no family. How could she forget? If only Lynette would keep her word and send the adoption consent, they could be truly mother and son and the boy would have some stability.

She made the tea and Cliff fetched the cake tin. Doreen had brought them a Victoria sponge in return for the cracked eggs May often sent her way. It seemed a lifetime since she'd done her own baking.

'If you carry the cake, I'll bring the tray,' she said.

They set the tea things out under the pear tree and May asked Cliff to serve. 'Ask Jesson if he would like some cake,' she murmured, before returning to her deckchair.

Cliff looked at her, unsure. She nodded.

'Would you like some cake, Jesson?'

'I would. Thank you kindly,' Jesson said, without a flicker.

May smiled inwardly as Cliff cut a wonky slice and passed it over.

'She knows you, doesn't she?'

Gracie had come running when May called. 'She and I are old friends, but she's getting on now.'

'How old is she?' Cliff asked, shooing the hen into her coop.

'Seth said a three-year-old chicken is equal to a thirty-year-old human. I've known her for about seven years, so she must be around seventy.'

'Cor! Older than Mr Arrowsmith was.'

May hadn't really considered Gracie's actual age. It wouldn't be too long before the old hen was no longer coming to her call. She wouldn't let her go for the pot. When the time came, she would be buried deep, safe from the fox.

What kind of farmer was she? She heard Wilf Kettle's voice in her head, 'Letting good food go to waste. Sentimental claptrap.'

They walked back to the house, laughing at Blossom. Upside down, huge white belly flopping from side to side, the mare was revelling in a roll.

'Sally'll love brushing all that dust off her in the morning,' Cliff said as they kicked off their boots in the back-kitchen.

May laughed as she followed him in to the kitchen. 'Right, time for – Jesson? What's the matter?' He was standing by the stove, staring out of the window.

He looked distraught as he turned to them. May's mouth went dry. She went to the sink and ran the tap to wash her hands. She didn't want to face whatever bad news was to come.

'The phone rang. I answered it – I hope you don't mind?'

She shook her head.

'It was my base. I have to get back. There's a ship sailing on Thursday.'

She closed her eyes and exhaled deeply. It couldn't have lasted: happiness, support from someone who helped her keep everything together. She'd only known him six days, but it felt like part of her life was being torn away. Again.

She dried her hands, took a deep breath and painted on a smile. 'Right,' she said turning to face him, 'we need to check bus times. I expect you'll want to leave tomorrow morning?'

Chapter 47

Spencer made the only sound other than the swish of pram tyres on the wet road as they walked to the bus stop. He gurgled and chattered to himself, reaching out to the yellow and red honeysuckle that laced the hedgerow.

May's mind held no comprehensible thought. Cliff, satchel slung over his shoulder, stared at his shoes. Jesson was silent. His lame leg seeming to pain him and he moved with a drunken roll. He hadn't met her eye as he handed her the cottage key. They walked abreast, May glad to have the pram to focus on.

'I hope the bus is on time—'

'What time is the bus—?'

They laughed nervously.

'We're ten minutes early,' May said. 'And they never run on time.'

'Okay.'

Cliff was trailing behind and Jesson slowed his pace.

'Summer vacation soon?'

'Um…? Oh, holiday. Yeah.'

'In three weeks,' said May. She broke off a piece of honeysuckle and handed it to Spencer. She mimed sniffing the flower.

The little boy copied her action and laughed in delight at the sweet scent.

It felt like a relief when the main road came into view but, as they stopped by the black and white bus stop post, May felt a surge of panic. This was the last time she would see him. She'd made him promise to write when he reached home. She'd told him she'd send one of the haymaking photographs when Rose had them developed. There seemed to be nothing else to say.

The bus rounded the bend and suddenly there wasn't enough time for goodbyes. Cliff threw his arms around Jesson, who clapped him on the back, speechless. May couldn't stop the pricking tears from escaping as he hugged her and kissed her cheek. She grasped him tighter than she should have and couldn't look him in the eye when she finally stepped back. The bus ground to a halt beside them, and Jesson laid his hand on Spencer's cheek. 'Goodbye little fella. Take good care of your brother and Aunt May.'

Spencer let out a squeal and held out the sprig of honeysuckle.

'For me?' Jesson's voice cracked. He took the flower and Spencer chuckled and waved his hand.

Jesson climbed on board and took a seat beside the window. For a second, May thought she saw the glint of a tear in his eye.

Chapter 48

She couldn't face work after seeing Jesson off. Sally had run through the day's jobs with her first thing that morning, and she'd left her to unload the hay into the barn.

After last week's fiasco in the post office they needed shopping, but she refused to give the Potts clan the chance to speculate on Jesson's departure and she was in no mood for more battles. There was no alternative but to stick with Parva for rations. It was a complicated process to transfer to a shop in a different village and would cause more gossip and bad feeling.

She left the pram by the gate that Jesson had cleared and collected a couple of shopping bags, her mac and a bottle for Spencer.

She pushed the pram quickly along the lane, past the farmyard. Had anyone spotted her? She thought not. She wanted a few hours of privacy; time to sort out her feelings and plan ahead, instead of floundering through each demand as it arose.

Thinking about Jesson was too raw; it clouded her mind. She pushed away the picture of him lifting his hand as the bus pulled away and began sifting through the jobs that formed a teetering pile in her mental in-tray.

'Wheee!'

She let the pram run on a little as they neared the bottom of the hill into Magna. Spencer roared with pleasure and, as she caught the handle, she noticed a speck of white on his gum. She looked closer. Yes, the tip of a lower front tooth.

'Your first tooth,' she said. The little boy grinned and waved his arms.

A pity Jesson hadn't seen it. She erased the thought and faced the realisation that teething was likely to mean a series of sleepless nights.

Even under the overcast sky, Magna's main street retained its grandeur. She pushed the pram along the wide pavement and nodded to a few people. Some she recognised from WI events, others were local acquaintances.

She went into the shops. The grocer's had a box of biscuits that were an expensive treat. In the butcher's she bought liver, heart and sausages – the cool dairy was a boon for keeping meat fresh. The greengrocer's had oranges for children. She showed the boys' ration books and got them one each. They had potatoes on the farm and plenty of vegetables in the cottage garden, so she moved on to the baker's. She bought two loaves and, passing the post office as she left, decided to get more stamps. At least she could avoid Victoria for a while longer.

The pram was heavy by the time she'd loaded everything, and she set off to scale the long hill.

'Mrs Sheppard?'

The Squire was walking up the path from one of the grandest houses in the street. She hadn't seen him since Tom's funeral.

'Good morning,' she said.

They exchanged pleasantries.

'I was intending to call on you,' he said. 'I understand you've decided to run Elem Farm yourself?'

The gossip machine again. 'Yes,' she replied, and realised she had, unconsciously, made that decision. Was he going to tell her what a fool she was?

'Marvellous,' he said, rubbing his hands. 'I wanted to make

a suggestion that may be mutually beneficial.'

May was flustered. He was speaking to her as if she were an equal. But you are, she told herself. Not aristocracy, but a fellow landowner. She smiled inwardly at her own audacity.

'The powers that be are hoping to derequisition The Park sometime this winter, but I am allowed full use of my grounds from September. I was hoping to organise a few shoots in the season. Some of my business connections have been stuck in the city for the duration and are longing for a spot of sport. I wonder, would you consider allowing a few drives across your land? You'd be remunerated, of course, and receive a brace of pheasants after each shoot.'

Pheasants. They haunted her.

She said, 'I hadn't thought of shoots. Pigeons are a real pest, just like the rabbits. They are decimating my crops. Perhaps I should learn how to use Tom's shotgun.'

He misunderstood her meaning and began to bluster, 'Um... well, ladies on a shoot... err, well, we've never...'

'No, No.' May felt herself blush. 'Sorry, I wasn't suggesting... I was thinking out loud. It's a good idea to include the farm in your shoots, but I won't be participating.'

He tried to conceal his sigh of relief as he held out a hand.

'There is one thing, though,' she went on. 'We discovered adders in Little Hill Field – at the top, where it adjoins your wood. You'd have to watch the gundogs there. I wouldn't want an animal injured.'

He frowned. 'Mr Arrowsmith did warn me about them some years ago. They should be hibernating by the time the season starts, but I'll remind the gamekeeper. I'm hoping it'll be my usual man by then – if he's demobbed in time. My old stager finds it a bit tough going nowadays. Anyway, thank you Mrs Sheppard. I'll be in touch.' He lifted his hat and made to leave, then hesitated. 'You could do worse than to get a four-ten for young Clifford to use. He'd be quite capable of knocking down pigeons and rabbits. And, once we start shooting, there'll be some beating available if he wants to earn some pocket money.'

May was flustered again. 'Um... I'm sure he does – he's saving for a puppy – although I'm not supposed to know that.' Why did she say that? He'd think her an idiot.

'Boys must have their secrets. Good day, Mrs Sheppard.'

She began the trudge up the hill. Cliff with a gun. Seth used to have one, though what kind she didn't know. Like Tom's shotgun, it was kept in a locked cabinet that she'd never opened.

Halfway up the hill, she turned and pulled the pram behind her, like a draught horse. She was wasting her energy and her time. Perhaps she would see about finding one of those child seats for the back of her bike.

She spread jam on the new bread: sandwiches for herself, soldiers for Spencer.

After quickly finishing her meal, she set out to track down Sally. The rain had held off and the girls had finished unloading the hay. The scent of summer meadows, now filling the barn, would last until the end of the year.

The girls were finishing their sandwiches in the harness room as Sally gave them instructions for the afternoon.

When they'd gone back to work, Sally said, 'A chap came to check on the flax. It's nearly ready to pull, and the team will be here within the next ten days. We need to get the Dutch barn cleared out, so I was going to start on that.'

May wheeled the pram beside her, past the new hayricks to the rusty old barn at the back of the stack yard. Open on all four sides, it had once been used for hay. Some years ago, the War Ag demanded Tom grow flax, and he'd reverted to using ricks for the hay that would later be sold, using the Dutch barn to store the flax until it was taken away for processing.

May hated the place. It was where Seth had had his accident, slipping on the loose hay he was stacking and hitting his head on the concrete base of one of the stanchions. She shuddered as she glanced towards the corner where it happened.

The earth floor of the barn was deep in debris: leaves, crumbling bits of last year's flax, odd tools and discarded implements were all scattered around.

'If you want to get on, May, I'll handle this,' Sally said.

'I really need to do some paperwork – it's getting out of hand. I've got to go and see Bill Tyler. He's promised to give me a bit more help.'

Sally's head snapped round. She said, 'When are you going?'

May frowned. What a strange question. 'Not this afternoon,' she said. 'He'll be busy. I'll ring him this evening and go over later in the week.'

'He works from dawn to dusk. He gets exhausted,' Sally said.

Was that a rebuke? May didn't like to think she was imposing on her neighbour, but he had offered. He'd been a good friend – until the last ten days or so. Since Jesson had arrived he'd behaved rather oddly. She'd tread carefully – perhaps ask him over for tea. He was usually keen on a family meal, despite his housekeeper's renowned cooking skills.

Sally headed over to the corner that May detested. She turned to go back to the house.

'May, these brambles are taking over a lot of the floor space.' Sally pointed to the pillar and the undergrowth that had encroached from the boundary hedge.

Tom couldn't bear the place anymore than May could. He must have deliberately ignored the vegetation. Reluctantly, she went over.

'It's that great thing there. It stops us getting to the hedges to cut down the briars. Tom always said to leave them, but it would be better to drag that out, cut the undergrowth back and clear out the ditch. What is it, do you know?'

They stared at the mildewed tarpaulin-covered form that filled the space between the building and the ditch. It blocked most of the end of the barn. The fabric was rotting where it was weighted down with bricks – themselves mostly hidden under leaf mould or entombed in bramble.

'No idea,' said May. 'Some antiquated piece of machinery, I suppose. Tom wasn't one for getting rid of things. We'll take a look one day when we've got more time.'

'I'll clear the floor. At least that'll be ready when the team turns up. They'll ring you a couple of days before they come.'

'Right you are,' said May, wheeling the pram around without glancing back towards the corner.

Chapter 49

Cliff scraped liver and mashed potato on to his fork. Having their tea in the kitchen with Mr Tyler wasn't new and exciting, like when Jesson cooked outside, but it was kind of cosy; like putting on your slippers.

Auntie May had given him a long list of rations to get from the shop tomorrow. He knew she didn't want to see the Pottys.

'Mr Tyler,' he said, when Auntie May was clearing the plates, 'what do you have to do when you go beating?'

'I heard the Squire's asked you to beat for him. Good for you. He must like you – he's quite fussy about his precious shoots.'

Cliff was pleased. The Squire did like him, he knew.

Mr Tyler went on, 'The guns – the men who are shooting – line up where the gamekeeper tells them, say facing a wood, and the beaters enter the wood from the other side. They beat sticks on trees and bushes to drive the pheasants towards the guns. As the birds fly out, the guns try to get a shot at them.'

Deliberately sending birds to their death. It sounded dreadful.

'It's not as bad as it sounds, Cliff. Most of those London gents couldn't hit a barn door with a shotgun. Nearly all the birds get away. You'll be all right. There'll be other lads, and you'll get paid. You usually get a lunch as well.'

Cliff wasn't sure. He loved animals and didn't want to be responsible for them being killed.

Auntie May said, 'The Squire suggested you learn how to use a gun to keep down the pigeons and rabbits on the farm.

They're causing a lot of damage to the crops. It would give us more meat and you could sell some to the butcher.' She put bowls of raspberries in front of them. 'I'll understand if you don't want to, but someone will have to tackle them and I'd rather not have Wilf Kettle with his nasty traps. He was quite rude to me when I told him I wasn't going to do anything about the adders.'

He'd seen the way the pigeons and rabbits destroyed crops on the farm. Last year, rabbits had eaten all the lettuces he'd sown in the cottage garden before they'd put wire around the beds. They couldn't do that in the fields.

'Can I think about it?' he said.

'Of course.'

'I can show you how to use a gun if you want to do it,' Mr Tyler said. 'We can take a walk round the farm at dusk one evening. I'll show you how to kill cleanly without causing suffering.'

He imagined holding a real gun, lining up the sights and firing. Hitting the target. An animal. An animal that would no longer be alive. He thought about how he felt when he saw the stumps of the lettuces he'd tended for weeks. He picked up a spoonful of raspberries. There were a great many rabbits and pigeons…

As Auntie May and Mr Tyler sat with cups of tea, papers strewn over the table, they began talking about tractors. Cliff, about to go and shut in the hens, pricked up his ears.

'I've heard the Americans aren't going to be sending them over like they did during the war, so I don't know how long you'll have to wait. Pity Tom didn't apply for one at the outbreak,' Mr Tyler said.

'He was against mechanisation. If Seth had been here it

would have been very different,' Auntie May said. 'By the way, do you know if they used to have a threshing machine – before the War Ag made Tom take on flax instead of wheat?'

'No. He had the gangs, same as me. They go to the farms in rotation, like the flax team.'

'In that case, what's that big sheeted-up thing at the end of the Dutch barn? Sally wants it out of the way, so I suppose I'll have to investigate.'

A big sheeted-up thing? A mystery at Elem Farm. He had to take a look.

He dragged on his boots, but his heart sank when Mr Tyler said, 'No time like the present,' and he and Auntie May followed him out.

The Dutch barn was gloomy with deep shadows along the back edge and he felt a prickle of excitement as they stared at the crouching green monster. Sally had left a billhook in her wheelbarrow, and Mr Tyler used it to slash the brambles that had grown into a thorny cage around the thing.

Auntie May stood outside by the hayricks. Was she scared about what they would find?

'That's about it I reckon.' said Mr Tyler. 'Come on, Cliff help me get these bricks off.'

They kicked the bricks away, the cloth beneath ripping in places and revealing straggly white weeds beneath.

'Ready?' Mr Tyler said.

Auntie May hovered just inside the barn. With Mr Tyler on one side and Cliff on the other, they dragged the tarpaulin back.

'O-o-oh no.' Auntie May clutched a hand over her mouth.

'Good God,' said Mr Tyler. 'I'm sorry, May, I had no idea.'

'What's the matter?' said Cliff. He was scared; Auntie May looked like she'd seen a ghost. It was only a lorry. Wasn't it?

***

252

Auntie May was making cocoa for all three of them because Mr Tyler was still sitting at the table. Auntie May kept telling him she was all right. Cliff could see she wished he'd go home.

Cliff had refused to leave the barn until she promised to tell him what was wrong, after he'd finished his work. Mr Tyler had taken her back to the house.

His mind whirled with ideas and he fed and bedded down the hens in record time. He almost ran back to the house, casting a fearful glance in the direction of the dark Dutch barn.

He crashed into the kitchen to see Auntie May, looking calm, chatting to Mr Tyler. The brandy bottle was on the table.

She stood up as he came in and put her arm around his shoulders. 'I'm so sorry for giving you a fright,' she said. 'It was just a shock. I thought that Mr Arrowsmith had sold that lorry years ago. It… it was Seth's and the last time I saw him before the accident, he was driving it.'

It was rather a let down after the things he'd been imagining – no robbers or smugglers.

He'd washed and changed for bed and come downstairs for his cocoa.

'There is something else, Cliff,' said Auntie May. 'I want you to know everything. The Dutch barn is where Seth died. Next to the where the lorry is parked.'

She looked at Mr Tyler, who continued, 'We think that's why Mr Arrowsmith left it there. Seth loved that vehicle, like you love your bike, and we think his stepfather meant it as some sort of memorial.'

They looked at him expectantly. He nodded and thought how silly it was they'd had to go everywhere on bikes, or buses, when there was a lorry here all the time.

'So, are we going to use it now?' he asked.

Chapter 50

'Driving? Are you sure you'll be able ter do it?'

She'd expected Rose to be more pleased. 'It's a lovely day. Shall we take our tea outside?'

Rose looked at her askance, but picked up her cup and saucer and followed May to the two deck chairs under the pear tree. May lifted Spencer from his pram and they watched as he shuffled around the grass on his bottom.

Rose began to laugh. 'Imagine Isabella seeing us drinking tea in the garden. She'd think we'd joined the gipsies.'

'Or the upper classes. Tea on the lawn. Pity we haven't got a butler!'

Rose laughed again. It was good to hear it. She hadn't been herself since she'd finished at the munitions factory.

'Any luck with getting a job?' May asked.

'Not so far. Too many people in the same boat as me. Ter be honest, I don't want ter be too far away. I don't want ter go on a bus everyday, but there's nothing round here. I'll help with the harvest in the short-term. Is Cliff going ter help at Magna Farm?'

'Yes. I'll lend a hand too, but I'm so caught up in the paperwork. Bill's explained it to me over and over and I've had a visit from the War Ag. The man seemed to think I was dim-witted. I nearly told him to try running a farm and a house, care for two boys and get his rotten forms in on time.'

'Look.' Rose pointed. Spencer was on all fours, trying to crawl, but moving backwards.

'Look out,' May called, as he bumped his nappy-padded

bottom into the tree trunk. 'That's torn it. He'll be everywhere now. I don't know how you coped with two.'

'I wasn't running a farm for one thing,' said Rose.

May moved Spencer away from the tree. 'What kind of job are you looking for?'

'Something in an office. It's what I did before I got married: secretarial and bookkeeping. But a lot of ex-civil servants will be picking up those jobs now. Women like me will only get cleaning or tea lady jobs when the men get back.'

'So many of the land girls are giving up, too. We're soon going to be stuck for workers until the men are demobbed. I don't know what the land girls will do – get married maybe?'

'Still need money, though. Len's Navy pay doesn't go far enough and, when he gets back, I've no idea what he'll do.'

Spencer shot off towards the runner beans. Rose jumped up and caught him. She tossed him in the air and set him giggling. She told him to try going forward and placed a hand against his bottom. The child sat down, a puzzled look on his face.

She was so good with children. Experience, of course, but patience too. Something May often felt she lacked herself.

'Rose, what would you say to becoming farm secretary-cum-bookkeeper-cum-nanny?'

'Very funny.' Rose hopped a knitted rabbit along the grass to Spencer.

'I'm serious.'

'Don't be daft.' She smiled, but her face changed as she saw May's expression. 'You're serious, aren't you?' Her eyes lit up. 'How would it work?'

They both sat down.

May, working it out as she spoke, said, 'Not full-time – I couldn't afford that – but say ten 'til three Monday to Friday? Farm paperwork, books and Spencer? How's that sound?'

Rose was incredulous. 'You do mean it, don't you?' she asked again.

'Of course. Now come on, I want to show you the lorry.'

'Bill was worried it might not run, after standing for seven years, but Tom had preserved it beautifully. All greased up, the wheels on blocks, everything just so.'

May opened the door of the green-painted cab. The musky smell of leather from the ruby coloured seats was strong after being enclosed for so long. The lorry was parked in the farmyard. They'd moved it so that Sally could clear out the corner she'd been fretting over. The barn was now full and the corner where Seth had fallen hidden behind tons of flax.

'Sounds like one of those Egyptian tombs – ready for the pharaoh ter travel ter the next world,' said Rose, putting a foot on the step and climbing in.

May stopped herself pulling Rose back. Stupid. It wasn't Seth who'd last sat on the driver's seat, it was herself, and Cliff, and Bill before them, and Tom must've driven it round to the Dutch barn all those years ago. Still, it *felt* as if it was Seth's seat.

Rose stretched her feet out to the pedals. 'Do you think you'll be safe on the road?'

'I drove it down the track and round the yard after Bill checked it over and pumped up the tyres. And put some petrol in it. I've applied for petrol rations – we can get them for the farm. I'll find out how safe I am when I get my license. Bill's promised me some lessons.'

Rose climbed out and walked round the back of the lorry. The green, open wooden body sat on a red chassis, which matched the metal wheels. The mudguards and radiator grille were glossy black. The word *Bedford,* in silver, angled across the top corner of the grille, which was edged with red. It looked as good as new, thanks to the hours Cliff had spent washing and polishing it – despite his disappointment when he found out the petrol ration was for farm business, not trips out.

'Very smart,' Rose said, 'I can see you driving it. I don't remember Seth using it. We hadn't lived here very long when he died so, ter me, it will be you; the lady farmer. My boss.'

May searched Rose's face. She was grinning from ear to ear.

Chapter 51

Outside the study door, heaps of boxes and bundles of paper blocked the hallway.

'Rose?'

'Hello. Hang on.' She stuck her head round the door. 'Sorry, May, it's not as bad as it looks. Come and see.'

May clambered over the piles and was amazed at the transformation. Without the curtains, which were blowing on the washing line, and the clutter, dust and dreary pictures, an abundance of light made the room appear large and inviting.

'I was just going ter move the desk over ter the other wall. That way, I'll get the daylight without being dazzled by the sun.'

'Hello, Spencer. Hello, Bunny,' May said, as Spencer offered her his rabbit. 'The playpen fits in well behind the door, Rose. Let me help with that monstrosity of a desk.'

Together they manoeuvred the unwieldy piece of furniture across the dark floorboards to the end wall. Beneath the cobwebs, the wallpaper in the corner where the desk had stood was brightly patterned with birds and flowers. The house must have looked lovely at one time.

'I'll get this finished this afternoon then make a proper start on the correspondence and forms tomorrow. Those papers in the hall seem very old, but you will need ter check through before we burn them.'

May groaned.

'A job for a winter's evening I would think,' Rose added.

'Can you stack all the junk in the dairy – that way I can try to forget it,' said May.

'As your right-hand woman, I'll remind you.'

May laughed.

'I left the post on the kitchen table, and there's a sandwich for you in the larder.'

Rose had only been doing the job for one day and already May's life felt easier. She started on her sandwich and sorted through the post: several circulars, they could go to Rose; a letter from Tom's solicitors in Dorchester – more forms regarding his estate; a letter with an American stamp. Her heart quickened and she looked up to see if Rose had noticed her flushed face.

Rose was apparently absorbed in making toast soldiers for Spencer, but May was sure she'd noticed the letter.

She scanned the single sheet. The handwriting was clear and confident, just like Jesson. He started with, *Dear Mrs Sheppard,* sent love to Cliff and Spencer, and signed it, *Yours, Jesson Cobb.*

May cleared her throat, 'A letter from Lieutenant Cobb.'

Rose turned round, eyebrows raised in false surprise. 'Is he back home already?'

'In New York, waiting for transport to Tuskegee to get his discharge. He thinks he'll be home by the middle of August.'

'Right. What's he going ter do? Work in the family business? Fruit growing, wasn't it?'

'I'm not sure. I think that's what he was thinking, but he left so suddenly...' Why did she have a lump in her throat. She folded the letter. 'I'll let Cliff read it. He sends his love to him.'

'Just to him?' Rose lifted a boiled egg from a pan and began industriously removing the top.

'Spencer as well.'

'Right.'

May pushed the pile of circulars to one side and noticed a badly written envelope caught between them.

It was addressed to *Mrs Sheperd, Crompton Village, Dorset,* and was postmarked a couple of weeks earlier in Southampton. Several notes had been made on the envelope: "Try Crompton Magna"; "Unknown"; "Try Crompton Parva".

Intrigued, she tore it open.

Dear Mrs Sheperd

I don't know if you remeber me. You came to my door looking for Lynette Erwin last year. She and Cliff lived next door before the bomings. I hope I haven't done the wrong thing but a darkie came to my door some weeks ago. He was asking for Lynette. He seemed very keen to find her and I told him your name and where you and Cliff live. It's been worying me in case I shouldn't have so if I did wrong I'm sory.

I hope little Cliff is all rite. I don't supose he'll be comming back to Southampton but if he does I'd be pleased to see him.

Bye the way, your village rang a bell and I couldn't think why but I found some old letters from when I was in service. My old mum kept me up to date on the news. A girl I went to schol with got in bother with the coppers over harming a nipper. I don't think there was much in it but mud sticks and she maried a soldier in a rush and moved to Crompton. Her name was Isobel Bullock. I wonderd if you new her?

Love to little Cliff.

Yours truly

April Wallbanks (Mrs)

'What do you make of this?'

May handed the letter to Rose. She held it with one hand,

the other dipping soldiers in the egg for Spencer.

'Isobel Bullock? You're not thinking it's Isabella are you? Bullock?' she began to laugh. May joined in. Within seconds, they were holding their sides, in hysterics.

When she could speak again, Rose said, 'She is such a snob. I once heard her ask Jean Smith in the baker's if her name was spelt with a 'y'. The poor woman was so confused, she said it was like "blacksmith". Isabella turned her nose up and muttered something about common roots.'

'I used to know a girl called Bullock. She was very sweet,' said May.

'I knew a Brian Bullock. He was a butcher – that made people laugh. Fancy preferring Potts. Think I'd prefer Bullock. At least the kids wouldn't call you Potty. But, what about "harming a nipper"? That's peculiar isn't it?'

Spencer began banging on his highchair tray.

'Sorry, Spencer,' said Rose. 'More soldiers?'

'I wonder whether she was prosecuted,' May said. 'Either way, she could have a police record. Maybe it explains why she doesn't like children. Why she doesn't like Cliff in particular. He comes from where she lived – if it is her. And Ephraim *was* in the Great War…'

'If this got out, Isabella could kiss goodbye to WI President,' said Rose.

'Kiss goodbye to Crompton Parva, I reckon,' May said. Her mind was churning. Could it be true? It could explain how they'd avoided having evacuees. She'd love to have some ammunition against the Potts. Something that was not their word against hers. Just to get them to leave her family alone.

Chapter 52

'Don't forget to signal.'

May thrust her arm out the window and self-consciously windmilled the left turn signal. She wrenched over the gear stick and released the clutch. So much to think of all at once. The lorry gave a grinding lurch, and she caught the grimace on Bill's face.

'Double declutch, May.'

'Sorry.' She felt the warmth in her face.

It would have been better to have her first lesson with Sally; Bill was in the middle of harvest and she hated making use of his free time. When she'd asked Sally – who had been so defensive of Bill's time – she'd just shrugged, saying Bill had agreed to teach her to drive and, anyway, he had dozens of POWs helping with the work.

That was true, but the weather hadn't been kind to the harvest this year and Cliff, usually full of news about cart rides and the competition the boys had carrying the sheaves, came home day after day, wet, muddy and fed up. He often arrived early as yet another shower had stopped the work. Most of the Elem land girls had been put on harvest duties at other farms, so May couldn't be spared and was struggling to keep up with the work.

Bill looked drawn and tired, but he'd insisted he needed a break from staring at wet stooks of corn and, having got her licence and petrol coupons, he said she must use them.

They reached a straight stretch of road and she began to relax, loosening her grip on the wheel. Tight, rather than desperate. Driving was really quite fun.

'That's good, May. You're doing thirty so keep it at that.'

Bill eased back in his seat. It was cosy in the cab and they chatted about everyday things. He asked about the boys.

'Cliff's a bit worried about moving to Grammar School in the autumn. They have to stay until they're fifteen and it's a bit daunting. It'll be a big change – going on the bus and being with children he doesn't know. The Gale twins are going too, so I hope he'll soon settle in.'

'I went to boarding school at first,' Bill said. 'Hated every minute of it and ran away. I only wanted to be on the farm, working with my dad. Fortunately, he was broadminded and let me leave and go to Bridport Grammar. That's where Seth and I got to know each other, before he moved to Parva. We're turning left up here. Mirror, hand signal, brake gently and change down.'

May completed the turn and accelerated into the lane that ran uphill.

She said, 'Can you remember when Ephraim and Isabella Potts came to the village?'

'Ephraim was born there. He was a real bully. Loved throwing his weight around, even then. I remember we boys cheered when we heard he'd been conscripted for the Army in 1914. We hoped he wouldn't come back. Careful on this bend.'

May slowed down and followed the steep lane as it ran through woods. 'When did Isabella arrive?'

'That was a bit of a mystery. He'd gone off to war an ordinary country bloke who no one liked, and turned up afterwards married to this glamorous young woman. There was all sorts of speculation about where he'd found her, but they played it very close to their chests. Isabella had no idea of country life, and my mother said she had ideas above her

263

station.'

'That hasn't changed,' May said.

Not much to go on, but it *was* possible Isabella used to be Isobel Bullock.

The woodland dwindled towards the summit of the hill and a spectacular view of the rolling Dorset countryside was laid out below them like a tapestry. The evening sun had broken through the clouds, giving the wheat fields a golden glow.

'Pull over, May.' Bill motioned to a gravelly area beside the road.

May checked her mirror, gave the hand signal and came to a graceful halt. She sat back with a sigh of satisfaction.

She turned to Bill. 'That was—'

His arm went around her shoulders. He pulled her towards him, his mouth seeking hers.

'No, Bill. Please.' She pulled away.

What on earth was he thinking of? That was pretty obvious. But she wasn't.

'Bill, I—'

'You must know how I feel about you, May. I thought you liked me.'

'I do. As a friend. As a friend of Seth's. I'm sorry, I had no idea—'

'Skin's the wrong colour. Is that it?'

'BILL. How dare you. I think we'd better go home.'

He straightened his jacket and sat mutely while she started the engine and pulled out.

She was fuming. How dare he imply there was anything between her and Jesson. She didn't want to hear any more from him and put every ounce of concentration into her driving. She'd prove she could do it and she didn't need his help.

She refused to ask him for directions. He said nothing and the atmosphere was stifling. She left the window open, ostensibly for the hand signals, but the cold air kept her alert. Eventually, she recognised the outskirts of Magna and stopped in the main street.

'You can walk from here. The farm is only round the corner. Thank you for the lesson.'

He opened the door. 'May, I shouldn't have said that. I'm sorry. It's just that you seemed so happy around him. I've never seen you like that. Not even with Seth.'

'Goodbye, Bill.'

She put her arm out the window and signalled right. He jumped down and slammed the door.

She pulled away, only then realising she had to face the horror of Magna Hill. On her own.

Chapter 53

Something had happened and he wasn't going to get the gun. He'd seen it in the cabinet in the study, although Auntie May kept the key hidden. But Mr Tyler wasn't coming round anymore. Auntie May said Mrs Gale had learnt how to do the forms and things and didn't need any help. And now she was driving the lorry, she didn't need him either.

Sometimes he thought she did need help driving. Like when they met a car on a corner and the lorry nearly went in the ditch.

He eased the lid off the biscuit tin. Mrs Gale was in the study, but she had ears like a schoolteacher. He stuffed a biscuit in his mouth and gently pushed on the lid.

It was raining again. At least, now the harvest was finished, he could stay indoors. It had been awful. They got all the sheaves in the dry eventually but it was a horrible time. Mr Tyler hadn't been very friendly and Cliff got hardly any rides on the carts, and none on the tractor.

The school holidays were miserable this year. It rained most days and Auntie May was always working. She hardly ever laughed with Mrs Gale anymore. The only time they had any real fun was on VJ Day, when the war in Japan ended. Mrs Gale and the twins were madly happy because Mr Gale was now out of danger and would come home soon. They invited all of them to a party at their house. Mr Gale's parents came, but they got a bit cross when Mrs Gale said she thought it was dreadful two huge bombs were dropped on Japan, killing thousands of people. Auntie May tried to speak up for Mrs Gale, but the parents soon left and everyone was miserable again.

'Cliff, can you answer the door, please?' Mrs Gale ran past, grabbing the washing basket.

The postman was on the doorstep, holding a rain-spattered parcel. 'I'll be gettin' webbed feet soon,' the man grumbled as he passed over the package. 'From The States. Hope it's some decent grub.'

It had to be from Jesson, unless… His mother? No, she'd forgotten about him. He searched round the parcel. Auntie May had let him read the letter from New York, but it was a different address that was scribbled on a corner of the package: *Houston Cty, Texas*. That was Jesson. Cliff had seen Texas in cowboy films. Cactuses like signposts; cows with huge horns stampeding on cattle drives; cowboys sleeping under wagons. He should have asked Jesson if he'd ever slept under a wagon.

Mrs Gale dashed in and dumped the washing basket on the draining board. She brushed rain off her jumper. 'Rotten weather. What's that?'

'From Jesson.'

'That might cheer up your aunt.'

'Postman thinks it's food.'

'As long as there's a letter,' she said, and went back to the study.

Was Auntie May missing Jesson then? She didn't talk about him. Sometimes she said Spence was getting to look like his dad, so she must've decided Jesson was his father. He just looked like a little boy to Cliff, a bit darker than normal, with curly hair.

There was no other post, not that he ever got, or sent, anything. He had put a note in Auntie May's letter to Mrs Wallbanks. He told her about his bike and Blossom and living on the farm. Auntie May asked him not to mention Spence, which was a shame because he'd wanted to put a crayon in Spence's hand and help him write his name at the bottom.

It was still raining. He was bored. He didn't want to go out on the bike in the rain. He'd get wet enough doing the hens later. Once he started at big school, he would only do them at weekends. Even though the school let you have time off for the potato harvest, Auntie May wouldn't allow it. She stopped the twins from doing it as well, saying they all needed their education, and anyway, some POWs would be helping.

The letter about the new school was on the dresser, the long list of uniform clipped on the front. He tried not to look at it as he picked up *The Beano*. He knew it off by heart anyway: blazer, cap, shirts, shorts, tie and PE kit. Auntie May was driving them into Dorchester to get it. It would use up all his coupons and he'd have none left to get long trousers on his birthday.

He picked up the parcel and shook it. It was heavy, but it didn't rattle. It would have chocolate inside, but what else? Americans had wonderful food – like the fish Jesson had cooked in the garden.

'Auntie May.There's a food parcel from Jesson. Can I open it?'

'Pardon?' She was taking off her mac and untying her scarf.

He pointed to the package. 'It's from Jesson. Can we open it?'

Mrs Gale came in. Spence crawled along beside her and stopped just inside the kitchen, sitting and gazing at them from the rug.

'It's from your dad, Spence – food. Chocolate maybe,' Cliff said.

'Cocco,' said Spence.

Cliff grabbed him and danced him round the kitchen.

'Cocco, cocco.'

Auntie May said, 'We don't know Jesson is his father, and we don't know what's in the parcel.'

Even though Auntie May was cross, Cliff had seen her eyes widen when he said it was food from Jesson. She was hoping for chocolate too.

She handed him a pair of scissors. 'Be careful how you open it.'

He cut the string and sliced through the paper tape. Inside was a cardboard box. Auntie May, Mrs Gale and Spence had their eyes fixed on it as he lifted off the lid.

The first thing was an envelope addressed to Auntie May. He heard Mrs Gale sigh.

Next, was something in paper with his name on. It was some kind of material: stiff blue stuff. He unfolded it. A pair of trousers. They had pockets, with metal rivets, on the backside.

He held them up. The ends of the legs fell over his shoes and several inches along the floor. Long trousers. Very long trousers. At last.

'Look, Auntie May,' he said spinning round and round, but she was reading the letter and took no notice.

'Smashing, Cliff. Auntie May will have to shorten them for you,' said Mrs Gale.

He laid the trousers aside and delved further into the box. Tins: ham, peaches, evaporated milk and minced steak. And, down the side, three large bars of Hershey's chocolate.

'I knew there'd be chocolate. Look, Spence. Cocco.'

He lifted everything out. Under a sheet of paper at the bottom was something hard, about a foot long. It had brightly coloured metal bars. Two wooden sticks lay underneath. It was labelled with Spence's name.

Cliff put it on the table.

'A xylophone,' Auntie May said.

'Everything all right?' Mrs Gale asked.

Auntie May nodded. 'He says thanks for the photograph, he's got it in his room.'

Cliff didn't know she'd sent Jesson the haymaking photograph, but he liked the idea of his picture being in Texas.

'Come on, Spence. Music.' He picked up the sticks, gave one to his brother and started banging the xylophone.

Auntie May sighed and said, 'Thank you, Jesson.'

Chapter 54

The potato harvest was becoming a nightmare. A major problem was that Sally was being very difficult. When May asked her when she thought they should start, she refused to give an opinion, saying it was really up to May. May could only assume she'd decided to leave and had lost interest. She did everything she could to lighten the atmosphere and make the girl's life easier.

If only the weather would improve; it rained almost every day. She was reluctant to have people picking potatoes in foul conditions, but if she left it too late, there was the possibility of rot, or frost, and the crop would be ruined.

The POW camp kept pestering for a date to bring the men and, when Sally finally volunteered that they should allow four weeks to get all the spuds out of the ground, bagged or clamped, she plumped for the second week of September. They should be safe from frost until the job was done, and she prayed for dry weather.

'It's like a battleground from the Great War,' she said, finishing off her sandwich. 'Everyone is wet and cold. The mud spreads right up to your thighs as you walk. My dungarees have permanently changed colour and it feels as if my hands haven't been dry for weeks.'

Rose passed her a cup of tea. 'I've made you a stew for tonight. I'll leave it in the oven and stay on 'til four for Spencer.'

'You're my saviour. Once the spuds are out of the ground,

we can go back to normal – I hope.'

'Cliff asked me to let him see that four-ten again. I said I didn't know where the gun cabinet key was. What are you going to do about it?'

'I don't know. I'm not going cap in hand to Bill. I haven't seen him since the driving lesson. I thought I might ask the Squire to teach him – it was his idea, after all. Cliff still hasn't spoken to him about beating and the first shoot's in a few weeks.'

'I think he'd like something to do. He's still getting used to school and, now he doesn't do the hens in the week, I think he's feeling cut-off from the farm. The twins keep inviting him to play football, but he's not keen. He wants to be here.'

'Point taken. I'll think about it, but the spuds have to come first – if we lose them, we'll be in serious trouble.' She drained her cup. 'Back to the trenches.'

Cliff seemed a bit more like his old self over the weekend, getting out his bike and cycling to the village wearing the new trousers she'd found time to shorten.

They fed the hens together, Spencer watching from the pram. It was like old times. She'd a called a halt to the potato picking over the weekend as everyone needed a break.

On Monday morning the sun came out. Only briefly, but the weather stayed dry until late afternoon. The potato fields seemed a different place. Although it was still muddy, the POWs were exchanging friendly remarks with the land girls, and a few jokes made the rounds. Perhaps they'd turned a corner.

As she dropped muddy potatoes into a wicker basket, she wondered when there would be a letter from Jesson. Her heart lurched every time she found the pile of post Rose left on the kitchen table. When there was nothing from overseas, she tried to hide her disappointment but recognised she probably did a poor job.

The letter in Jesson's parcel, weeks ago, had said that his family had welcomed him home. His leg was still painful when he over-taxed it, but he was helping his father on the fruit farm. He said he missed them and looked at their photograph every night. She had her framed copy of the photograph on the kitchen dresser and often found herself staring at it, remembering the week they'd shared as a family.

She tipped the potatoes into the cart. Blossom stood patiently, waiting for Sally to drive up to the clamp. Lorry loads of bagged potatoes had gone to market, but the rest were being put in storage in earthed-over up clamps, to keep them frost-free until they were needed.

Cliff's twelfth birthday fell on the last Sunday of September. Peter and Bob came over for tea, and May made a sponge cake with mock cream inside and candles on the top. After they'd eaten, she lent them her bike so all three could go off for a ride. Her present had been a saddlebag and the twins had given him a bicycle tool kit. Once again, nothing had arrived from Lynette, but the look on Cliff's face when she passed over a card she'd put aside from the Saturday post had made up for that. It was from Mrs Wallbanks, his only connection with his old home.

The good weather lasted until the final load of potatoes had been hauled and stored. There had been a feeling of the last day of school – everyone happy and smiling. May had never been happier handing out money than when the workers queued up for their final hard-earned wages.

'You sit down,' she told Rose, 'I'm making the tea and we're having that last bar of chocolate to celebrate the end of four weeks back-breaking work.' She called up the stairs, 'Come down, Cliff. Tea and chocolate.'

He clattered down, carrying Spencer.

May broke the bar and they wolfed the chocolate. She didn't feel guilty guzzling rather than savouring, just pleased that they were sharing the feeling of accomplishment.

Rose was getting ready to leave when they heard a tap on the door.

'I'll get it,' Rose said, pulling on her coat. 'I'll see you in the morning.'

Sally came in. One look at her face and May knew there was trouble. 'You'd better get on with your homework, Cliff,' she said, 'and take Spencer with you.'

'Sit down, Sally. Cup of tea?'

'No thanks, May. I've got some news. I didn't want to tell you until today was over, but… I shall be leaving at the end of the year.'

Damn, damn, damn.

'I'm sorry to hear that. I know a lot of the girls have gone back to their old jobs, but I thought you might have stuck with farming.'

'I am.'

She was going to another farm? That was a bit rich: May had treated her like an equal. Maybe if she suggested taking her on as an employee, not a land girl…

Sally was grinning and holding out her hand, a diamond ring sparked on her chapped finger.

'My goodness. You're engaged? Congratulations. Who's the lucky man?'

Sally's face matched her red hands. She dropped her gaze

274

and said quietly, 'Bill. Bill Tyler. He asked me last night. This is his mother's ring.'

May opened and closed her mouth, goldfish-fashion. *Bill Tyler?* No wonder Sally had got moody when he spent time at Elem Farm. It was only a couple of months since he'd made a pass at her. Should she say something? No. She couldn't spoil the girl's happiness.

'That's wonderful news,' she said, 'I'm sure you'll be very happy. He's a lovely man – Seth was very fond of him. They were best friends.'

She was rambling. Would they be happy? Did she actually mind that he was marrying Sally? Actually, no. Pride a bit dented, perhaps.

'Yes, he's told me all about Seth. He misses him still. That's why he's been so protective of you.'

Protective. That's what he called it?

'He's been very good to me since I took over the farm. He's helped me so much – like you.'

She wished Sally would go, let her think. 'We'll miss you, but you'll only be down the road. We'll sort out your leaving date another time. I expect you want to get over to see Bill and celebrate?'

'His housekeeper's cooking us a special meal,' Sally said, a dreamy expression on her face as she paused in pulling on her gloves to stare at the ring.

'Pass on my congratulations to Bill,' May said, as Sally closed the door.

Chapter 55

May pushed the pram down to the barn. Rose wouldn't be here for another couple of hours, and she had to run through the day's work with Sally.

Hell. Voices in the harness room. The girls were still there. Sally was sure to be telling them about her engagement dinner last night.

They were clucking around Sally, poring over the ring.

'You'd better take care,' May said. 'You don't want to lose it in the muck heap.'

'I'll take it off for work,' Sally said. 'Bill would never forgive me if I lost it – he's waited a long time to find the right person.'

Point taken.

The girls went out in flurry of wedding talk and May felt obliged to ask about the date.

'Easter, we think, when the weather is better. I'll leave here as planned, spend some time with my folks and then help Bill with the poults,' Sally said.

'Right,' said May. 'So, what's on the cards for this week?' She pulled the farm diary from the pram bag. Seeing Sally's questioning look she said, 'I've been keeping a record of what we've done each week, but now I'm going to write down what we plan to do. That way I can pick up on anything we miss.'

'Mmm,' said Sally, flexing her finger to flash the diamond in the sunlight.

'I never thought of Bill Tyler as a cad,' Rose said.

'I don't think he is, at heart,' May said. 'I've thought about it all night, and I wonder if I misinterpreted the situation?'

'You can't mistake someone trying to kiss you.'

'I know that, and his remark about Jesson was unforgivable, but maybe it was just on the spur of the moment. You know, both of us close together in the cab, the romantic evening light…'

'Pah! He knew what he was about. If you'd complied, Sally would have been out of the picture.'

Good. Rose thought she hadn't imagined it. He *had* liked her. She'd lost her chance now. She could have been a farmer's wife, spending time baking and making chutney. With a man who thinks skin colour is important. What would have happened to Spencer? To Cliff? Bill hadn't cared enough to honour his promise to show the lad how to use the gun. No, she was well out of it. Better to run her own life than be bound to a man who wasn't who she thought he was.

'Will you go to the wedding?' Rose asked.

'I can't avoid it, can I? I'll have to make my peace with him – he's a neighbour and I'm not interested in getting into a feud.'

'Git orf ma land,' Rose drawled.

May couldn't help but laugh.

The weather broke again on Saturday evening and Cliff went to get the hens in early. The purple in the sky was spreading like a bruise and she hoped he'd soon be back.

A huge crash seemed to shake the farmhouse and Spencer began to cry. A flash of lightning lit the stairwell as May ran upstairs.

Cliff was still not back as torrential rain hurled itself against the kitchen windows. Spencer was on her knee; she couldn't leave him and go to find his brother. She jiggled the child to distract him as another thunder crack bounced around the hills.

The back door crashed open as the wind whipped it back.

'*Auntie May,*' Cliff shouted, coming into the kitchen. His boots were filthy and water cascaded from his head to his feet, washing mud across the floor. She was about to tell him to get the boots off, when she realised the water on his face wasn't just rain.

'It's Gracie. I think she's dead,' he sobbed.

May ran towards the coop, her boots spraying muck up her legs as she ploughed through the runnels of water flowing across the poultry yard. Beneath black clouds, stacked like giant hayricks, the light was an eerie yellow.

In Gracie's run, she unlatched the coop door and there was the hen, wet feathers plastered down, lying on the straw where Cliff had placed her.

Eyes closed, she was still warm. May spoke her name, but she knew it was useless. That first thunderclap must've given the old hen a scare that her heart couldn't take.

May pulled off her headscarf and used it to wrap Gracie. She carried her tenderly, tucking her under her arm as she locked the gate.

In the barn, she sat on a feed bin. She pulled back the scarf and stroked the russet feathers. Tears flowed. It wasn't just Gracie, although she'd loved the hen, it was the wreck of their lives: Cliff was rootless and she couldn't resolve it; Spencer could barely speak but was castigated for the colour of his skin; she'd got serious staff problems on a farm she didn't know how to run and she'd thrown away probably the only chance she'd ever have of a good life for them all.

She laid Gracie on the tobacco-scented hay, buried her face in her hands and submitted to the flood of self-pity.

Blossom whickered and the sound brought her back to reality. Animals always knew when you were upset.

An arm wrapped itself around her shoulders. 'Cliff,' she sniffed, 'you shouldn't have left Spencer.'

'Spence's safe in the house, Mam.'

In the dark barn, he was barely visible, but she could smell him. She'd forgotten the woody scent of him. Soap? Hair oil? She didn't know. Didn't care. She turned and buried her head in his chest and sobbed. He was back.

The rain had stopped and the clouds were darker shadows against the deep blue sky. The setting sun cast a reddish glow as they walked to the house. Jesson had gently placed Gracie in a sack. He promised to bury her in the orchard the next day.

As they stepped into the kitchen, Cliff's jaw dropped. She realised what a fright she must look. She'd pulled herself together in the barn and apologised to Jesson for her loss of composure. 'It was the shock,' she said, 'I've loved that hen for years. She was one of my last connections with my husband.'

He'd stepped away and she'd felt cold without his arms around her. She began to shiver and he closed up the barn, before taking her arm to steady her through the treacly mud.

'Where's Gracie?' Cliff asked.

'She's in the barn,' May said. 'Thank you for putting her in the coop. It was exactly the right thing. We couldn't have done any more for her. She just got too old.'

Cliff nodded.

'Could you run some water in the tub for Aunt May to take a bath, please?' said Jesson. 'And do you know if there's any brandy in the house?'

***

The hot water, sprinkled with lavender flowers, restored her. The murmur of Cliff and Jesson's voices downstairs was comforting and things began to slide into proportion. What must Jesson think of her? Flinging herself on him like that. She couldn't deny the surge of relief she'd felt when she realised he was there. In her hour of need. Again. Mind you, there had been plenty of hours of need when he wasn't there. She hadn't asked why he was here or how long he was staying. He'd just fitted back in to the family. Right now, while she was lazing in a bath, he was making her a sandwich and checking Spencer was asleep in his cot.

'You will stay at the cottage, won't you?'

'I was hoping you'd suggest that, Mam. Just 'til I get a job.'

'It's May.'

'Sorry, May. I don't know how long it'll take. Word is there are plenty of jobs in England right now as your boys aren't back yet.'

'Demob seems to take forever,' she said, sipping her tea and getting a shock as she realised it had brandy in it. 'But I thought you were going to work for your father.'

'He doesn't really need me. He was just making a job. I decided I really liked the UK. And the people.' He grinned at her. She blushed.

'We need someone on the farm,' Cliff piped up. 'Sally's leaving to marry Bill Tyler.'

'Bill Tyler?' Jesson looked at May again. Her colour deepened.

'They've been seeing each other for some time,' she said. 'We're very pleased for them, aren't we, Cliff?'

''S'pose so, but he hasn't shown me how to use the gun.'

'What's this?'

May explained about the four-ten and the idea of Cliff keeping down the vermin.

'I can show you how to handle a gun,' Jesson said. 'I've been potting rabbits since I was knee high.' Seeing May's doubtful expression, he added, 'And we did get weapons training in the army.'

'Wizard,' said Cliff. 'I'll get to shoot like a soldier.'

There was so much she wanted to tell him. She hadn't asked about his leg or what kind of job he was looking for, but he put up a hand to stop her.

'Now Cliff's in bed, I have to show you something.'

He went to the hall door and switched on the light. He was moving easier. She saw no sign of a limp as he went to the heap of cases just inside the front door. He looked different in civilian clothing. The tan pullover he wore complemented his skin tone and his hair had grown out from the draconian army cut. Now, it formed a neat black cap that framed his face.

He brought in the holdall that she recognised from his previous visit. 'I took a cab from Bridport station – I didn't want to tackle a British bus with all my bags.'

No fuel for the gossipmongers, then.

He opened the bag and laid a folder on the table.

'Take a look at this.' He handed her some thick papers.

She unfolded them and ran her hand across to flatten the creases. It was some kind of legal document.

She saw Spencer's name in curly black lettering and her heart lurched. Had they been wrong; was he in collusion with Lynette?

Her hand shook as she tried to read the words, but the phrases swam past without meaning: Legal Guardian. No further claim. Parental Right. At the bottom, a signature,

"Lynette (something illegible) née Erwin".

She couldn't take in the legal jargon. Did it mean Lynette was taking Spencer? Is that why Jesson had come, to take the child to America? She stared at Jesson, lip trembling. 'I don't understand. Why have you got this? What does it mean?'

'I'm sorry, I shouldn't have sprung it on you like that. It's just that I couldn't wait to show you. I'll start at the beginning. Here.' He poured a brandy and handed her the glass.

She took a mouthful. If she was losing Spencer, she needed anaesthetising.

Jesson said, 'When I left here, I had one day before my ship sailed and I spent that time asking around the base if anyone knew of a call girl called Lynette who'd hooked up with a Southerner invalided out in '44. I hit a lot of false trails until a guy told me about an old gatekeeper who'd worked there for years. He came on duty at six the morning I left, but I tracked him down. He remembered Lynette and the name of the guy.'

Jesson pointed to the brandy bottle. 'May I?'

May gestured to help himself.

He poured a measure and continued, 'When I got to New York, I had time to kill before I got transport to Tuskegee, so I asked around about this lieutenant. Eventually, after a few dollars changed hands, I got his address.'

'The man Lynette was going to marry?'

'Yes, leastways, that's what I hoped. Anyhow, when I got back to my folks, I borrowed the farm truck and headed out to South Carolina.'

'How far is that?'

He shrugged. 'Few hundred miles.'

Many hundreds of miles, she suspected.

'I found the family's place. It's a fancy plantation house with servants – black, of course. I set to watching it, hoping to see Lynette.

'After a few hours a woman drove out. I couldn't be sure, so I followed and she stopped in town outside the beauty parlour. I wouldn't have recognised her if I wasn't expecting to see her. Her hair's gingery brown and the red lipstick's pink. And the snappy clothes – she looks like a senator's wife.'

A senator's wife. Lynette? She still knew how to impress the men though; he'd remembered every detail.

'I waited until she came out. When I spoke to her, she looked at me as if I was something she'd stepped in.'

Same old Lynette under the snappy clothes, then.

'Until I mentioned Spencer's name. She took me more seriously after that. She dragged me off the sidewalk into an alley. I told her I'd seen Spence and Cliff, and Cliff was unhappy because he wanted you to adopt him but she hadn't agreed. She laughed it off, saying she'd write to you. She started to walk away. That was when I said maybe I'd call at the house and ask her husband if he'd like to take in the son his wife had off a black man.'

He sipped more brandy.

'She said her father-in-law would have me whipped. I said I'd be willing to risk it. I could see her working it out; she'd lose everything if it backfired. After a minute, all her fancy manners left her. Her face turned ugly and she told me to say what I wanted. I said she couldn't just abandon two children and not make proper arrangements for their future. I asked her, did she want the children back, said I could bring Spencer and Cliff over – sorry, May, I was flying a kite there.'

Her mouth went dry. How could he gamble with the boys' future?

'She looked stunned. I said if she didn't want Spencer back, could she read the papers I gave her and I'd be back the next day, same place. If she agreed with my proposal, she was to sign the documents, with a witness, and bring them back.'

'She could have torn them up.'

'I'd had the lawyer draw up two copies. One was safely under the seat of the truck.'

She wasn't sure where this was leading. She was desperate to read the papers again, but he had his hand on them and he hadn't finished his story.

'She was there the next day. I admit I was scared she'd ask for the boys.' He lowered his eyes.

May's hand shook as she took a gulp of brandy. She winced as it burned her throat.

Jesson went on, 'First, she made me give my word I'd never contact her again, then almost threw the papers at me.'

'But what do the papers mean? How do they affect me and the boys?'

He spread the document on the table between them. May gulped the rest of the brandy in her glass. Her head spun and she noticed the brandy bottle was almost empty. She tried to stand and immediately sat down again.

Looking down at the table, he said quietly, 'In that alleyway, I asked her straight out, was Spence my son. She thought she'd got an ace in the hole. I could see the way her eyes narrowed, she thought she could bargain her way out, the way she did with you over Cliff. I let her know I meant it about going to her husband if she didn't come clean and, finally, she admitted it. Spence is my son. There's no doubt apparently, she says I was her only slip off the path.'

A likely story.

'She wants nothing to do with him and she signed this confirming I am his natural father. She's handed all rights to him over to me.' He shook his head. 'She didn't even seem sad she was letting him go. A lawyer in the States has legalised it; it's a complete break from her.'

'But what about Cliff? Has she sent anything about him?'

'Sorry, May, I could do nothing to persuade her. She gave me her word she'd write and confirm she was happy for you to adopt him, but…'

Back to square one, Lynette had the upper hand. 'What are you going to do about Spencer? How will you work and—'

He must've come to get Spencer. To take him back to America. Cliff would lose a brother. She'd lose her baby.

'Hold on, May. I have something to ask you.' He cleared his throat.

Was he was going to propose? She looked round for an escape. She didn't want to be tied down. It was too soon and she was horrified about him gambling with the boys' futures.

'I knew before I got to Tuskegee that I couldn't live back in the States. I can't handle segregation again – sitting at the back of a bus; in the smoky part of a train, with no toilets; kept apart from "decent white folks". I'm making Great Britain my home.'

He cleared his throat. 'May, would you consider continuing to raise Spence? As his foster mother. I can't look after him and hold down a job. You're the only mother he's known and I think you care for him.'

She wanted to laugh. Proposal? Yes, but not the one she'd thought.

She couldn't stifle a yawn. 'I need to think about it,' she said.

Chapter 56

May woke in the early hours, surprised to realise she must have fallen asleep instantly. She needed to think, but her mind kept sliding away from the issues. It was like trying to grasp egg white. She tried to get back to sleep. Finally, in a mass of tangled sheets, she gave up, sat up and forced herself to focus on her problems.

Did she want to keep Spencer? Yes, she loved him like a son and it was unthinkable that she wasn't going to bring him up. Also – this was difficult to admit – the child was a link to Jesson and one that she dearly wanted to maintain, despite his cavalier handling of their lives. If she was honest, she'd have known which way Lynette would jump, too. But she wouldn't have risked the gamble.

As Spencer got older, he'd face more problems fitting in and she wanted to be the one to protect him – along with his father, of course.

She'd need to confirm what it involved, legally, before making a promise but, effectively, she'd made up her mind; she would agree to be Spencer's permanent foster mother.

Her shoulders were chilly and she shuffled further down the bed, tugging up the eiderdown. The major issue still loomed over her. Cliff. Jesson had seen Lynette several weeks ago and there had been no contact regarding the adoption. It wasn't going to materialize unless she did something and the only way to get Lynette to do anything was to force her hand. So far, she'd held the power. Could May turn the tables?

She mulled over the options until a line of light outlined the curtains. She had a plan. Underhand it might be, but Cliff must be given a secure future and, if Lynette would only respond the ultimatums, so be it.

'I don't want you to mention anything about Spencer until I've tried to sort something out about Cliff's adoption. He will be poleaxed if he finds out his brother's future is settled while his is still in the balance. I need to know where both boys stand before I make a final decision. Is that all right?'

'Sure,' Jesson said, pouring water on to instant coffee that he'd brought from America. 'Take as long as you need.'

'For the time being, you could stay on here and work on the farm. We can make some decisions in a few weeks' time, if you're happy with that?'

'Sounds fair. Thanks.'

He gave May one of his disarming grins and she felt herself flush. She looked around the room. It was strange sitting in her old kitchen, but she'd wanted to talk to Jesson without fear of being overheard. Realising he had no food in the cottage, she'd brought him a bag of staple groceries.

'Would it be possible to look at that document you showed me last night? I was too tired to really take it in,' she said.

He took the document from his holdall, which was by the stairs door. May scanned it for the information she wanted.

'Is it all right if I copy out her address?' she asked.

'Of course. What're you planning?'

'Not sure, although it's obvious that Lynette...' she looked at the "parties" listed at the top of the paper. 'Vickersan?'

Jesson nodded.

'...that Lynette Vickersan isn't going to respond voluntarily.' May wrote the details in a notebook she took from her pocket. 'I've got to get back. Join us for dinner. You can start work tomorrow.'

Once May was alone that evening, she began writing the letter she had been composing in her head all day.

Dear Mrs Vickersan

I have been given your address by Lieutenant Cobb, who tells me he is Spencer's natural father and has been given sole parental rights over the child.

Spencer was put into my care, but I have had no word from you about this new arrangement. I am planning to contact my solicitor to ascertain the legal position and also what rights I have over Cliff's adoption that you agreed to when I took in Spencer but have never confirmed, despite your promise.

As it takes several weeks for post to travel back and forth to America, I will wait a month but, if I do not hear from you by then, you can expect to hear from my solicitors.

I am enclosing a picture, which I thought you might like – there are plenty more I can send.
Yours faithfully
May Sheppard

Was that last phrase too heavy-handed? When she thought of how Spencer had turned up without warning, she decided Lynette didn't deserve kid glove treatment.

She signed the letter, addressed the envelope and removed the picture from a photograph frame on the dresser. She looked at the two grinning boys, arms around each other, and wrote *Cliff and Spencer Erwin, June 1945* on the back. She tucked it in the envelope and sealed it.

'Explain that dropping on to your breakfast table,' she said.

Chapter 57

'You can't shoot on a Sunday afternoon, Cliff. It's bad enough we don't go to church every week, I don't want to upset the vicar even more.' Auntie May had that look on her face, and he knew it was no good arguing.

Jesson was drinking something called "instant coffee". He'd brought more chocolate, but Auntie May had put it away in the dresser.

Spence was banging his xylophone by Jesson's feet. Cliff smiled as he thought about the joke he and Auntie May had shared that morning. Jesson had come in by the back door, and Spence was sitting on the floor. He crawled over to Jesson and said, 'Da-da.'

Jesson thought it was especially for him. Auntie May winked at Cliff, and he knew not to say it was Spence's favourite word that he'd been saying to everyone for weeks.

'You wouldn't be able to fire the gun today, Cliff. It has to be cleaned and oiled. I guess it's been in that cupboard for a long time. When I've had my coffee, we'll get out from under your aunt's feet and I'll show you how to dismantle it.'

'Is it true that soldiers have to be able to do that in the dark?' Cliff said, imagining how fast he could take it apart and put it back together again.

'Yeah, but I think we'll stick with daylight today,' Jesson said.

'Jesson...'

Auntie May looked round, suspicious.

'What sort of job are you looking for?'

'Cliff, that's none of your business,' Auntie May said.

'It's okay. I don't know, Cliff. It depends what's available. Why?'

'Cliff…'

'We need someone now Sally's leaving. And you know about horses and tractors and—'

'Clifford Erwin. That's enough.' Auntie May had the red spots on her cheeks.

He bit his lip.

'Outside. Go and do something until Jesson is ready to do the gun.'

As he went out he heard her apologise to Jesson. But what would Jesson say? He'd looked quite interested when he said about Sally's job – a proper one, not just helping out like Auntie May said he was going to. He pretended he couldn't get his boot on, straining his ears to hear.

'What experience are you looking for, May?'

'Cliff? Are you still there?'

Rats. He shoved his foot in the boot and went out, slamming the back door.

He mooched around the stack yard, digging out mud between puddles with his boot, making the water run between them. He was concentrating on making the water circle a hayrick when, with great squawk, a hen pheasant flew up and startled him.

He watched her skim the hedge into the field beyond and knew he'd made the right decision.

Paul Mountjoy had answered the door of The Lodge when Cliff had tapped, hesitantly, the previous week. Cliff hadn't been there for months and was relieved the Squire's family were still living there and hadn't moved back to their big house.

'Wotcha, Cliff.'

It sounded stupid from someone with his posh accent.

'Thought you'd be away at school.'

'Exeat.'

'Right.'

'Come in. The parents've laid in some ginger beer – prefer the real thing myself, but you know how it is...'

Who was he kidding? He was the same age as Cliff.

'Pa will be back in a mo.'

Cliff wiped his boots on the doormat and stepped warily into the hall. It was nowhere near as grand as the Squire's big house, but it felt strange enough. A big oil painting of a riderless horse held by a man in a striped waistcoat and red cap, took up most of the right-hand wall and a great glass case, brimming with china figures, protruded from the left. Cliff stepped around it with great care although Paul charged on into the dark kitchen.

'Take a pew.'

Cliff sat at a table far smaller than the one at Elem Farm and was surprised to see the kitchen was old-fashioned, with a range. Elem Farm kitchen was much more modern.

Paul carried two pint tankards to the table, frothy liquid spilling over the top.

'How's your pony?' Cliff asked.

Paul, who'd grown taller and skinnier in the past year, shrugged. 'He's been passed on to my little cousin. He was too small for me anyway, and he wasn't a challenge to ride anymore.'

It hadn't looked that way on the dark evening last autumn when Cliff had picked Paul up from the ground. Without his glasses, dazed and crying that his pony had broken its leg and would have to be shot, the boy had been distraught. In fact, the animal's reins had become entangled in a branch and its saddle had slipped to beneath its belly, making it kick out and try to pull away. Once Cliff had righted the saddle and released the reins, the pony had calmed down enough to allow itself to be led home with a traumatised Paul aboard.

'When we get back to the Park – that's our big house, you know – Pa's buying me a hunter. A proper horse, not a *pony*.'

'Will you try jumping that over logs in a wood, in the dark?'

Paul's face flushed crimson and Cliff smothered a satisfied smile with his tankard.

The back door opened and the Squire came in. Cliff stood up. Paul looked pleadingly at him and he got the message not to mention the accident. Mr Mountjoy had been livid with his son, telling him that he could have killed both himself and the pony, all for some schoolboy bet.

The incident had resulted in a flow of pheasants to Elem Cottage from the Squire's estate, but landed Cliff in hot water with Auntie May.

'Hello, young Clifford. Come to firm up the arrangements for the beating, have you?'

'Um... yes. Well, no.'

'I see.'

Heck. He looked at Paul who was flicking his gaze between the Squire and Cliff, biting his bottom lip.

'I came to tell you that I can't do the beating,' Cliff blurted. 'Thanks for asking me, though.'

The Squire said, 'I'm surprised, I thought you would have liked to earn some pocket money.'

'I would of. But it's... it's just I don't think it's right to scare birds into the guns. It doesn't seem fair.'

Paul's sharp intake of breath sounded like a whipcrack.

Cliff stared down at his boots.

There was a long silence.

'You are an unusual lad. I knew that last year when you

brought Paul home,' the Squire said.

Paul had discovered something interesting to pick at on his finger.

The Squire continued, 'In my own defence, I would say that we breed the pheasants especially for the sport.'

Cliff didn't think that was any better and said nothing.

'Well, I understand your reservations, and I respect your judgement. Thank you for coming to tell me, Clifford.'

He'd done it. He wanted to shout hurray but he said goodbye to Paul, who looked at him with wide-eyed respect, and followed the Squire to the doorstep, where they shook hands.

Cliff wanted to skip down the drive, but the Squire was watching. As he let himself through the gate into the road, Mr Mountjoy put up his hand. Cliff waved back, only to jump out of the way of Old Potty. He was trunking so hard, he nearly fell off his bike. He'd be dying to know why Cliff was at The Lodge. Hard cheese.

'If we don't knuckle down to it, we will be taking this apart in the dark.' Jesson was carrying the four-ten.

He passed it to Cliff. 'What's the first thing you do when you're handed a gun?'

'I know that. Break it. But you've already done that,' he pointed to the gun barrel, hanging down at an angle to the stock.

'Correct, but what else?'

Cliff shook his head.

'Check it's empty. Look down the barrel.'

Cliff raised the gun and looked. He grinned. This must be what it was like to have a father.

Chapter 58

There was a lot of traffic on the road from Dorchester. May was stuck behind a coal lorry, hanging back as gritty dust blew on to her windscreen.

From the number of black clouds on the horizon, they were due for a soaking. She'd be too late to collect Cliff from the school bus and she'd wanted to talk to him, alone, to give him the news. The letter had arrived that morning, less than three weeks since she'd written to Lynette.

She'd persuaded the solicitor to see her right away, before the weekend. He confirmed the document she'd received, sealed by an American lawyer, was sufficient to begin the adoption process.

In the envelope, hand-addressed to May, Lynette had included a note confirming Jesson had all rights over Spencer. She gave a vague apology for not contacting May sooner about Cliff and hoped that the document her husband's lawyer had drawn up would *"finalise Cliff's future so you won't need to contact me again"*. May had slammed down the letter at that point, appalled that the woman could throw off her son so heartlessly.

She'd placed a small white envelope, bearing Cliff's name, in the dresser drawer with the other papers. As she slid the drawer closed, she realised how much weight had been lifted from her, now that Lynette was out of their lives forever.

Jesson was marking time until she gave him her final decision over Spencer. The solicitor's advice was to make the foster agreement official, and she'd asked him to draw up the paperwork.

She let her thoughts wander as she drove. Would Cliff call her 'Mum'? It was a strange, but delicious, thought and she realised she was grinning madly.

Heavy raindrops hit the windscreen, sending black streaks down the glass. She switched on the wipers. When was the coal lorry going to turn off? The spray was making it difficult to see.

They were on the road to Crompton Parva, the rain coming down faster than the wipers could clear it, when the coal lorry made a violent swerve. A figure was pushing a bicycle along the roadside and May was forced to swing the steering wheel hard over, praying there was no oncoming traffic. There was no verge on this bit of the road and the cyclist was in danger of being run down. She checked her mirror. Nothing behind. She pulled over and waited for the caped figure to catch up. She leant across and wound down the passenger window.

'Put your bike in the back and jump in,'

The bedraggled figure heaved in the bike and then clambered into the cab, water streaming off him. May put her arm out of the window, signalled and moved off. She could smell the acrid scent of the rain cape. It reminded her of the rubber hot water bottles that were now impossible to find.

'Thank 'ee. Bliddy chain gave out a mile back.'

Hell, hell, hell. That's what you get for doing a good turn. Ephraim Potts.

He pushed back his hood. ''tis you, May Sheppard. I hope 'ee knows how to drive this thing?'

'Too late now if I don't, Ephraim.'

How far was it to the village? She supposed she'd have to drop him at his cottage. Bloody little man.

She asked how Isabella was and they managed to make

small talk until she turned into the village.

'I 'ears that nig— darkie's back workin' on the farm?'

May seethed. This had to stop. Occasional ignorant comments they'd have to put up with, but not concerted attacks on Jesson and Spencer.

She stopped the lorry just short of the Potts' cottage. She turned to him before he could get the door open. 'Ephraim. I will not put up with any more comments about my family, my friends or my employees. It stops right now.'

He looked at her, scorn on his face. 'If 'ee associates with them sorts—'

'I know about Isobel Bullock.' What had Jesson said? Flying a kite?

For a minute she thought he'd had a heart attack. His body jerked violently and, in the dim light, he seemed quite green.

'I dunno what 'ee's on about,' he said eventually, reaching for the door.

'Yes you do. And if your attitude doesn't change, so will the whole village.'

''ee'd better keep 'ee's mouth shut, May Sheppard. It'd kill my Isabella.'

'In that case, Ephraim, I think we understand each other. Take your bike, I want to get home.'

Chapter 59

Blossom and Ben were eating their hay on the ground beside Cliff as he perched on the orchard gate. The sound of their chomping was one of his favourite farm noises, and now he would always hear it. He was going to stay here and Auntie May would be his proper mum.

He would be in a family, especially now Jesson wasn't going to go away to work. He really was Spence's dad and Auntie May was going to keep looking after his little brother.

Auntie May had told him about his adoption when she got in last night, just the two of them, upstairs in his room.

'Is it real? It can't be changed?' he said.

'No, Cliff, it's real. You'll soon be my son.'

He fell on her in a huge hug. When they parted, he saw Auntie May wipe her eyes and realised his own face was wet.

They came downstairs and she let him tell Jesson and Spence the news. She got out some cowslip wine and let him have half a glass. Jesson toasted them and even Spence lifted his beaker to join in. Cliff look a big gulp of wine, only to splutter so much they all roared with laughter.

This morning, Auntie May and Jesson were talking about Jesson's new job. When Sally left, he was going to be farm foreman and live in the cottage.

Cliff pulled a white envelope out of his pocket. It was from his old mum, but he was getting a new mum now and he didn't want to read it. Blossom stuck her head over the gate and began snuffling at his pocket. He gave her half a crust and threw the rest to Ben, who didn't want to leave his hay.

Blossom pushed at the letter with her nose. 'All right, I'll read it,' he said.

He ripped open the envelope. It was written on stiff white paper, not like the thin lined stuff she used to use:

Dear Cliffy

I'm sorry I haven't written before but I was very busy with my wedding. I've got married to a nice American and we live in a big house. We have servants which is very nice, I just have to tell them what to do. The food is lovely, too.

I know you love living with Mrs Sheppard and want to stay there so I've signed some papers to let her adopt you. It's for the best, I don't expect you really remember me anyway.

Mrs Sheppard is a good woman and I hope you and Spencer have a happy life.

With love from

Mum

P.S. I'm sorry I wasn't a better mother.

He stroked Blossom's nose. 'That's that, Blos. The last of me Ma.' He leant into her neck, smelling her sweet horsey smell.

The mare snorted. He sat up. 'Yeah, you're right, I got another one now. A better one,' he said.

He looked in the envelope. No luck; she could have sent a dollar or two.

Chapter 60

They'd just finished eating, when a figure passed the kitchen window.

'Cliff, the Squire's here. Open the back door,' May said. He must have come about the next shoot. Jesson helped her grab bowls and plates off the table and pile them by the sink.

The Squire came in and they exchanged greetings. 'This is Jesson Cobb, soon to be my foreman,' May said.

The Squire held out his hand. 'Mountjoy. Pleased to meet you, Mr Cobb.'

Not a flicker of hesitation, May noted. Would she always think of that now? She had been a little worried that Jesson's farming experience may not be a great deal more than her own, but he'd been keen to take the foreman's job, on condition they got a tractor. They'd arranged a trial period of a year and she'd promised to follow up Bill's initial enquiries about tractors.

The Squire refused a cup of tea. They briefly discussed the shoot – the first one had been successful and they agreed a date for the next.

'You'd be welcome to join us on the landowner's shoot at the end of the season, Mr Cobb. Unless Mrs—?'

'No, thank you. I'm leaving that to Jesson and Cliff,' May said, as Jesson thanked him.

'Clifford is the reason I'm here,' the Squire said. 'Although, not to ask him to alter his decision not to beat,' he added, at Cliff's alarmed expression.

May looked at Cliff. He'd presented her with a fait accompli and, while she was proud that he'd faced the Squire and

299

presented his arguments, she wasn't sure how unequivocally they had been received.

Mr Mountjoy continued, 'I don't think we've thanked him well enough for last year, and I thought he might like something... One second.'

He walked out of the back door, leaving everyone bemused, and returned carrying a lidded picnic basket.

He opened the basket and lifted out a blonde puppy.

He handed it to Cliff. 'It's not a purebred – father unknown – but its mother is a cracker. Belongs to my gamekeeper. If you train her, she'll retrieve your pigeons.'

Cliff had been buzzing with excitement ever since May had told him the adoption news and that Spencer and Jesson were staying, but this...

His face shone, glowed, with delight as he held the pup.

The Squire went to leave. Cliff, nursing the puppy, thanked him, then turned to Spencer. 'Look, Spence. Dog,' he said. 'Dog.'

As May showed the Squire out, he said, 'I thought he'd appreciate that – more than those pheasants.'

The pheasants. The darned pheasants. This time, she would find out why he'd got them.

Acknowledgements

I owe huge thanks to my dear friend, Edward Field, for his freely given advice, support and refusal to let me dwell on the false dawns that plagued the route to finally seeing this work in print. Also, for his editing, proof-reading and ruthless culling of my errant commas.

Without the unceasing support of my husband, Mike, and our daughter, Katheryn, this book would never have seen the light of day. Thank you for your belief in me through the bad times and for sharing in the good ones.

I am indebted to the Dorset Federation of WIs for granting me access to *The Dorset Federation of Women's Institutes War Record Book (1939-1945)*. This wonderful, inspiring and unique book details life on the Dorset Home Front in personal, often handwritten and hand-illustrated, reports from those women who experienced it.

Thanks too, to my cover designer, Stefan, at Spiffing Covers for bringing May, the boys and the pheasants to life. Also, to my friends Carole, Jean, Sue and Wendy for their invaluable help and encouragement.

Finally, thank you, the reader. I hope you enjoyed your visit to Crompton Parva. If, on your way home, you could take a short detour to Amazon or Goodreads and leave a review, it would be very much appreciated.

Coming soon

May's Stony Road

Eighteen months after VE Day, life is hard. Then, the worst winter of the century sets in.

May's problems are intensified by a threat to her home, family and reputation.

How many battles can one woman tackle? If she loses a fight, the family loses everything.